Shakespeare in the Theatre: The Stratford Festival

SHAKESPEARE IN THE THEATRE

SERIES EDITORS

Peter Holland, Farah Karim-Cooper and Stephen Purcell

Published titles

Nicholas Hytner, Abigail Rokison-Woodall
The American Shakespeare Center, Paul Menzer
Mark Rylance at the Globe, Stephen Purcell
Patrice Chéreau, Dominique Goy-Blanquet
Peter Sellars, Ayanna Thompson
The National Theatre, 1963–1975: Olivier and Hall,
Robert Shaughnessy
Trevor Nunn, Russell Jackson
Cheek by Jowl, Peter Kirwan
Peter Hall, Stuart Hampton-Reeves
Yukio Ninagawa, Conor Hanratty
The King's Men, Lucy Munro
Sir William Davenant and the Duke's Company, Amanda
Eubanks Winkler and Richard Schoch
Sarah Siddons and John Philip Kemble, Fiona Ritchie
Tina Packer, Katharine Goodland

Forthcoming

Shakespeare Theatre Company, Drew Lichtenberg and Deborah
C. Payne
Satoshi Miyagi, Mika Eglinton
Phyllida Lloyd, Elizabeth Schafer
Kathryn Hunter, Stephen Purcell
Reduced Shakespeare Company, Ronan Hatfull

Shakespeare in the Theatre: The Stratford Festival

Christie Carson

THE ARDEN SHAKESPEARE
LONDON • NEW YORK • OXFORD • NEW DELHI • SYDNEY

THE ARDEN SHAKESPEARE
Bloomsbury Publishing Plc, 50 Bedford Square, London, WC1B 3DP, UK
Bloomsbury Publishing Inc, 1359 Broadway, 12th Floor, New York, NY 10018, USA
Bloomsbury Publishing Ireland, 29 Earlsfort Terrace, Dublin 2, D02 AY28, Ireland

BLOOMSBURY, THE ARDEN SHAKESPEARE and the Arden Shakespeare logo
are trademarks of Bloomsbury Publishing Plc

First published in Great Britain 2024
This paperback edition published 2026

Copyright © Christie Carson, 2024
Foreword © Neil Carson, 2024

Christie Carson has asserted her right under the Copyright, Designs and Patents Act,
1988, to be identified as author of this work.

For legal purposes the Acknowledgements on p. xi constitute
an extension of this copyright page.

Series design by Dani Leigh
Cover Image: Christopher Plummer as Prospero and Julyana Soelistyo as
Ariel in *The Tempest* 2010, (Courtesy of the Stratford Festival)

All rights reserved. No part of this publication may be: i) reproduced or transmitted in any form, electronic or mechanical, including photocopying, recording or by means of any information storage or retrieval system without prior permission in writing from the publishers; or ii) used or reproduced in any way for the training, development or operation of artificial intelligence (AI) technologies, including generative AI technologies. The rights holders expressly reserve this publication from the text and data mining exception as per Article 4(3) of the Digital Single Market Directive (EU) 2019/790.

Bloomsbury Publishing Inc does not have any control over, or responsibility for, any third-party websites referred to or in this book. All internet addresses given in this book were correct at the time of going to press. The author and publisher regret any inconvenience caused if addresses have changed or sites have ceased to exist, but can accept no responsibility for any such changes.

A catalogue record for this book is available from the British Library.

Library of Congress Cataloging-in-Publication Data
Names: Carson, Christie, author.
Title: The Stratford Festival / Christie Carson.
Description: London; New York: The Arden Shakespeare, 2024. |
Series: Shakespeare in the theatre; vol 14 | Includes bibliographical references and index.
Identifiers: LCCN 2023055184 (print) | LCCN 2023055185 (ebook) |
ISBN 9781350380806 (hardback) | ISBN 9781350380844 (paperback) |
ISBN 9781350380813 (ebook) | ISBN 9781350380820 (pdf)
Subjects: LCSH: Shakespeare, William, 1564-1616–Stage history–Ontario–Stratford. |
Shakespeare, William, 1564-1616–Dramatic production.
Classification: LCC PN2306.S77 C37 2024 (print) | LCC PN2306.S77 (ebook) |
DDC 822.3/3–dc23/eng/20240216
LC record available at https://lccn.loc.gov/2023055184
LC ebook record available at https://lccn.loc.gov/2023055185

ISBN: HB: 978-1-3503-8080-6
PB: 978-1-3503-8084-4
ePDF: 978-1-3503-8082-0
eBook: 978-1-3503-8081-3

Series: Shakespeare in the Theatre

Typeset by Deanta Global Publishing Services, Chennai, India

For product safety related questions contact productsafety@bloomsbury.com.

To find out more about our authors and books visit www.bloomsbury.com
and sign up for our newsletters.

To my parents who instilled in me at an early age a love of the theatre, with special thanks to my father who has helped me at every stage of researching and writing this book.

CONTENTS

List of Figures ix
Acknowledgements xi
Series preface xii
Preface by Christie Carson xiii
Foreword: 'The Miracle of 1953' by Neil Carson xv

Introduction 1

Foundations 17

1 The Stratford myth retold 19

2 Openings, beginnings, origins – Tyrone Guthrie (1953–5) 33

3 Establishing a new theatre building and an institutional structure – Michael Langham (1956–67) 51

Achieving 'maturity' and stability 75

4 Canadian expansion and British reinvention – Jean Gascon, John Hirsch and Robin Phillips (1968–80) 77

5 A challenging time of change – John Hirsch and John Neville (1981–9) 103

6 From festival to corporation – David William and Richard Monette (1990–2002) 122

Moving towards a new model 141

7 The Stratford Festival in the twenty-first century – Monette, McAnuff and Cimolino (2003–22) 143

8 The search for a Canadian *Hamlet* at the Festival 164

9 Creating a legacy with *The Tempest* at the Festival 190

Conclusion – A moment of reorientation for the company (2022–3) 215

References 223
Index 236

FIGURES

1 Set from *Richard III*, 2022. Photograph by David Hou. Directed by Antoni Cimolino. Designed by Francesca Callow. Lighting design by Michael Walton. Courtesy of the Stratford Festival 3
2 Tom Patterson walking before Tyrone Guthrie and Cecil Clarke as they disembark from a train. Photograph by Peter Smith. Courtesy of the Stratford Festival 29
3 Architect Robert Fairfield (far left) marking construction blueprints at the worksite for the Festival Tent auditorium. At his left stand Cecil Clarke, Tanya Moiseiwitsch and Tyrone Guthrie. Photograph by Peter Smith. Courtesy of the Stratford Festival 31
4 Alec Guinness as Richard III with members of the company in *Richard III* (Stratford Festival, 1953). Photograph by Peter Smith. Directed by Tyrone Guthrie. Designed by Tanya Moiseiwitsch. Courtesy of the Stratford Festival 37
5 Alec Guinness as King of France and Irene Worth as Helena with members of the company in *All's Well That Ends Well* (Stratford Festival, 1953). Photograph by Peter Smith. Directed by Tyrone Guthrie. Designed by Tanya Moiseiwitsch. Courtesy of the Stratford Festival 41
6 Christopher Plummer as King Henry V, with members of the company, in *Henry V* (Stratford Festival, 1956). Photograph by Herb Nott and Company. Directed by Michael Langham. Designed by Tanya Moiseiwitsch. Courtesy of the Stratford Festival 55
7 Festival Theatre Stage, 1962. Photograph by Peter Smith. Courtesy of the Stratford Festival 66

8 William Hutt as Duke (in disguise) and Martha Henry as Isabella in *Measure for Measure* (Stratford Festival, 1975). Photograph by Robert C. Ragsdale. Directed by Robin Phillips. Designed by Daphne Dare. Lighting design by Gil Wechsler. Courtesy of the Stratford Festival 92

9 Nicholas Pennell as Hamlet and Richard Monette as Hamlet in *Hamlet* (Stratford Festival, 1976). Photograph by Robert C. Ragsdale. Directed by Robin Phillips and William Hutt. Designed by John Pennoyer. Lighting design by Gil Wechsler. Courtesy of the Stratford Festival 171

10 William Hutt as Prospero and Martha Henry as Miranda in *The Tempest* (Stratford Festival, 1962). Photograph by Peter Smith. Directed by George McCowan. Designed by Desmond Heeley. Courtesy of the Stratford Festival 194

11 Josue Laboucane as Spirit, André Morin as Ariel, Martha Henry as Prospero and Mamie Zwettler as Miranda in *The Tempest* (Stratford Festival, 2018). Photograph by David Hou. Directed by Antoni Cimolino. Designed by Bretta Gerecke. Lighting design by Michael Walton. Courtesy of the Stratford Festival 209

12 Jessica B. Hill as Helen in *All's Well That Ends Well* (Stratford Festival, 2022). Photograph by David Hou. Directed by Scott Wentworth, Designed by Michelle Bohn. Lighting design by Louise Guinand. Courtesy of the Stratford Festival 216

ACKNOWLEDGEMENTS

This book has involved many conversations with family, friends and friends of family, all of whom have attended the Festival for many years. The staff at the Stratford Festival Archive has also been incredibly helpful, in particular Christine Schindler, who was instrumental in obtaining permission to use the images included. I am indebted to the series editors Peter Holland, Farah Karim-Cooper and Stephen Purcell for giving me the opportunity to write a volume on a topic that is close to my heart. Thanks goes particularly to Peter for providing feedback on the introduction and giving me general guidance along the way. In addition, I would like to thank Margaret Jane Kidnie and Karen Fricker, who both took the time to talk to me at key moments in the writing process and whose scholarship has informed this volume enormously. I would like to express my gratitude to the staff at the Arden Shakespeare, Mark Dudgeon and particularly to Ella Wilson, for answering my many queries with patience and good grace. My most heartfelt thanks go to those closest to me who have supported the writing of this book over the past three years, listening and providing unending encouragement: Lynne, Mark, Anna and Cameron Rickards, Liz Fisher, Jane Gawthrope, Susan Brock, Susan Bennett, Tania Dacre-Ord, Nicoleta Cinpoes, Gillian Carlisle and Di Walden.

SERIES PREFACE

Each volume in the Shakespeare in the Theatre series focuses on a director or theatre company who has made a significant contribution to Shakespeare production, identifying the artistic and political/social contexts of their work.

The series introduces readers to the work of significant theatre directors and companies, whose Shakespeare productions have been transformative in our understanding of his plays in performance. Each volume examines a single figure or company, considering their key productions, rehearsal approaches and their work with other artists (actors, designers, composers). A particular feature of each book is its exploration of the contexts within which these theatre artists have made their Shakespeare productions work. Thus, the series not only considers the ways in which directors and companies produce Shakespeare but also reflects upon their other theatre activities and the broader artistic, cultural and sociopolitical milieu within which their Shakespeare performances and productions have been created. The key to the series' originality, then, is its consideration of Shakespeare production in a range of artistic and broader contexts; in this sense, it de-centres Shakespeare from within Shakespeare studies, pointing to the range of people, artistic practices and cultural phenomena that combine to make meaning in the theatre.

Series editors: Peter Holland, Farah Karim-Cooper and Stephen Purcell

PREFACE BY CHRISTIE CARSON

This volume is designed to investigate the Festival's artistic history and legacy, both in its own presentation of that history and in the critical reception of its work in the press and scholarly analysis. My association with Stratford goes back to its beginning, even though I was not born until a decade after its founding. My father was an actor in the first two seasons and then worked in public relations for the Festival before becoming an academic. Growing up just an hour away from Stratford, I attended performances nearly every summer of my life. As a result, the unique thrust stage, and the very particular acting style it encourages, defined my vision of what a Shakespearean performance should look like.

From the outset, the Stratford Festival invited the involvement of British theatre artists. It would never have happened without the input of Tyrone Guthrie, Tanya Moiseiwitsch, Irene Worth and Alec Guinness. But neither would it have come about without the inspiration of Tom Patterson and the dedication and hard work of the community in that small Ontario town. As a second-generation member of the Stratford Festival community, who has studied and taught in the UK for over thirty years, I feel well placed to compare these two national Shakespeare performance traditions and to comment on their interactions and exchanges over the years.

These comparisons became particularly interesting during the years of the pandemic when companies on both sides of the Atlantic faced unprecedented challenges. Shakespeare's Globe, the Royal Shakespeare Company (RSC) and the Stratford Festival were all in the middle of documenting the entire

Shakespeare canon on film and had been screening this work in cinemas for over a decade. However, what happened during the ongoing theatrical and global health crisis differentiates the Stratford Festival from the two UK-based companies. The site StratFest@home not only developed into a testament to the way this Festival works but also demonstrates the place it holds in the community of which it is a part. As the largest classical theatre in the country, the Stratford Festival has a unique position in Canada and even in North America. The performance of the texts of Shakespeare's plays is what unites this Festival with other dedicated companies across North America, as well as the Globe and the RSC, but the means of production and the motivation to attain that end are entirely bound up in the cultural, social and political environment that engendered them.

FOREWORD: 'THE MIRACLE OF 1953' BY NEIL CARSON

The Canadian Stratford Festival began on a warm July evening in 1953. Members of that opening night audience had come from many parts of Canada as well as the United States. Since public transportation to this small rural town was irregular, most visitors had arrived by car, driving through the lush green Ontario farmland past cities called London or Windsor or Breslau or New Hamburg, commemorating the British and German settlers who had cleared the land scarcely 150 years ago. The Festival visitors had come because of their interest in Shakespeare, but also out of a sense of curiosity or even outright incredulity.

Before the performance there was a sense of excitement among the nearly 1,500 ticket holders who thronged to the theatre. They realized they were taking part in a very special event. Already they had been overcome by the warmth with which they had been welcomed by the local community. Those who were planning to stay overnight but found that all the local hotels had been unable to accommodate so many unexpected tourists were billeted in private homes. Others who lived within driving distance but could find no table in any of the few Stratford restaurants were served meals in a local church basement. Disorienting as all of this was, however, everyone was excited by the extraordinarily improbable gathering they had been persuaded to attend. Thanks to an excellent wire service linking newspapers from Halifax to Vancouver and many centres in the United States, the remarkable story of the Stratford Festival had been featured in news articles from coast to coast. It recounted how a Stratford journalist by the name of Tom Patterson had convinced first the town council and then an internationally celebrated British theatre director that the way to save an economically depressed town, with the auspicious name of Stratford, was to organize a local Shakespeare Festival. More astonishing still was the fact that the star of the proposed enterprise was to be the world-famous film actor Alec Guinness. As the curious first-nighters filed into the very large circus tent which was to serve as the theatre, none of them knew quite what to expect.

For many, it proved to be an overwhelming experience. Beneath the billowing blue ceiling of the tent was a compact, steeply raked amphitheatre. Portable seats were arranged on jute matting to help with the acoustics and to soften the appearance of the bare concrete. Four large tent poles and several lighting standards interfered with some sightlines, but the overall feeling was of amazing intimacy. The focus of this encircling auditorium was a stage unlike anything anyone had ever seen before. Uncomfortably close to the front circle of seats was a forty-foot circular acting area consisting of a small upper level and what looked like a series of four platforms of increasing size beneath it. Jutting out from the back wall was a triangular balcony supported by pillars and looking like the prow of an approaching ship. Staircases on either side of the balcony led down past two rear entrances to the main-stage level. Most surprising of all was the total absence of any curtain to hide the stage prior to the performance. Looking more like a welcoming front porch than the usual theatrical setting, the stage seemed at once naked and mysterious. When the last of the audience members was seated, a huge bell sounded and the play began.

Richard III opened quietly with a soliloquy, spoken conspiratorially by Alec Guinness as the hunchbacked King, perched on the front of the balcony in the exact centre of the amphitheatre. It was one of the few quiet moments in a production filled with swirling banners, gorgeous pageantry, stunning medieval costumes and a climactic battle that threatened to endanger the perilously nearby spectators. The reception of the audience was rapturous. The next night could not have been a greater contrast. Whereas *Richard III* had been a crowd-pleasing historical melodrama, frequently performed and a standard star vehicle, *All's Well That Ends Well* was a practically unknown, not very funny, 'comedy'. The Stratford performance was to be the first professional production of the play in North America. Most astonishing of all it was to be done in 'modern dress', set sometime in the Edwardian period in a kind of Ruritanian neverland. It is hard to imagine a riskier choice for a newly created company. Whether it was the dazzling performance of the British actress, Irene Worth, or the greater comfort of the Canadian actors in a more contemporary setting, the production was a revelation. With the imported male actors (including Alec Guinness) taking smaller roles, it was possible for the Canadian performers, including several who would later become prominent members of the Stratford company, to shine.

That summer of 1953, Canadians on both sides of the non-existent Stratford footlights felt they had witnessed a miracle.

June 2023

Introduction

On 18 June 2022, I entered the Tom Patterson Theatre at the Stratford Festival to be confronted with a replica of the Coronation robe worn by Alec Guinness as Richard III in 1953. The play I was about to see, with my father who had been on stage with the original robe and actor, was again *Richard III*, this time starring the beloved Stratford actor Colm Feore. This production was directed by the artistic director of the Festival, Antoni Cimolino, as part of the first full season of plays to be mounted after the pandemic hiatus, a season entitled 'New Beginnings'. In the programme for the production Cimolino states that the 2022 season was 'A fresh start: an opportunity to reassess ourselves in the world today, reaffirm what we value and take the best path to an extraordinary future' (*Richard III* Programme, 2022b: 1). The new theatre, which had its opening delayed by the Covid crisis, is a testament to the history of the Festival in a number of ways. First, it is named after the Stratford founder, Tom Patterson, and not the man usually seen as the father of the Festival outside the country, Tyrone Guthrie. Second, it occupies a location which has been integral to the development of the Festival since the very beginning, although at first it was the venue for the concert hall which housed the Music Festival. And third and finally, the stage at the heart of this new theatre was created with the iconic Festival Theatre in mind but with its own unique character, boasting an extended thrust stage which requires most of the audience to face one another, with the actors working in the middle of this sea of observers. Activity has taken place in this space (and the adjacent car park) since the 1950s, and while not all of it was Shakespeare-related, it was always groundbreaking and innovative. This theatre and this season typify the legacy of the Stratford Festival, standing as they do for longevity, community and a sense of continuity, looking to both the Festival's history and its future.

Given this sense of a new beginning with a building that was constructed sometime before it was unveiled to the public, it is no wonder that the Festival was keen to make an occasion of the new production of the first play performed in 1953. Linking the past and the present was an element of every aspect of this visit to Stratford. The wall of donors proudly displays the public as well as private funders who made the theatre possible and enabled the Festival to endure the two years of reduced activity. But the fact that much of the funding for the Tom Patterson Theatre was in place before the development campaign for the new theatre even started illustrates something quite significant about this Festival: it is an institution which holds a great deal of cultural capital for those involved. The size of the names on the wall indicates the level of the donation and government funding ranks at the top of this scale. The Stratford Festival, like the Royal Shakespeare Company (RSC), has a government-funded mandate to maintain cultural standards for the nation.

Just along from the donors' wall is a display of images of the key events which have taken place at this location. An image of the first Festival Concert Hall shows a barn-like building, but the images which accompany it indicate that this was a place of serious intent musically. Duke Ellington and Billie Holliday both performed in this makeshift space in the 1950s. Later, when the building was replaced with a new Community Centre, it was the City of Stratford which had top billing on what was to be a shared space that contained the first experimental theatre (initially called the Third Stage) when it opened in 1971. Like The Other Place at the RSC, this theatre was designed to give the Company a space for experimental work. When it was renamed the Tom Patterson Theatre in 1991, it was in recognition of the intrepid spirit of innovation that the Festival's founder represented (Figure 1).

FIGURE 1 *Set from* Richard III, *2022. Photograph by David Hou. Directed by Antoni Cimolino. Designed by Francesca Callow. Lighting design by Michael Walton. Courtesy of the Stratford Festival.*

Entering the theatre space itself I was struck by a pre-show set that highlighted both a real event and the research of a British university. The Crest and name of the University of Leicester featured on square structures surrounding two lit holes in the stage. On the panel facing my seat was a drawing of a figure wearing a hoodie, created in the style of Banksy. In large red letters, seemingly spray-painted onto the false wall, were the words 'SPREAD ANARCHY'. But ANARCHY had been crossed out and in smaller black letters underneath was written 'DON'T TELL ME WHAT TO DO!!' Around what was clearly meant to be the excavation site of the real Richard III in a car park in Leicester, there was a red and white cordon which prevented anyone from approaching.

When the actors entered, they appeared to be both those working on the site and those opposed to this activity. It was a twenty-first-century framing of the events of the play, leading to a great reveal. Suddenly the stage floor opened up behind the panel walls and the lit figure of Colm Feore, as Richard III, ascended the stairs from beneath the stage. The walls around the former excavation site were hastily removed and in an instant the past became the present and the audience was taken from twenty-first-century Britain to the Britain of Shakespeare's constructed past. Applause greeted the actor and the stage wizardry that lit not only the body of the newly reborn Richard but also a series of translucent tiles that resembled stained glass windows, which were embedded in the floor and ran almost the length of the extended thrust stage. It was a dramatic entrance that contrasted, but remembered, Alec Guinness straddling the balcony for his solitary opening soliloquy in 1953. Both actors were keenly aware of being part of an event that was larger than themselves and both understood the importance of unveiling the potential of the theatre space that they were there to highlight.

The production which followed neither vilified nor glamorized a despicable Richard. The manipulations of the would-be monarch seemed to elicit sneering laughter rather than appreciation or disgust. There was very little passion in the wooing scene and elsewhere. Where the passionate centre of the play rested was with the women of the court. In terms of the Festival's history the characters of Queen Margaret (Seana McKenna), Queen Elizabeth (Lucy Peacock) and the Duchess of York, (Diana Leblanc) represented cumulatively sixty-nine seasons of performances. McKenna has a strong attachment to the Tom Patterson Theatre since it was both where she first performed Shakespeare at the Festival in 1982 and where she performed as the Madwoman of Chaillot, the last production staged there before the refurbishment (*Richard III* Programme 2022b: 19). A list of her other roles on this stage gives a clear indication of the way it has figured as a site of experimentation with both Shakespeare's work and other classical writing: Medea, Mother Courage, Queen Elizabeth I, Phèdre, Constance, Lady Tolerance, Andromache and Klytemestra, to name a few. But perhaps most importantly, McKenna also performed the role of Richard III herself on the same stage in 2011. For a regular audience member of the Festival, Peacock's performance as Queen Elizabeth might also be seen as the culmination of her work on all four of Stratford's stages (Ophelia, Rosalind, Viola, Portia, Desdemona, Lady Macbeth, Titania, Beatrice, Gwendolyn, Helena, Duchess of Malfi, Masha, Regan, Mary Stuart, Volumnia and Satan). Leblanc is better known for her directing of work at the Festival and elsewhere, but she played Katharine in two important productions of *Henry V* at the Festival (1966 and 1980). In these women there was the gravitas and passion required to command the stage, but they also seemed more comfortable with the extraordinary intimacy of this space.

Feore, while hugely experienced as a Shakespearean actor, having taken on many of the key roles at Stratford and elsewhere, has largely performed on the more expansive Festival Theatre stage. His Richard on this occasion (he last played the role in 1988) was understated and almost off-hand vocally in this smaller space. Most of his effort went into the extraordinary physicalization of the part. With a brace on his back, that seemed to speak to the discovery of a scoliosis in the skeleton of the real Richard, Feore effected a strange sideways limp that involved his whole body. Given the current debate around whether an actor should be affecting a disability in this part, and the performance by the disabled actor Arthur Hughes at the RSC in the same summer, this seemed a strange choice (see Tracy 2022), one which forced me to recognize that I had applauded performances in the past for exactly the thing that now made me uncomfortable. But perhaps the key to Feore's underpowered vocal and overpowering physical performance lay in the direction. In his programme notes Cimolino writes, 'His rivals are certain that he cannot have achieved his own success nor will ever be able to wield power on his own. Consequently, they believe that he can be used for their own purposes. His rise is enabled by their own ambitions' (*Richard III* Programme 2022b: 5). The justification for this in the text is slim but it speaks more clearly to the case of Donald Trump, as well as to Prime Minister Boris Johnson in that summer, both men whose apparent lack of ability fooled their rivals into complacency. Cimolino's notion that 'Richard plays along with their plans and then upends their narratives' (*Richard III* Programme 2022b: 5) goes against the character's clear articulation of his motives in his opening soliloquy ('I am determined to prove a villain [. . .] Plots have I laid, inductions dangerous' (1.1.30, 32)) but this directorial choice made the play speak to the cultural moment of the summer of 2022.

The production completed the twenty-first-century framing of the main narrative with the characters of Richmond and Elizabeth appearing in modern dress, delivering the final speech together, flanked by their two adorable children. Union Jacks were draped on either side of the main central entrance with 'Jerusalem' played at speed, setting up the unusual sense that the next generation of leader would be quite different but somehow more threatening. Cimolino writes, '[Richard] was replaced by a much more sophisticated police state, under regimes that were more cruel and more effective at political manipulation' (*Richard III* Programme 2022b: 5). The image presented on stage (a vision of William and Kate as the next Royal rulers?) seemed to contradict in profound ways the reverence for the Queen and her descendants which had been displayed in the UK for the Platinum Jubilee just a couple of weeks before this production opened and again for her funeral a few months later. If the Tom Patterson Theatre presents the true spirit of Canadian Shakespeare at the Festival, it appears to be more concerned with its own history than Britain's, past or present. If this is the case then perhaps *Richard III* is a truly representative play for a Festival which has fought valiantly for many years, been battered by criticism locally, while being largely ignored by the international critical debate about Shakespeare in performance. The ascendancy of the Stratford Festival to the throne of online recognition, as the only North American company to attempt to present the entire canon on film, might well mean that the title of Cimolino's notes is particularly apt: 'A Template for Tyranny?' (*Richard III* Programme 2022b: 5).

But the key to this performance, as with every performance at the Festival, was not so much the director's interpretation as it was the interaction between the audience and their own history with this cultural institution. The audience listened intently and greeted rustling or talking in their midst with hostility. This audience was acutely aware of its involvement in the celebration of what, for Canada, was a cultural event of great significance. There was a very Canadian sense of familiarity with the actors on stage, which was more like the interaction seen at Shakespeare's Globe than at the RSC. The Tom Patterson Theatre embodies the feeling of the Festival, which is that the audience members are not passive observers of the performance but active participants in creating the event of the play in the present moment.

To attend the Festival regularly, as I have done, is to become invested in the unlikely project of creating Canadian Shakespeare. But history weighed a bit too heavily on this production. The violence on stage in Guthrie's 1953 production, and in Doran's 2022 production at the RSC, drew laughter by presenting black humour with a serious undertone. In Cimolino's production the violence came across as cartoon action, which did not move the audience to anything but cynicism. Quite unusually the two Princes were murdered on stage in this production. Rather than evoking horror and pity this choice placed these murders into the general melee, stripping away the power of the description of the deed by Tyrell. The final moment of unnecessary brutality came at the end of the final battle when Richard was stabbed in the back by one of his own men who then turned to Richmond for appreciation of the deed. Rather than taking him into his service as the text suggests ('Proclaim a pardon to the soldiers fled/ That in submission will return to us' (5.5.16–17)), Richmond slit the young man's throat, leaving him to die on stage without ceremony. There is no doubt that *Richard III* is a bloody, brutal play, but this production left the audience with a sense that it was watching a pageant designed to highlight the Festival's history and the capabilities of the performance space.

While this *Richard III* may well have conveyed an accurate vision of the views of the actors and director in the post-Covid political world in North America, it made for disappointing live theatre. The task of paying homage to the Festival's history, while also satisfying an audience hungry for cultural affirmation after two years of terrible struggle, was never going to be easy. Moving forward, the Stratford Festival needs to reassess its position within the Canadian cultural landscape to ensure that it continues to provide the best training ground for new generations of theatre makers as well as rewarding experiences for audiences.

Professional theatre in Ontario prior to 1953

To understand the Festival's current predicament it is necessary to give a sense of the cultural environment which engendered this endeavour. Theatre in Canada has had a long, and at times complex, relationship with Shakespeare's work. Throughout the nineteenth century local stock theatre companies were common, often boosted in their efforts through the support of the British Garrisons (until the withdrawal of British troops in 1871). After this time the development of the railway lines allowed for visiting troupes to be brought in, making Canadian cities stops on the international touring circuit (Wagner 1989: 397). However, by the beginning of the twentieth century the demand for Canadian content was on the rise. Lavish imported productions continued to draw audiences, but this was countered by a growing desire to see a distinctly Canadian theatre develop. In Toronto this goal was supported by wealthy families such as the Eatons and the Masseys, who encouraged more 'local artistic self-expression' (Wagner 1989: 399) before government support for the arts was available. Elsewhere in the country throughout the 1920s and 1930s the first flourishing of theatrical activity took place through the extremely popular Little Theatre movement. This amateur activity was regionally based but was drawn together to create a sense of national identity and an autonomous Canadian culture through the Dominion Drama Festival, which ran from 1933 to 1970, almost continuously. However, Anton Wagner highlights that the assessment of this Festival was left to experts from outside the country; 'Companies were encouraged to improve artistic standards through adjudications by leading figures from both European and American professional theatre' (1989: 400). This Festival took the form of a competition, but it also allowed for a showcasing of talent from across the country, giving theatre artists the opportunity to learn from one another as well as from external expertise.

After the Second World War the Canada Council, following the British model, was set up to support the work of Canadian artists. In English Canada government-funded professional repertory theatres across the country began staging English classics, with the work of Shakespeare figuring most prominently. In French Canada it was often the work of Molière and Racine which stood as a testament to the abilities of home-grown actors. According to Irena R. Makaryk, 'The real explosion of interest in Shakespeare, both in English and French Canada, occurred after 1945 and coincided with the growth of cities, the influx of immigrant groups, the rapid development of technology, and debates about national identity and culture' (2001: 64). The Canadian Broadcasting Corporation (CBC) from its inception in the 1930s had a mission to support Canadian drama. In fact, a national public service radio system was developed in direct response to the American domination of the theatrical circuits, and its focus on drama was designed to help nurture the country's first professional actors. Therefore, somewhat unusually, a national professional theatre in Canada was aided by the development of both radio and film, which took the popular audience away from the imported productions, making theatrical touring less profitable.

The decline of foreign tours after the Second World War allowed the burgeoning Canadian professional theatre to prosper. However, the form that theatre would take was strongly influenced by the requirements set down by The Royal Commission on the National Development in the Arts, Letters and Sciences and its resulting Massey Report of 1951, which describes the need for a strong national theatre which would rely on the performance of classical theatre to train local talent. While the 'miracle' of Stratford was made popular by the accounts of the Festival's opening by Guthrie, Patterson and others, the report of its opening in *The Times* points out the context for its inception; 'there is no doubt that Canada has been presented with a cultural enterprise of the kind which the Massey Report blessed in principle before its inception' (1953: 11). The arrival of Tyrone Guthrie and the establishment of the Stratford Festival fulfilled a national mandate.

Critical reception of the Stratford Festival

The entry for the 'Stratford Festival Theatre, Ontario' in *The Oxford Companion to Shakespeare* reads simply 'See Canada; Guthrie, Sir Tyrone' (Dobson and Wells 2001: 451). This vision of the Festival, as a stepping stone on the quest to articulate Guthrie's ideas about an open stage which was to revolutionize the performance of Shakespeare worldwide, is widely adopted within the British tradition of performance history. A key text in perpetuating this idea of the Festival is Robert Shaughnessy's *The Shakespeare Effect* (2002), which recounts the events of the opening of the Festival in a way that relies very heavily on Guthrie's own account and only briefly discusses the Canadian social, political and economic context. More recently the British theatre producer and designer Iain Mackintosh, in *The Guthrie Thrust Stage: A Living Legacy* (2011), argues that the Stratford Festival Theatre is one of several experiments in stage architecture, including the Olivier Theatre and Shakespeare's Globe, which eventually led to the reconstruction of the Royal Shakespeare Theatre in Stratford-upon-Avon in 2011. Even Cimolino when interviewed repeats this version of the role of the Stratford stage in international performance history (2022). All of these accounts strip the Canadian Festival of its seventy-year production history. Makaryk concludes: 'On the whole, Stratford's influence has been architectural rather than theatrical' (2001: 64). It is this position that this volume seeks to challenge.

However, it must be acknowledged that these dismissive readings are countered by volumes which have been published in Canada to celebrate the work of this Festival and construct its history, starting with the three books written by Guthrie and Robertson Davies (1953, 1954, 1955) which document the Festival's first three seasons. Later accounts produced by those directly involved recreate the founding of the Festival in their own image (Whittaker 1958; Guthrie 1959; 1987, Raby 1968; Patterson and Gould 1987; Reid and Morrison 1994). There was a concerted effort to involve audience members in the foundation story and so *The Stratford Shakespearean Festival of Canada, 1953-1959* (Stratford Festival 1959), a booklet produced by the Festival's publicity department, was updated and re-released every year until 1982. A romantic vision of the Festival has been reinforced by volumes created to celebrate the anniversaries of the Festival. The Festival's thirtieth anniversary was heralded by John Pettigrew and Jamie Portman's two-volume *Stratford: The First Thirty Years* (1985), which contains a detailed analysis of each season followed by an appendix which lists the complete details of the cast and crew of every production staged. The Festival's fiftieth anniversary was marked by the publication of three volumes: Martin Hunter's *Romancing the Bard: Stratford at Fifty* (2001), Robert Cushman's *Fifty Seasons at Stratford* (2002) and Richard Ouzounian's *Stratford Gold: 50 years, 50 Stars, 50 Conversation* (2002), which again all provide in-depth information about individual productions and the experience of individual theatre artists, alongside stunning images of the plays on stage. In Canada the myth-making and remaking of the Festival is well established and supported by a range of print publications both from the publicity department and beyond it.

However, the vision of the Festival as a miraculous occurrence that created the first flourishing of a Canadian professional theatre has also been widely criticized in the country. In fact, criticism of the Festival in the press began shortly after it started, but more recently a body of critical writing on Canadian theatre history has developed which takes the position that the Festival was a colonial imposition on the country at a time when it needed to develop its own creative voice. This voice was not heard, so the argument goes, for several decades because of the dominance of the Festival and its imported ways of working. Two key figures in this debate, Alan Filewod (1987) and Robert Wallace (1990), stress the importance of a politically motivated alternative Canadian theatre, created to counteract the imposition of a colonial model. In the early 1990s Richard Paul Knowles applied this criticism to the story told by the Stratford Festival to its audiences in print. Knowles has consistently examined the Festival's work with a critical eye, highlighting 'the role that Shakespeare has played in the constitution of postcolonial Canadian subjectivity and nationhood' (2004: book cover). This study of the Festival's history aims to both acknowledge and question this position.

Two more recent collections of critical essays entitled *Shakespeare in Canada* in 2002 and 2017 look at aspects of the Festival's creative output and its influence, as well as the economic model it puts forward of a tourist-oriented presentation of Shakespeare's work as part of a summer Festival. In *Shakespeare in Canada: A World Elsewhere?* (2002) editors Diana Brydon and Makaryk draw together seventeen essays divided into four parts, covering the establishment and development of critical arguments about the productions and adaptations that Shakespeare's work has inspired across the country. As the editors point out in their Preface 'this study addresses the local uses of "Shakespeare" in embodying cultural value and creating communal identities both under empire and after its dissolution' (2002: ix). By 2017 when the second *Shakespeare in Canada* collection was published, it came with the subtitle *Remembrance of Ourselves*. Again Makaryk was one of the editors, this time with Kathryn Prince. This volume contains fourteen short essays which came out of a project run by the editors' own institution, the University of Ottawa, designed to celebrate the 400th anniversary of Shakespeare's death in 2016. The tone of this collection is less optimistic in terms of Canada's potential to have an international impact and even more self-referential. The use throughout both collections of the pronouns 'we' and 'our' seems to suggest that these critical essays are aimed primarily at a Canadian audience. Together these accounts provide a less celebratory vision of the work achieved.

Ian Rae sums up the situation of the critical reception of the Festival in the following way:

There are two grand narratives of the founding of the Stratford Festival, North America's largest repertory theatre: the story of the 'Stratford Miracle,' which is an outgrowth of the Festival's publicity machine, and the critique of that story by the alternative theatre community, which emphasizes national factors in the founding of the Festival (e.g. the thwarted mid-century drive to establish a national theatre in Canada) even as it rejects the Festival on nationalist grounds. (2017: 50)

Suffice it to say that the Festival has never had an unproblematic or uncontested critical retelling of its history. Therefore, in the chapters that follow I proceed chronologically to situate the work of the Stratford Festival in a Canadian social, cultural and political context, engaging with the wide range of critical writing it has inspired. Inevitably this approach questions both what makes Shakespeare Canadian and conversely what constitutes Canadian Shakespeare. The Festival has been accused of shying away from politically oriented Shakespeare production but I argue that given its role in debates about

Canadian cultural identity, the Festival has had a profoundly political, as well as theatrical, impact.

The final two chapters of this study re-examine the history of two plays at the Festival, *Hamlet* and *The Tempest*, making the argument that the generational power shifts in these texts provide an opportunity to explore Canada's changing cultural climate. In the conclusion I consider the 2022–3 seasons as a moment of reorientation. Just as the new Tom Patterson Theatre was nearing completion, the pandemic made it necessary to cancel the 2020 season. In 2021 outdoor spaces were created to accommodate in-person audiences on a small scale, and these performances were made available online to international audiences. The Stratford Festival returned to its roots in 2021, since the season was performed in marquee theatres, reminiscent of the original tent and the 'adventure' was recorded for those not able to attend. Therefore, the history of the Stratford Festival is one that has come full circle, starting and ending with the local community but now with a global presence and influence. The single thrust stage that Guthrie envisioned is, in the twenty-first century, augmented by three other stages: the Avon proscenium arch theatre, the small black box Studio space and the extended thrust stage of the newly renovated Tom Patterson Theatre. This array of performance spaces puts the Stratford Festival in an unparalleled position of flexibility to experiment with the relationship between the stage and the text with an established repertory company, in collaboration with the loyal Festival audience.

This study cannot be exhaustive but instead aims for coherence through articulating and illustrating what this Festival has contributed to the wider understanding of Shakespeare in performance through the consistent examination of the plays on stages that bring the audience and actors together with a sense of shared responsibility for the meaning generated. To provide a throughline in this complex history I highlight the work of three actors who have had a lifelong association with it and with each other: Christopher Plummer (the Festival's first Hamlet), William Hutt and Martha Henry (the Festival's first Prospero and Miranda, see Figure 10). These three actors not only performed in early productions at the Festival but also featured in its most recent productions of *The Tempest* as Prospero (see Chapter 9). Looking at the careers of these actors, alongside the development of the Festival under each of its artistic directors, demonstrates how the Festival has acted as a catalyst for creativity and a magnet for talent, which has often resulted in binding connections lasting many years. Plummer achieved some of his first triumphs and ended his onstage career at the Stratford Festival. While his career is unique, in some ways it speaks to an underlying trend of actors and directors to take what they have learnt in this small Ontario town on to other areas of work, then to return with knowledge and skills from 'a world elsewhere' (Cor. 3.3.134), with influence travelling both from the Festival and back to it in equal measure.

Foundations

1

The Stratford myth retold

In *The Guthrie Thrust Stage* Mackintosh charts the progress in theatre architecture from the Assembly Hall in Edinburgh in 1948 to the Royal Shakespeare Theatre in 2011, with the Stratford Festival Theatre presented as the second of twelve stages built to satisfy Guthrie's vision of the open stage. He asserts: 'Epic thrust stages, inspired by Tyrone Guthrie, have been built in many countries over the last fifty years. In these playgoers have rediscovered the immediacy of Shakespeare and other classics.[. . .] On all these stages theatre makers have forsaken illusion and allowed audiences to relate to the ritual of real performances mainly because they are so close to the performer' (2011: 5). By contrast, Cushman proclaims the building of the Stratford stage as more singular event: 'Of the theatres erected in the English-speaking world since 1953 only a few have been designed in direct imitation of the Stratford Festival but all – certainly if they were intended to house a classical repertoire – have had to take notice of its existence' (2002: 11). These two quotations nicely sum up the opposing visions of the founding of the Festival and its impact from the view of the British performance tradition and from a Canadian perspective. For Mackintosh the epic stage was developed in response to British Victorian pictorialism and modernist ideas of naturalism, influenced by the advent of film. In Canada the Stratford Festival was founded at a time when there was an international desire to put in place political structures and cultural initiatives that would continue the Allied war effort.

In the years between the end of the war and the founding of the Festival there had been a lively debate about the future of Canadian culture across the country. There was a desire to consolidate and expand on Canada's growing international reputation and theatre was seen as one clear way in which this might be achieved. Canadian luminaries such as Robertson Davies and Dora Mavor Moore, both colleagues of Guthrie's, contributed to the Massey Report of 1951, which called for several key reforms to extend Canada's cultural life. Guthrie's intervention in the history of performance in Canada undoubtedly pushed Canadian actors and audiences into a global world of Shakespeare performance that they might not otherwise have had access to, but the moment of its creation was complex.

Margaret Groome in 'Stratford and the Aspirations for a Canadian National Theatre' (2002) points to the work of Dora Mavor Moore, in founding the New Play Society in Toronto in 1946, as the beginning of the first stage of developing a truly Canadian drama. She highlights the Society's extraordinary record of producing Canadian plays, with forty-seven of the seventy-two plays put on stage over a ten-year period being by Canadian playwrights. Moore's insistence that Canadian plays be set beside the classics helped to bring about a new generation of actors who aspired to perform to professional standards (even if the Society remained a non-profit organization), making the quick assembly of the Stratford Festival possible. But the New Play Society is just one example of the exciting semi-professional work that was going on across the country in the late 1940s and early 1950s, moving Canada a step closer to establishing a national drama. Moore encouraged Guthrie to come to Canada because she believed, as he did, that a Canadian professional theatre had to be cultivated by training actors using the best material available to them.

This approach to creating a native drama was directly opposed by Earle Grey, a British actor whose festival of

Shakespeare performance in Toronto bore his name from 1949 to 1958. Grey felt that Canadian actors and audiences should experience 'what Shakespeare had in mind' in a way that illustrated the 'extraordinary timeless quality' (qtd in Groome 2002: 118) of the plays. Grey put forward a position that many at the time found appealing. He states; 'As far as possible twentieth-century notions would not be permitted. Stunts, fashionable slants, Freudian implications, and silly-clever ideas which are the bane of the contemporary Shakespeare theatre would be ruled out' (qtd in Groome 2002: 118). Groome argues that this position was one that was taken up by the Stratford Festival and was given further authority through the engagement of successful theatre artists from England. She insists that the two festivals accepted 'Shakespeare as [a] cultural authority and Shakespearean production as a soothing entertainment, a form of commodity, through which one can escape from the "outside world"' (Groome 2002: 119). Given the horrors of the Second World War it is hardly surprising that there was a desire to establish a cultural life for the nation that would bring about harmony, but the privileging of British values over Canadian home-grown visions was not what Guthrie and the Stratford Festival set out to do. In the terms set out by the Massey Report theatre provided an opportunity to demonstrate Canadian artists' abilities on the world stage, but in order to achieve this end, Shakespeare was seen as the country's best ambassador and teacher. The Stratford Festival was successful not only in developing a new stage space and audience relationship, but it trained actors, directors, designers and theatre technicians, as well establishing a professional theatre with a self-sustaining infrastructure.

This infrastructure allowed for a permanent building in 1957 and has sustained the Festival through each new project and financial crisis, (including the Covid pandemic). While the Stratford Festival recruited artistic and production staff from the UK in 1953, the appeal of coming to Canada for many of these artists was the chance to escape the restrictions of the established British theatrical tradition. This was certainly the case for Guthrie, and he invited others to follow his lead. The image of a great director imposing his will on a pliable new nation quickly breaks down in the face of the contradictions which were inherent in Guthrie's own life and work. Due to his experience working in both Ireland and Scotland Guthrie understood the issues at stake in creating theatre that could support a developing national identity. He was impressed by the conviction of Patterson and his Canadian committee, but the request came at an opportune moment. In 1953, Shakespeare's work was seen by both Guthrie and the Festival's Founders as the best source of material to train actors and directors who would then go on to develop a Canadian theatre of which the country could be proud. In theory the Stratford Festival provided a blank slate for creating a new way of working. In reality a number of competing approaches to classical theatre in Canada were at play, which could have influenced the general direction of development. The notion of an apprenticeship model, as mapped out by the Massey Report, was key to the way the Festival was conceived. The local community and the imported experts were, from the beginning, working together for a common cause to upend the theatrical norms of British theatre (rather than to reinforce them), with the aim of creating Canada's own national theatre tradition.

The Guthrie/Patterson myth: Two unlikely allies working towards a shared goal

According to Guthrie's telling of the tale, Patterson was inspired by the cultural life of the many small towns he visited while travelling in Northern Europe and England during the war. But Patterson had no love for the theatre and by the time he contacted Guthrie had only seen two professional productions, neither one a Shakespeare play. Patterson's family was well established in Stratford. His great grandfather,

Thomas Patterson, had arrived in the town from Scotland in 1870 to work with the Grand Trunk Railway (GTR) locomotive repair shop, the town's largest employer. A general strike in 1933 and the ravages of the Second World War made Patterson worry for the future of the town. He came up with the idea of a Shakespeare Festival early on simply because of the city's name, its park system along another Avon river and the existence of 'wards and schools with such names as Hamlet, Falstaff, Romeo and Juliet' (qtd in Riedstra 2010: 3). His vision was born out of civic pride and a desire to encourage visitors to the town; 'The picture I had in my mind was not of a building nor of a stage, as I knew absolutely nothing about theatre, or how it worked. Rather I had an image only of lots of people pouring in' (qtd in Riedstra 2010: 3). He first spoke to the Mayor of Stratford about his idea for a Shakespeare Festival in May 1951. Then in January of 1952 Patterson approached the Stratford City Council for a grant to pursue the idea. With civic support and a grant of C$125 Patterson headed to New York to try to speak to Laurence Olivier. While he never met the actor the *Stratford Beacon Herald* announced, 'Council told of Idea to Make Stratford World Famous Shakespeare Centre' (1952). This article was picked up by other newspapers across Canada and the idea began to seep into the popular imagination. On his return to Stratford Patterson was able to gain a commitment from the city and so set up a festival committee. It was at this point that Dora Mavor Moore suggested that Guthrie might be the right person to approach to further the committee's goals. And so it was that Guthrie made a trip to Stratford, Ontario in July 1952 to provide advice.

Mackintosh's account of Guthrie's development of the thrust stage begins with his first experiment in 1937 when his Old Vic production of *Hamlet*, scheduled for performance at Kronborg Castle in Elsinore, Denmark, had to be moved indoors due to rain. Anthony Quayle, who played Laertes in that production, recounts how this impromptu performance 'planted in Tony's mind the idea that Shakespeare could not be acted in a proscenium-arch theatre, but demanded presentation almost in the round' and that this event inspired 'the theatres he built with Tanya Moiseiwitsch' (qtd in Mackintosh 2011: 7). The key to this initial experiment, according to Mackintosh, was the 'triumphant congress of actor and audience' (2011: 7). Guthrie felt certain that he had discovered something new about the plays through the interaction that resulted in a shared space. So, his next encounter with the thrust stage was more carefully planned. In 1948 he was asked to stage an old Scots text called *The Satire of the Three Estates* at the Edinburgh Festival. For this production he created a purpose-built stage in the Assembly Hall of the Church of Scotland. Mackintosh recalls how '1,350 spectators were arranged on benches around a raised platform stage, thrusting out from the fourth of four galleries' (2011: 8). He claims that every 'spectator participated in the ritual' and the result was that 'theatre architecture was transformed' (2011: 8). Guthrie returned to the Edinburgh Festival for several years to direct plays at the Assembly Hall, and this experience seems to have convinced him of the value of this new approach. So, rather than happenstance, Patterson's invitation gave Guthrie the opportunity to build a stage and auditorium to suit his vision, shaped by years of practical experimentation.

Guthrie was also more invested in the idea of creating a Canadian theatre than he is given credit for since his encounters with the theatre in Ireland, through his work at the BBC in Belfast (1924–5) and with the Scottish National Players in Scotland (1926–8), gave him an appreciation of the importance of the theatre in national self-fashioning. His work as the artistic director of the Festival Theatre in Cambridge (1929–30) introduced him to the rigours of the weekly repertory system and working at the Old Vic Theatre during the war gave him extensive experience directing Shakespeare. But Guthrie had also visited Canada in the 1930s to develop a radio broadcast for the Canadian National Railway (CNR) entitled *The Romance of Canada*, a series that took him across the country by rail in 1931. The CNR wanted to produce a broadcast series that would draw the expansive nation together through the medium of radio. What Guthrie found attractive in terms of Canada's developing cultural life was an appreciation of the rhythm of language, more apparent on the radio than on the stage, and the wonders of nature, two things which are amply supported by Shakespeare's texts. Rather than a stroke of luck, the invitation to Stratford Ontario in 1952 was the culmination of decades of work and experience. Herbert Whittaker recalls, 'Guthrie stated his vision of the Festival as a Canadian project, with Canadian actors presented properly to a Canadian audience' (1958: xxiii–iv). Guthrie's tenure was both brief and crucial. He knew better than the committee he served, the importance of creating something that was made by and for the local community but which had international appeal. Directing at the Edinburgh Festival exposed him to the idea of conscientiously combining international stars with local talent to create a sense of occasion.

In 1958 Whittaker believed Guthrie was responsible for a great step forward in Canada's cultural self-determination; suggesting it was 'Guthrie who established the Festival's particular flavour of Canadianism, which suited the sudden need for a national expression by a country thrust into the international scene without a characteristic to call its very own' (1958: xxiii). In fact Whittaker credits Canadian nationalism as the key factor in the venture's success. The Festival committee was transformed into a Board of Directors of the Stratford Shakespearean Festival Foundation of Canada in October 1952, with Harrison A. Showalter as President and A. M. Bell as Vice President. Their commitment to the project inspired Guthrie's dedication to help them realize their goal but as Cushman points out, 'he saw his job as being to get in, get started, and get out' (2002: 19). Guthrie wanted to create an innovative theatre space that would capture the imagination of the nation, train local theatre artists and gain international attention. Post-war prosperity made it possible for the people of Stratford to imagine, along with Patterson, the transformative power of a local cultural endeavour that could provide 'a rallying point for Canadian theatre' (Cushman 2002: 19). The stage space Guthrie created with Moiseiwitsch provided a focus for the development of a new kind of Shakespeare performance, fuelled by Canadian determination and talent, which established the fledgling Festival as an event of international importance.

The Stratford community and the British visitors

Patterson put his faith in Guthrie, and as a result the faith of all who had been convinced of the viability of the venture followed the pair willingly. The committee, according to Guthrie, was 'extremely intelligent, realistic and most surprisingly of all – humble' (qtd in Patterson and Gould 1987: 93). In a letter to Alec Guinness in September 1952 Guthrie writes: 'We (you and I) have in this project a chance to make an exceedingly conspicuous and therefore potentially *useful* gesture in favour of Anglo-Canadian co-operation' (qtd in Patterson and Gould 1987: 94). The committee was not afraid to ask questions, but Guthrie's authority held sway. From the outset Guthrie dismissed the idea of performing in the open air because he felt the 'works of Shakespeare require, if they are to be intelligible, the close and undistracted attention of every member of an audience' (1959, 1987: 284). Guthrie warned the committee that staging Shakespeare was an expensive business and that it 'would be a wild extravagance' (Guthrie 1959, 1987: 284) to build a theatre before an audience had been established. The initial budget the committee had agreed to with Patterson of C$30,000 was raised dramatically to C$150,000 at Guthrie's insistence. The idea of a tent theatre was put forward and the conversation soon turned to Guthrie's experiences with a thrust stage.

It was decided that two plays would give the Festival the best chance of establishing itself without overstretching the budget or the limits of time. The committee also discussed what role would be filled by experts from outside the country. Guthrie recounts:

> Finally, we decided that the project must be demonstrably a Canadian one, carried out not merely by Canadian initiative, and with Canadian finance, but by Canadian actors. But this need not prevent the committee from seeking the assistance of a limited number of people from Britain or elsewhere. Not merely the sale of tickets, but the whole status of the project, would be greatly assisted if we could obtain the services of an actor of the highest quality and international fame. (1959, 1987: 285)

The project, therefore, was predicated on a vision of a Canadian venture with the support of international experts, 'a corps – or core' (2002: 19) as Cushman puts it. This model served the Festival well over the first three years, during which time Guthrie relied on his regular collaborators to achieve a harmony of visual aesthetic. Moiseiwitsch, in particular, was key since she designed, not only the set, props and costumes for each production in the first three years, but the iconic stage itself. Her work at the Abbey Theatre in Dublin (a revolutionary nationalist theatre where she designed over fifty productions in three years) as the resident designer at the Oxford Playhouse (where she designed over 150 productions) and with Guthrie at the Old Vic Theatre formed the cornerstone of the creative project.

Before coming to Canada Guthrie and Moiseiwitsch had worked together at the Shakespeare Memorial Theatre in Stratford-upon-Avon on a production of *Henry VIII* (1949 and 1950) which Dennis Kennedy notes integrated elements of an Elizabethan stage within the proscenium arch: 'On the regular stage a gallery and inner stage were built to one side, surrounded by multilevel acting spaces, a variety of entrances, changeable units, and swirling banners' (1993: 155). This production was so successful that it was mounted a third time at the Old Vic in 1953, in honour of Queen

Elizabeth's coronation, immediately preceding the opening of the Stratford Festival. Elements of the design for *Henry VIII* were soon to appear in Stratford Ontario, including elaborate and detailed costumes that 'accented the reality and vitality of the play's fiction' (Kennedy 1993: 155). Therefore, the new Canadian Festival benefitted from a relationship between a director and designer that was well established and internationally renowned, making it possible for, as Kennedy puts it, the 'most important development in Shakespearean scenography of the modern age' (1993: 152) to take place outside Britain.

Alec Guinness was an internationally recognized film star when he agreed to headline the first season, and he worked closely with Guthrie to choose the plays to be staged. A star vehicle, it was agreed, was needed and *Richard III* seemed an obvious choice. To create a contrast both in terms of tone and subject Guthrie and Guinness wanted a second play that would rely on an ensemble cast. Guthrie writes: 'We also felt that it would make for a better team-feeling between the British and Canadian actors, if one of the two plays were as new to us as to them' (1959, 1987: 286). *All's Well That Ends Well* was chosen as a good option because, while its unfamiliarity would be a hurdle in London, that seemed less of a problem in Stratford, Ontario. By Christmas 1952 Guthrie was ready to start casting. He returned to Canada and interviewed three hundred and seventeen people in five days, moving from Montreal to Ottawa and finally to Toronto. While acting talent was available, what Canada lacked was sufficient support backstage to create the elaborate costumes, props and sets designed by Moiseiwitsch. Cecil Clarke, the production manager at the Old Vic at the time, was engaged to join the Festival as Guthrie's assistant (Figure 2) and Clarke brought with him two other experienced professionals, Ray Diffen, a theatrical cutter, and Jacqueline Cundall, a prop maker. It was Clarke's task to create a workshop for the theatre, and with Cundall and Diffen, he quickly trained local cutters and sewers to generate the Festival's elegant onstage attire.

FIGURE 2 *Tom Patterson walking before Tyrone Guthrie and Cecil Clarke as they disembark from a train. Photograph by Peter Smith. Courtesy of the Stratford Festival.*

Guthrie's account of the artistic development of the first season is peppered with intriguing detail, but he breezes over the two major crises of finances which could well have derailed the whole project. Accounts by Patterson and Gould (1987), and Reid and Morrison (1994), make it clear just how precarious things became in the run-up to the opening of the Festival. A great deal more money was needed than had been budgeted (nearly C$50,000 more) but the local community came to the rescue of the enterprise, both in terms of financial support and in terms of a renewed faith that the undertaking was possible. National and international press coverage of the event was engaged in every step of this journey and Patterson's hometown was not going to be seen to fail. Invitations had been sent out, contracts had been issued, not only for Guthrie, Guinness and Moiseiwitsch but also for British actors Douglas Campbell, Michael Bates and the star of the West End who was to play opposite Guinness, Irene Worth. The board and the community would not countenance delay or abandonment of the project, both of which were considered in the lead-up to opening night. When the money ran out for the building of the stage and the cost of the enormous tent, it was the people of Stratford who saved the day. *The Times* proclaimed in July of that summer that; 'In all, $70,000 has been raised in the town, including an anonymous gift of $25,000. A further $80,000 has been raised elsewhere in Canada, chiefly in Ontario' (1953: 11). Oliver Gaffney, the local contractor charged with the task of building the stage and the auditorium, agreed to continue working without payment (Figure 3). The tent was being constructed in the United States, and it was feared that it would not arrive on time for the opening, if at all. But once tickets went on sale the response was enormous. The first season had to be extended from four to six weeks of performances. The money to secure the delivery of the tent was soon raised, and the board of directors was able to meet its financial obligations, just in the nick of time. Guthrie had taken Patterson's vision and elevated it to one of seriousness and purpose, linking it to an international movement to improve the cultural lives of ordinary people in a post-war world that was longing for positive models for the future. The people of Stratford made sure that Guthrie's vision became attainable. Opening night was a triumph, or so the story goes.

The mythologizing of its origins began at the same time as the Festival, in large part due to the Academy Award-nominated National Film Board documentary created during the summer of 1953 entitled *The Stratford Adventure*. This short film re-enacts the image of Patterson as the determined founding father and stalwart of the community (he is seen playing with his children by the river Avon, as well as in the meeting where he convinces the Stratford Council to give him funding for a trip to New York). The film recreates Guthrie's

FIGURE 3 *Architect Robert Fairfield (far left) marking construction blueprints at the worksite for the Festival Tent auditorium. At his left stand Cecil Clarke, Tanya Moiseiwitsch and Tyrone Guthrie. Photograph by Peter Smith. Courtesy of the Stratford Festival.*

arrival and his first interaction with the board. The doubts and fears of the locals are depicted, as well as the influence of the free-wheeling actors arriving from Britain (both Alec Guinness and Irene Worth are literally seen with bicycles). The town's idyllic riverside setting, its parklands and its swans all feature to create the vision of what this Festival was to become. The voice of God narrator, who introduces the story, and the image of Guinness as Richard III, which forms the film's finale, all work to make a myth from an event that was still in progress. The publicity of the Festival, the writings of Guthrie and Davies and the national and international press which supported the myth as it came into being, all demonstrate one aspect of the

Stratford story. But the flurry of early critical attention quickly dissipated and in many ways the Festival has been chasing that first moment of international attention, which seemed to raise Canadian Shakespeare to the level of a global star, ever since.

The later accounts by members of the company, actors, directors, designers but also stage managers and local supporters, all work to expand and problematize this initial narrative. In 1994 Barbara Reid, a long-time Festival employee and supporter, and Thelma Morrison, a journalist at the *Stratford Beacon Herald*, published their account of the balance of influence in the founding of the Festival:

> If we compare the beginnings of the Stratford Festival to that of a great feast, Guthrie, Guinness, Worth, Moiseiwitsch, Clarke and others were perhaps the roast beef. But it was the people of Stratford who were the vegetables, the potatoes, the gravy, the brandy, the pie, the china, the crystal, the cutlery, the tablecloth, the napkins, the table, the chairs, the oven . . . Well you get the idea. (1994: 143)

This assessment of the Festival is placed in their volume above a photo of Stratford's 1953 autumn parade, depicting two coronations side by side, Queen Elizabeth II on television and Richard III in the theatre. The Stratford Festival without the people of Stratford would not have come into being. While the Guthrie 'Miracle' myth endures in performance histories written in Britain, in Canada it is the name of Tom Patterson that encapsulates the community spirit which brought about this unlikely venture.

2

Openings, beginnings, origins – Tyrone Guthrie (1953–5)

The Festival's cultural moment

In 1953 the relationship between Canada and Britain was influenced, on the one hand, by the collective memory of joint participation in the Allied Forces and, on the other, by the current experience of a new monarch who highlighted the international importance of the Commonwealth. George VI was associated with the war, while the accession to the throne of Elizabeth II marked the dawn of a new era of optimism. The two productions which opened the Festival spoke directly to this political and cultural moment. Guthrie's choice of a well-known play that reflected Britain's past and a play that was new to North American audiences helped to solidify the Festival's position both as a preserver of tradition and a supporter of innovation for a new generation; attributes which continue to be central to the Festival's identity. Guthrie's direction on the thrust stage, particularly in the case of *All's Well That Ends Well*, also provided evidence for editors and scholars of a practical approach to textual problems. The impact and influence of this new venture had repercussions which far exceeded the imagining of its founder, Patterson, who simply wanted people to visit his hometown.

With the opening of the Festival two of Shakespeare's plays were seen from a new North American perspective. Whittaker writes: 'The first season's *Richard III* provided the most exciting night in the history of Canadian theatre but the second night's *All's Well That Ends Well* topped it, and every other performance at Stratford since, in sheer theatrical magic, in its discovery of breathless beauty in a dark old Shakespearean comedy' (1958: xiv–xv). The work of Guthrie and his British co-collaborators imbued the new Festival with a sense of authority, but these productions had a lot of cultural work to do. The Massey Report spelt out the need for 'permanent institutions which give meaning to our unity and make us conscious of the best in our national life' (Royal Commission 1951: 275); unusually placing cultural institutions on a par with military capabilities in defending the country's sovereignty. The arduous political battle for a National Theatre in London, which Guthrie was deeply involved in, brought with it a contentious political climate that was different, but not entirely removed, from the work going on in Southern Ontario in the 1950s. The choice of *Richard III* was inevitably linked to the real-life transition of power witnessed by millions in the first internationally televised coronation ceremony. As such it was a bit of a gamble opening the Festival with a play that did not reflect well on the House of Windsor. Televising Elizabeth II's investiture was designed to make the Royal Family more approachable, but the broadcast was seen by some as a step too far in popularizing this centuries-old ceremony. Such a break with formal protocol meant that this Queen would be seen in close-up by her people from the very start of her reign.

Similarly, Richard III, as played by Alec Guinness, was an altogether more approachable king than had been represented on stage in London. Factual and fictional monarchs were strongly linked in this moment through Shakespeare's work and the Guthrie and Moiseiwitsch production of *Henry VIII* at the Old Vic in 1953. Representing another English monarch on a Canadian stage, only a month after this production and the televised coronation, gave Guthrie the chance to put forward a different vision of the British royal family. The intimacy of the newly created Festival stage provided the opportunity to comment on the potential danger of granting greater access to Royal ceremony in London. The two opening productions quickly established Guthrie's approach to the space, which kept the actors moving on stage from start to finish; 'both to open their faces to different sections of the house and to prevent one actor from masking another' (Kennedy 1993: 161). Guthrie would stay at the Stratford Festival longer than he intended, three seasons from 1953 to 1955, but in that time, he would establish both the benefits and the pitfalls of the thrust stage he had long envisioned, which would become his legacy on both sides of the ocean.

Richard III

The opening production of *Richard III* was designed to highlight the architecture of the space and its possibilities in terms of audience interaction. This was a performance environment no modern Shakespeare audience had experienced before. Neil Carson notes: 'For the director, the principal problem was controlling the focus in a space without a common perspective. With no background but the unadorned permanent setting (or, for some members of an audience, a sea of opposing faces), it was impossible to create the sense of a circumscribed environment, such as was possible behind a proscenium arch' (2010: 66). The necessities of the space made costume design, movement, sound and spectacle all key elements of the performance. The magnificence of the court was provided 'by elaborate banners, crucifixes, halberds, torches, and especially by sumptuous costumes made to be seen in the round and from a short distance' (Carson 2010: 66). For Kennedy the 'coronation was the climax of the visual experiment, with giant crosses and rich costumes making a grand show, yet on a human scale and in the round' (1993: 160). The pageant master Guthrie created a production that could be linked directly with the ceremony of the real coronation of Queen Elizabeth, although whether the tone was reverential or sardonic depended on the audience member in this small Southern Ontario town, where the two coronations were seen to have almost equal weight.

The excitement, or indifference, felt within a Commonwealth country towards a new monarch could have easily divided critics and audiences, but Guthrie's choice of plays cannily hit opposing notes of caution and optimism. While Robert Shaughnessy makes much of the masculine nature of the ritualistic performance style of *Richard III* as it contrasted the free-flowing dance-like feminine performance style of *All's Well That Ends Well*, I suggest that such a gender divide is a simplification of the performers' presentation and the audiences' response. Carson cites two key examples of how 'the necessity for the actors to play to all parts of the house' manifested itself in a ritualistic way for the female characters in *Richard III*: 'Guthrie had Lady Anne circle the bier of her father-in-law as in a formal ritual. Similarly, the three wronged queens – Margaret, Elizabeth, and the Duchess of York – circled one another, "curling and writhing in an agony of hatred"' (2010: 67). In these two instances it was the women in the play who commanded the stage with their movement and words. The circling ritual, as well as the robes, crown and sceptre used by Richard in his coronation all inevitably brought to mind not just the power of this usurper but the arresting influence of the watching ladies of the court. Whittaker recalls: 'Around the central figure – sly, humorous, full of insinuation, yet audacious and capable of rage – swirled such a production as none of us had ever seen in Canada before' (1958: xiii). In particular, the battle scenes produced a profoundly visceral response. According to Pettigrew and Portman: 'The cast, including a bevy of Stratford choirboys, who made their entrance for the coronation down the aisles and through the audience, seemed overwhelming to playgoers of the day. The build-up to the final battle, as opposing forces moved slowly and ritualistically to the beating of a single drum, was thrilling' (1985a: 1:5). The interactive nature of the performance was both terrifying and exhilarating for audiences unaccustomed to live theatre of epic proportions.

Queen Elizabeth's long robe and the stately formality of her televised coronation were invoked in the mind of the audience through the design of Richard's opulent ermine-trimmed cloak. Moiseiwitsch describes how by 'the time Alec Guinness got to the throne, the whole of the stage was covered in the 40 yards of his red velvet cloak [. . .] The thought behind it was to get to the throne he had killed a lot of people, and this was an ocean of blood that he was carrying as a burden on his shoulders' (*Tanya Moiseiwitsch* 2003: 4) (Figure 4). The appearance on stage of a monarch dragging a blood-soaked cloak of care may not have been obvious to audience members,

FIGURE 4 *Alec Guinness as Richard III with members of the company in* Richard III *(Stratford Festival, 1953). Photograph by Peter Smith. Directed by Tyrone Guthrie. Designed by Tanya Moiseiwitsch. Courtesy of the Stratford Festival.*

but the idea of Royal responsibility for the young Canadians who had served their King and country and returned (or not) to build their own national institutions could not have been far from the surface. Cushman describes the brutal physical nature of the performance which included members of Richard's court being dragged on stage 'having clearly been tortured, and then dropped to their fate through trap-doors' (2002: 20). The ghosts who appeared to Richard before the Battle of Bosworth, emerging from the trapdoors, included the decapitated Buckingham holding his own head. Guthrie and Guinness took the opportunity presented by the opening of the Stratford Festival to put forward this cruel leader as a means of dissipating the anger and despair of the war years, while highlighting the innovative stage which this small Canadian town had facilitated.

A spirit of optimism and unabashed physical prowess was the source of a darkly comedic interpretation of the play which used the stage space and particularly the balcony to great advantage. According to Cushman, 'Alec Guinness as Richard presided gleefully over the bloodshed, literally over it [. . .] allowing the architecture of the Festival stage to declare its crucial importance from the very first moment of the very first show' (2002: 20). The upper level was used throughout the battle scenes with one soldier being memorably thrown off it. At the end of the play Richmond was hoisted onto the upper platform by his soldiers to signal his victory (Pettigrew and Portman 1985a: 1:5). The stars of this show were not just the actors but the stage itself, with its exceptional proximity to the audience. Shaughnessy writes, 'In *Richard III* the King's rising and falling fortunes were exhibited through his fluctuating mastery of the balcony and platform: opening the evening with one leg hooked arrogantly over the balcony, Alec Guinness's Richard ended it sprawled ignominiously across the steps linking the platform to the auditorium, a liminal and ambiguously-defined *platea* space' (2002: 142). This opening production established the Festival style through sound, spectacle and vigorous dramatic action. Taking control of every surface and entrance the stage had to offer, the production created meaning through its spatial relations.

All's Well That Ends Well

Thinking through the implications of the concurrent performances of *All's Well*, in semi-modern dress, the link between Shakespeare's work and the new monarch might be extended. A parallel could be drawn between Helena's struggles and the challenges facing Queen Elizabeth; partly in their mutual desire to modernize the existing male hierarchies but also in the fact that the queen famously set her sights on Prince Philip and would not be dissuaded from her choice, despite censure by other members of her family. As Shaughnessy highlights 'Guthrie's production was an attempt to negotiate the theatrical reputation of *All's Well* within the framework of an abbreviated post-Victorian history of sexuality' (2002: 138). The strong and forthright nature of the young queen might well have been in the minds of audience members not familiar with the story of Helena's fight for a destiny she controls. In Shaughnessy's words the 'abolition of the proscenium arch, and the encirclement of actors by audience, had been conceived in the spirit of egalitarianism and democratic inclusiveness; it now seemed that Guthrie and Moiseiwitsch had created the conditions for a physically literal state of perpetual revolution' (2002: 135). Movement was again the key to the success of this production; Brooks Atkinson calls it 'an elegant ballet which discloses the accomplishments of an excellent acting company' (1953). But while the 'state of perpetual revolution' (2002: 135) Shaughnessy refers to seems to focus on the physical turning of the actors, he also points out that reviews of the production likened it to Wilde, Ibsen and Shaw, all social innovators of the Victorian period. He argues that the late nineteenth-century European setting helped to promote 'the Old World/New World dynamics of the production's situation, in that it suggested a Euro-Canadian axis connecting the past, present and future' (2002: 139). The audience attending this production were engaged in a wider debate about post-war Canadian political engagement and cultural self-determination which involved a reassessment of the relationship with the allegiances of the past.

Guthrie's use of the vomitoria, the tunnels under the auditorium, allowed the actors to populate the stage quickly, producing the choreographic movement on stage he sought in an illusionistic and melodic production. Atkinson writes, 'Guthrie's performance flows without effort across the apron stage up and down the stairs, through the forest of columns and out of the ports in the pit' (1953). Shaughnessy notes the audience's need to learn from the space; '*All's Well* both offered a demonstration of the representational potentialities of the stage space and provided a lesson in how to read them' (2002: 142). He highlights the way that Worth's movement on stage reflected Helena's growing sense of freedom of action; 'Guthrie's production liberated the play which had been closeted and repressed by Victorian prudery, in a dynamic movement from shame and concealment to frankness, openness and visibility' (2002: 137). He goes on to note how the balcony, which in Richard III was a male space of conquest, in this production was 'a space of optimism, transformation and hope' (2002: 143). Shaughnessy describes how Worth's Helena gained access to the physical territory of the stage as her confidence increased (2002: 145) (Figure 5). Walter Kerr suggests that 'Guthrie has transformed a puzzling patchwork into a consistently wry and unbelievably delectable comedy of character' (1953). Like the heroines of Wilde, Ibsen and Shaw, Helena was given the opportunity to challenge the established hierarchies, while making optimal use of the stage space. Guthrie's direction used the physical environment to speak to the issues of age, class and gender at the heart of this difficult play.

Carson recalls how the gentlemen of the court were differentiated by age and allegiance; 'On the one hand, a group of mature counsellors aligned themselves with the King and

FIGURE 5 *Alec Guinness as King of France and Irene Worth as Helena with members of the company in* All's Well That Ends Well *(Stratford Festival, 1953). Photograph by Peter Smith. Directed by Tyrone Guthrie Designed by Tanya Moiseiwitsch. Courtesy of the Stratford Festival.*

Lafew. Opposed to them was a group of young soldiers who befriended Parolles and Bertram' (1974: 60). Shaughnessy points out how the stage space and actors' movement were used to create meaning; 'the men are afforded an athletic mobility which gives them the freedom of the steps between platform and audience; thus the mass entry of the court of the King of France in the second scene brings with it a confident occupation of every level of the performance space by the stratified ranks of male figures' (2002: 144). The female characters did not initially have this freedom, but Helena's struggle for increased social and physical mobility formed a key element of the onstage action. The fact that the implications of age, class and gender roles could be created spatially helped to make this stage revolutionary and this production a revelation.

The hyperbole which surrounds these productions makes their importance in the minds of the cultural elite of the day clear. Robertson Davies writes 'This country now finds itself in the forefront of a development of the theatrical art which has its roots deep in what is best in the classical theatre, and which sweeps aside much of the accumulation of rubbish which has cluttered the theatre' (qtd in Groome 2002: 127). Canada, which had played a strategic role in the Allied Forces, would now provide an example of how a new approach to Shakespearean performance could contribute to a model of post-war harmony. In other words, as Groome puts it, 'the Festival had revolutionized the theatre worldwide' (2002: 127) or so its organizers were keen to believe. She quotes Davies's notion that the Festival stage presented 'the theatre of the future' and 'an artistic bombshell' as well as the idea that this new performance style had come along 'when Canadian theatre is most ready for a break with the dead past and a leap into the future' (qtd in 2002: 127–8) indicating a war-weary nation looking for something new to believe in. The link I make between the ceremonial production style of *Richard III*, the fantasy of thwarted love enacted in *All's Well* and the coronation broadcast of the same summer illustrates the desire of both the cultural creators and commentators to bring the monarchy, high culture and British influence closer to the people of Canada through Shakespeare's plays. Rebirth and regeneration after years of terrible conflict internationally were sought by many. The innovations of the television broadcast and the new theatre were heralded as overwhelmingly successful by their producers.

However, while for some critics the closeness to the actors created a bond of trust, the stage and its intimacy was also seen as a source of some contention, since there were times when the actors and audience were nearly touching. Even Alec Guinness performing Richard found the space unwieldy to work in and, according to Carson, 'missed the physical barrier between actor and audience' (2010: 67). The shift in emphasis from the text to performance was also too much for some. Atkinson in *The New York Times* writes, 'the drama came off second best amid such powerful externals' (qtd in Carson 2010: 69). Even Guthrie himself felt the experiment was not wholly successful: 'In our desire to be intimate, we have overdone it. The stage is a little too small and the people are a little too near. There are times when this makes things a little too embarrassing for the people in the audience and for the actors too' (qtd in Pettigrew and Portman 1985a: 1:81). But the discomfort felt by Guinness in the face of this new intimacy raises questions about the inherent danger of opening up a formerly formal practice to general view. It has taken the classical British stage rather longer to accept the informality that the thrust stage implies. Giving authority over to an audience, as Prospero makes clear, puts the actor in its power.

So, even if the leading actors, the designer and the director of the 1953 productions were intent on imposing their vision of Shakespearean performance on the company and the audiences, the Stratford stage in that first season was not a clean slate on which to write. The cultural moment, the experience and training of the Canadian actors, the bearing and presence of the audience, and the investment physically and financially of members of the Stratford community made this production uniquely Canadian and of its moment culturally. The role of Queen Margaret, and her ritualized curses about past sacrifices in war, made for a presentation of *Richard III* which was not just comedic. King Richard, a man plagued by social, physical and cultural insecurities, could be seen to be a parallel for the Queen's father, in that he also carried the weight of the losses in a brutal war. The exuberance and lightness of *All's Well* showed a vision of the future in which young women might have greater agency. The birth of the Festival at the moment of the crowning of a new Queen was above all a reassessment of Canada's place in the world, looking back in memory of the sacrifices made at home and abroad, and looking forward with optimism for a new beginning as part of a united project to improve the cultural lives of those who had returned from the war, but were changed by it.

Later critical reassessments of the opening season

There is no doubt that Guthrie brought a new kind of professionalism not seen before in the Canadian theatre and Moiseiwitsch's stage and designs raised the bar for local performance. But, according to Makaryk, there was a cost to this approach: *Richard III* 'was greeted with wild enthusiasm and set high standards of acting, directing, and production, but it was also regarded by some as initiating a three-decade tradition of dependency upon "hired hands"' (2002: 24). Knowles expresses this opinion more strongly: 'The founding of Stratford, then, was discursively constructed as the founding of a Shakespearean National Theatre in Canada after the British (imperialist) model, [. . .] Canadians provided the capital and the labor, but the lead roles both onstage and off were played by the British' (2004: 35). As a result of Guthrie's intervention, the longed-for international attention was finally paid to Canadian performance, but this came at the expense, Groome argues, of the development of a truly Canadian theatre: 'the efforts to foster Canadian playwriting would be undermined by the postwar emphasis on Shakespeare and the Massey Report's vehemence concerning the classics, and then eclipsed by the favouring of Shakespeare at the Stratford Festival. The cause would not be revived until the early 1970s' (2002: 117). The two sides of this debate, those who believed in Guthrie and his vision of how to build a national theatre through Shakespeare and those who felt that reliance on Shakespeare demonstrated a cultural inferiority complex, were not given equal weight or attention at the time of the opening of the Stratford Festival. The Massey Report had strong and eloquent supporters who insisted on the training potential for Canadians of working with classical texts. So, it seems in the moment of conception the universalist position won out. But did it? Looking at the productions themselves, it is possible to highlight the way that the Festival represented not simply an imposed vision of the world coming from Britain, but an interaction with a new form of monarchy, made possible through the optimistic and enthusiastic way that Guthrie's ideas about Shakespearean performance were embraced by a new group of actors, many of whom came to the texts as new works. The reaction of the largely Canadian audience, combined with the predominantly Canadian cast, created an event that was very much of its place as well as its time.

Guthrie's legacy: The 1954–5 seasons

The second and third seasons of the Festival did not attract the same level of critical hyperbole, either at the time or later. But they did attract audiences and establish a solid reputation for the Festival, which embedded many of Guthrie's principles as its foundational mandate. The 1954 season involved three plays: *Taming of the Shrew*, *Measure for Measure*, and *Oedipus Rex*, which ran for nine weeks and sixty-nine performances, boasting 97 per cent attendance. While Moiseiwitsch designed all three productions, Guthrie moved forward with his intention to extricate himself slowly by handing the reins for *Measure for Measure*, and nominally for the season as artistic director, to Cecil Clarke. The headline star for this season was British actor and Hollywood star James Mason, who took on the roles of Angelo and King Oedipus. However, disappointed not to be directed by Guthrie in *Measure*, Mason made Clarke's task more difficult and may well have contributed to Clarke's decision to leave the Festival at the end of the season. Cushman notes the sombre nature of the production and the cast's dislike of Clarke's more rigid approach (2002: 25). Nevertheless, Whittaker says 'his *Measure for Measure*, if clouded in motivation, was sharp in its picture of a murky, sinister Vienna' (1958: xvi). Another difficult play was given a new perspective on the thrust stage in the second season.

But the triumph Guthrie achieved with *All's Well* was not repeated with his *Taming*. Kennedy points out that this production contained the 'best and worst of his visual habits'; the play within a play 'was treated as a wild west medicine show at the turn of the century' (1993: 162). With its 'eclectic costumes' and comedy that relied on 'vaudeville pranks and pratfalls' (Kennedy 1993: 162) Guthrie's production was not admired by critics. Cushman suggests that whereas in *All's Well* the plentiful anachronisms were used to make the meaning of the play clearer, in this production they were inserted purely for entertainment value (2002: 24–5). This lack of seriousness in intent caused Robert Speaight to write: 'the production lacked a certain dimension of humanity and depth of humour' (1973: 236). The North American setting allowed Guthrie to show his playful side and his flair for the dramatically absurd, aspects of his personality which would become a calling card in later years, particularly in the productions of Gilbert and Sullivan he directed at the Festival in the early 1960s. However, placing the plays in a North American setting did not guarantee audience empathy. In fact, if done thoughtlessly, in a way that generated no engagement with local issues, the director could be chastised for flippancy and irreverence.

The surprise addition to the season, which demonstrated Guthrie's dedication to a ritualistic theatre, was Sophocles's *Oedipus Rex* but this production suffered from a mismatch between Guthrie's vision and the cast's abilities in execution. Cushman suggests that Mason's cinematic style was not well suited to the epic grandeur of the design (2002: 27). Again, the director relied on spectacle to inspire awe in the audience but the grandeur of the costumes, which included full Greek masks, required a ritualistic style of acting unknown to the actors. Whittaker writes, 'the superb figure of the King conjured up by Miss Moiseiwitsch – a great golden figure, enlarged into heroic size by mask, crown and cothurni – was not filled out by Mr Mason, vocally or in emotional projection' (1958: xvii).

With this criticism begins another refrain that has plagued the Festival, that the spectacular costumes and action have the potential to dwarf the actors' efforts. But significantly this production made critics consider a different aspect of the stage space. As Kennedy points out, the auditorium 'was indebted more to ancient Epidaurus than to any theatre in the sixteenth- or seventeenth-century London' (1993: 158). The grand vision of the first season was not quite matched by the efforts of the second season. However, it did achieve financial success. Attendance at the Festival reached 125,155 and ticket sales raised C$392,000. The annual influx of visitors to Stratford Patterson imagined was firmly established in 1954.

The 1955 season

In 1955 Guthrie took back the leadership role of artistic director but also invited a new director from Britain, Michael Langham, who was again being tested for his ability to take on the top job. Langham was entrusted with *Julius Caesar,* starring Lorne Greene as Brutus, Donald Davis as Mark Antony and a young William Shatner as Lucius. Langham fought against a similar antipathy from the company, however, he was clearly a very good director in the making. This production was an audition of sorts which convinced both Guthrie and the board that he was the right man to take over as the artistic director. But there was a significant difference between working as a visiting director under Guthrie and tackling the role himself. Langham recalls: 'It was still regarded as an adventurous novelty bursting with possibilities for the flowering of untapped Canadian talent – an artistic manifestation at last of national maturity – and both press and public were right behind it' (1968: 6). The young director was not impressed with his cast's abilities; 'the company that year was very uneven in skill and diverse in approach. Much talent existed, but [. . .] it was raw and confused in expression. Some were bent on an introspective American style' (Langham 1968: 6), an interesting observation given the Festival's nationalist claims. Guthrie had filled the enterprise with his enthusiasm and, according to Langham, 'imbued everything with a theatrical panache so stirring that it successfully distracted the senses from perceiving much else' (1968: 6). Langham, like Clarke, had to persuade his cast that Guthrie's approach to Shakespeare was not the only viable one on the thrust stage. Langham's approach, which was more intellectual and textually centred, would take time for the company to appreciate.

Guthrie, who directed *The Merchant of Venice* in 1955, with Frederick Valk brought in to play Shylock, continued to draw remarkable performances from the actors so had the impression of an increasingly confident and competent Canadian ensemble. According to Martin Hunter in this production; 'Antonio was openly in love with Bassanio, an interpretation which at the time was groundbreaking' (2001: 31). The fact that British critic Speaight writes; 'Antonio's affection for Bassanio was given a gratuitously homosexual motivation' (1973: 237) supports the suggestion that Guthrie was willing to make interpretative decisions in Stratford, Ontario, that he might have found more difficult in the UK. The third production of the 1955 season was a revival of Guthrie's *Oedipus Rex* with British actor Douglas Campbell taking on the role of the king, making up for Mason's untrained vocal display the previous year. With another year of training both the costumes and the theatre were adequately filled, demonstrating Guthrie's vision of a ritual performance style in the space.

In addition to the three mainstage productions 1955 was the first year that a Music Festival, under the direction of Louis Applebaum, was added to the programme. The Stratford Music Festival was ambitious, drawing together acclaimed musicians such as Elisabeth Schwarzkopf and Glenn Gould to give concerts and conduct Masterclasses, with members of the main company performing in the first musical drama produced. The programme for 1955 combined Canadian talent (the Hart House Orchestra performing with a range of soloists, and the Festival Chorus conducted by Elmer Iseler) with a production of Stravinsky's *A Soldier's Tale*, directed by Campbell, with Douglas Rain playing the Soldier, William Needles performing the Narrator and the internationally renowned mime artist Marcel Marceau taking on the role of the Devil. The Music Festival productions went on to expand the scope of what was seen in Stratford, as well as the stages that were used for performance. The Avon Theatre, a pre-existing proscenium arch venue in the centre of town, was rented by the Music Festival for the first time. The season of 1955 was in many ways the beginning of a period of expansion and consolidation.

But one key issue plagued the venture: the fact remained that it was a summer Festival, with no work for the actors during the rest of the year. This issue was addressed at the end of 1954 by Patterson and Campbell, who together founded the Canadian Players, a touring company that employed actors from the Stratford Festival (although it was in fact a separate entity). Pettigrew and Portman note how the sixteen actors carried everything they required in a bus, performing all over Canada (1985a: 1:114). The focus of the Festival on developing Canadian talent was hampered by the short season it was able to sustain in Stratford. Being a professional actor at this time was a financially precarious pursuit. Taking on the responsibility of building new audiences, as well as creating work for the actors, the Canadian Players was remarkably adept at developing touring circuits in Canada and the United States. However, the company ran into conflict with the Festival's own touring plans in 1957 and eventually merged with the Crest Theatre in 1966.

By the end of the 1955 season it was clear that audiences enjoyed the Stratford productions because of the way the stage and auditorium engulfed them in dramatic spectacle, music and movement. To a large extent Moiseiwitsch as designer and Applebaum, the Canadian music director, devised many of the elements that won over the Festival audiences so entirely. While Guthrie's intention to hand the levers of power to another director was resisted by the actors, the continuity created by other members of the production team meant that a strong foundation existed to support Langham as he moved into the post. Langham was quick to understand the dynamics of the stage and the actor/audience relationship it established. He embraced both it and his creative collaborators and went on, after a bumpy start, to preside over one of the longest and most successful periods of the Festival's history when he became the artistic director the following year. Guthrie left the Festival a hero, showered with praise and critical acclaim. Langham, Moiseiwitsch and Applebaum stayed on to build on the foundations he left behind, both physically and in the minds and hearts of newly devoted Stratford Festival audiences. In fact, Applebaum's fanfare heralds the beginning of every performance at the Festival Theatre to this day.

3

Establishing a new theatre building and an institutional structure – Michael Langham (1956–67)

Moving the Festival from a bold experiment to an established theatrical institution was the challenge set down for the incoming artistic director. His task was one of moving from adolescent exuberance and optimism to a mature state of stability, where governance of the enterprise required restraint and persistence. Guthrie had hand-picked Langham for the job, yet it was an uphill struggle which battered the younger director's confidence and compromised his health. But ultimately Langham put in place much of the infrastructure which now can be seen as the bedrock of the company by focusing on three key areas. First, he worked with Christopher Plummer, among others, to develop productions which created the Festival's first Canadian stars. Second, he worked with Moiseiwitsch and Robert Fairfield, the architect of the original auditorium space, to create a permanent theatre for the Festival which retained 'Tanya's' stage and the festive feeling of the tent. Third, he worked to develop the careers of Canadian directors, to expand the company's repertoire and to take on the leadership of the Festival after his departure. Langham stayed on longer than he initially intended, but his loyalty to the Festival was rewarded with the success of a wide range of productions he both directed himself and instigated. The inspiration and support he gave to others created a coherent approach to working on the open stage, which has since become a defining characteristic of the Stratford Festival.

Langham was born in England but had a strong association with Scotland, where he grew up. His experiences in the Second World War, as a prisoner of war for five years, demonstrated to him the power of the theatre, when he produced plays for his fellow officers. After the war he directed first in Coventry (1946–8), then at the Birmingham Repertory Theatre (1948–50) and then in Glasgow (1953–4). In 1950 he directed John Gielgud in *Julius Caesar* at Shakespeare Memorial Theatre in Stratford-upon-Avon and in 1951 he made his West End debut. The first three years of the Festival benefitted from a release of pent-up energy to create, and demand to consume, culture in Canada. But the idea of a tradition which could sustain itself was something that Langham had to work with the company and the board to create. As in Guthrie's time, the board of directors and the people of Stratford continued to be intimately involved in supporting the Festival through this period of growth. There was a rising sense of what it was to be Canadian and Langham's bilingual *Henry V* was seen by critics as the first truly Canadian production of Shakespeare. To maintain its place on the international stage the Stratford Festival began touring, both nationally and internationally. The Canadian government was invested in highlighting the work of Canadian artists abroad during this decade to help expand the country's international reputation. The beginning of Langham's tenure coincided with the establishment of the Canada Council and ended with the Centennial celebrations of Canada's founding, a landmark event in terms of establishing cultural enterprises across the country. Langham oversaw not only the move into a permanent building in 1957, but also its redevelopment in 1962 and the acquisition of a second theatre, the proscenium arch Avon Theatre in 1963. The creation of the Chichester Theatre in England in 1962 and the Guthrie Theatre in Minneapolis in 1963 resulted in a miniature touring circuit which highlighted the work instigated in Ontario. In these three theatres, audiences discovered new approaches to Shakespeare's work.

The Music Festival, which began in 1955, was building in strength by combining international stars with local performers, in a way that would create long-term change for Canadian artists. These musicians played in the orchestra for the musical dramas only because they could also work on rarely performed chamber pieces, which were presented in concert throughout the season. The Festival was a training ground for a generation of multi-talented artists who would go on to help the company, and the Canadian cultural environment as a whole, grow and develop. When the Festival bought the Avon stage in 1963 and renovated it for the performance of drama, there had already been several years of experience of creating outstanding musical theatre in the space. For the performers the practice of working in contrasting styles, in more than one performance space, began to influence the performance of Shakespeare. Starting as an apprentice to Guthrie, Langham eventually became the master of the Canadian space he helped to build and the captain of the company that he created, through the careful curation of a programme that challenged the actors to become adaptable and fearless on the open stage.

1956 – A turbulent but triumphant final year under the tent

Guthrie's bombastic directorial style was so different from Langham's quiet intellectual approach that the transition between the two was never going to be easy. Despite the huge success of the productions under the tent, nothing mounted at the Festival was seen outside Stratford until 1956 when suddenly the company toured to Toronto, New York and Edinburgh in one year. The excitement and enthusiasm of the critics and audiences in the first three seasons made invitations to these centres possible but it did not assure success. Drawn away from Southern Ontario, the Festival productions were exposed to new scrutiny. Guthrie's extravagant and spectacular production of Marlowe's *Tamburlaine the Great*, toured to New York after opening in Toronto in early 1956. This hugely ambitious venture, which employed 76 actors to play the 125 speaking parts, stretched the company's abilities both creatively and financially. While it drew a great deal of attention, the production was withdrawn from its run at New York's Winter Garden Theatre after just twenty performances (sixty-eight performances were scheduled), leaving the Company with a deficit of C$51,000, a serious financial blow when there was a campaign under way to establish a permanent theatre building. The financial troubles of the members of the board were exacerbated by the fact that the architect, Fairfield, presented an initial cost estimate that was less than half of what the theatre building would ultimately cost. The exciting artistic decision to bring in musicians of the highest quality to Stratford upset the local musicians' union, and Langham's choice to employ French-Canadian actors for his cast of *Henry V* created another difficult set of contractual negotiations (Pettigrew and Portman 1985a: 1:115–17). The box-office sales for the 1956 season were not as robust as they had been for 1955, and Langham himself was absent in the first part of the year, directing in Stratford-upon-Avon. When the young director did return and began rehearsals for *Henry V* the company found him demanding, even tyrannical, compared with Guthrie. Langham's second production, *The Merry Wives of Windsor*, although not as successful, was cross-cast with *Henry V* providing opportunities for the actors to develop their range.

Henry V, which opened the 1956 season, was immediately embraced by the critics and became a significant triumph, heralding the beginning of a new era for the theatre. Christopher Plummer in the leading role drew considerable attention. Kerr writes in the *New York Herald-Tribune*: 'With his vigorous, varied and unexpectedly moving Henry, he has clearly established himself as the most promising classical actor on the continent today' (1956). In *The New York Times* Atkinson enthusiastically reports: 'He plays Henry magnificently [. . .] this is an intelligent, clean, vibrant versatile performance' (1956). These accolades from international critics helped to establish Plummer and this production as serious contributors to the debate about Shakespearean performance (Figure 6). But for Canadian audiences and critics it was the involvement of the French-

FIGURE 6 *Christopher Plummer as King Henry V, with members of the company, in* Henry V *(Stratford Festival, 1956). Photograph by Herb Nott and Company. Directed by Michael Langham. Designed by Tanya Moiseiwitsch. Courtesy of the Stratford Festival.*

Canadian actors, playing out the national opposition of the two founding languages and cultures, that really made this production stand apart from others which had come before it. Hunter describes how the 'ailing, wild-eyed king of France, Gratien Gélinas, was backed up by the acerbic power of Jean Gascon's Constable; the rest of the French court was a band of capering, mercurial young actors from Montreal's Théâtre du Nouveau Monde' (Hunter 2001: 18). The presence of Gratien Gélinas, a leading political playwright in Quebec, as the King of France and Jean Gascon, (one of the founders of Théâtre du Nouveau Monde who would go on to succeed Langham as the Festival's artistic director) as the Constable, gave English Canadian audiences a new sense of what Canadian theatre had to offer. The arrogance of the young king was met with genuine hostility but the resolution of the play looked to a future where compromise between the warring factions was possible. The fact that Langham engaged the French-Canadian actors to perform three Molière farces, in French, at the Avon Theatre as part of the summer season, gave audiences the opportunity to see the other theatrical tradition of the country at work.

For Langham the casting of *Henry V* was obvious, rather than provocative or an act of showmanship: 'It was plain common sense to use French Canadian talent like this, for its involvement could help realize some of the national identity which Stratford was instinctively beginning to seek' (1968: 7). Coming from outside the country Langham saw an opportunity and seized it in a way that a Canadian director, knowing the hurdles involved, may not have done. The result was the first step in establishing Langham as a serious director who had the Festival's best interests at heart: 'the production was a success, an emotional and political hit, eliciting eulogies in the House of Commons, leading articles in the New York press, and allowing Stratford to pay Guthrie the happy compliment of surviving his absence' (Langham 1968: 7). The board, the company and Langham all needed the success of *Henry V* to steer the Festival on to its next phase, a permanent home and a director of considerable skill who could speak to a range of audiences through his intelligent direction of the plays.

Retrospectively, the reception of *Henry V* was not universally positive. Knowles argues that '*Henry V* in 1956 was perhaps the most cynical attempt to exploit the rhetoric of national unity' (2004: 34). He quotes Guthrie's letter to Alec Guinness; 'Canada is busting with money & more importantly, busting with a sort of XXth century nationalism' (qtd in 2004: 34). According to Knowles both Guthrie and Langham felt privately that there was no distinctively Canadian way to produce Shakespeare, yet this *Henry V* when it toured to the Edinburgh Festival was credited with a sort of raw energy and passion that was often lacking in British productions of the history plays. However, Kenneth Tynan saw it as entirely derivative; 'A bold new venture stood revealed as Old Vic writ large: and one looked in vain for something indigenously Canadian' (1956). Touring helped to establish the Festival's work internationally but also brought new scrutiny and pressure to succeed. Groome asserts that through 'the Broadway and Edinburgh tours of the mid-1950s, the Festival was conflated with the nation [...] the Festival's fame was billed as the artistic voice of the country' (2002: 129). But while Langham managed to bring actors from Quebec and take the company to Edinburgh, in Stratford the audience continued to be largely local. In 1956, 85 per cent of the audience came from Ontario, with only 12 per cent travelling from the United States (Pettigrew and Portman 1985a: 1:122). Imaginatively the Festival 'was now declared to be *the* institution at the centre of Canadian cultural life' (Groome 2002: 129) in reality it was still very much an Ontario-focused cultural event at this stage.

The Festival Theatre, a permanent home

The campaign to build the permanent theatre produced a booklet entitled *An Appeal to Pride* which presents the idea that 'Canadians no longer accept undigested the standards of taste set elsewhere. They have placed their own criterion of excellence on the world stage' (qtd in Groome 2002: 129). Again, this ideal was belied by the reality in Stratford. As soon as the company flew to Edinburgh following the closure of the 1956 season, the tent came down for the last time and work began on the permanent building. Despite an extremely tight schedule, the new building, which took its inspiration from the original tent, was ready for the 1957 season. The auditorium space in the new building was augmented by a balcony, much better acoustics and professional lighting equipment. The capacity of the theatre was increased from 1,500 to 2,192 (with 858 seats in the balcony) and the audience sweep around the stage was reduced from 260 to 220 degrees. The aisles and exits were widened and permanent seats were installed, with the furthest seat being just sixty-five feet from the stage. An orchestra chamber was built above and behind the stage to accommodate fifty musicians. The audience access was dramatically improved by the promenade areas around the seating and the large foyer, a terrace was extended out from the balcony. Multiple doors on the ground floor level allowed audiences to leave the hall quickly at the interval, and after the show, to enjoy the gardens outside. Behind and below the stage there was ample space for dressing rooms, workshops and rehearsal and administrative spaces, all with a view of the River Avon. Arnold Edinborough reports: 'From the outside, with its circular scalloped roof fluting into deep folds like some great nun's coif and topped by a jaunty coronet flying two flags, it still retains the carnival atmosphere which the tent had' (1957: 511). However, the rudimentary nature of the tent space was replaced by a purpose-built auditorium.

Langham reflects: 'I think this kind of stage and Shakespeare's writing ask for a degree of honest interplay between actors. [. . .] The extraordinary discovery is that if actors do really play to each other, [a] degree of truth of relations develops [which . . .] does not exclude the audience but brings them even more into the experience of the play' (1982: 418). This young artistic director's optimism worked well to launch the Company internationally but in Canada the shadow cast by Guthrie was a challenge for Langham when it came to building the permanent theatre; the board, as well as the company, were devoted to Guthrie's vision for the space. Langham felt that the new theatre should have fewer seats and they should not circle around the stage to the same degree. But the board, being afraid of not repaying the cost of the theatre, felt the need to add in additional rows. Langham says: 'It was allowed to be too big. I was artistic director when those decisions were being made and Guthrie had just left. If I said things [. . .] that the board didn't like to hear, they'd phone him up and he'd say the opposite [. . .] and so it got bigger and bigger' (1982: 419). Langham was faced with taking on a project that was formed in his predecessor's image, and Guthrie's influence was persistent.

But the new theatre was also caught up in the story of building a national theatre which the campaign, led by board of directors, pursued: 'When Canadians watch the Stratford stage, they see the reflection of their own deepening perception and judgement. It is their own growth . . . the growth of their country . . . which is mirrored in the performances before them' (qtd in Groome 2002: 130). Donations came from across the country and donors were rewarded with snippets from the original tent (46,000 were sent out to supporters). The precedent of significant public funding was also established; C$250,000 was provided to highlight the potential of the newly established Canada Council and C$150,000 was contributed by the Provincial Government. The contractor, as with the original auditorium, agreed to build the new structure at cost, a stipulation put in place by Fairfield. The theatre was a local project that would bring national and international attention and, therefore, the views of the artistic director were perhaps less essential than national pride and balancing the books. The constraints on construction were extreme, with just 276 days to complete the project in a particularly bitter winter (with a stated prerequisite of using local materials and suppliers) but the corner stone was laid on schedule on 26 January 1957, covered by a banner that came from the 1953 production of *Richard III*. The theatre was officially opened by the Premier of Ontario, Leslie Frost, on 30 June and opening night, 1 July 1957, fell on Canada's ninetieth birthday. Before the first performance Robert Christie, wearing his Duke of Buckingham costume from *Richard III,* read out a Prologue written by Guthrie and Langham, which welcomed the gathered dignitaries before 'God Save the Queen' was played. The pageantry of this opening was designed to establish the Festival's 'authoritative cultural voice' as the 'supplier of the nation's cultural respectability' (Groome 2002: 130) despite having a second British director in charge.

Langham's first burst of energetic activity (1957–9)

The first season in the new theatre, which featured *Hamlet* and *Twelfth Night*, was not well received critically, but Langham recognized that the new building would inevitably be the star of the show. Greater praise was given to Francis Hyland as Ophelia than to Plummer in the title role and to Desmond Heeley's Dürer-inspired design (see Chapter 8). Heeley, who had designed Langham's Stratford-upon-Avon production of the play, would go on to become an established part of the Stratford design team, creating a new partnership between a director and designer. Guthrie and Moisewitsch worked together on their last Shakespeare play with *Twelfth Night*, in a melancholic production which did not live up to the expectations of the reviewers. However, despite the lacklustre critical response there was, as Langham puts it, a 'joyful orchestration of the cash registers that summer' (1968: 7) due to curiosity about the building and investment in the idea of making the Festival permanent.

The Shakespeare performances were accompanied by music concerts by Billie Holliday, Count Basie and Duke Ellington. The first international film Festival was launched, and the well-loved parody *My Fur Lady* came from McMaster University to occupy the Avon Theatre. Langham expanded his responsibilities by becoming the general manager that year, adding to the strain he already felt. The board, the company and the country were all impatient to have a venture that would continue Stratford's early success, but Langham was keenly aware that an infrastructure was needed to allow this to happen: 'We needed the opportunity to make the natural mistakes of growing up [. . .] we needed training schemes and, above all, a continuity of work, winter tours, a winter home' (Langham 1968: 7). While all of these things proved more difficult to establish than Langham had imagined, his vision for the Company was to prove instrumental in the years to come.

In 1957–8 the Festival moved forward with his ambitious plans and set up a winter tour of two plays, creating conflict with the Canadian Players. Without established audiences Langham's production of *Two Gentlemen of Verona* and Don Harron's Canadian setting of *The Broken Jug* by von Kleist lost money on tour and took up the time and energy of the company. The 1958 season demonstrated Langham's commitment to an apprenticeship model, with George McCowan co-directing *Henry IV Part 1* with him and Moiseiwitsch co-designing with Marie Day. Unfortunately both this production and Douglas Campbell's *The Winter's Tale* were widely criticized. So, it was Langham's solo direction of *Much Ado About Nothing*, with Plummer as Benedick, that saved the season and established this director's command of the stage. Berners Jackson proclaims: 'It was with this *Much Ado* that the Stratford audience saw for the first time that sharp etching and delineation of a play by an acute intelligence that gives a Langham-directed comedy the sparkle and vitality of crystal' (1968: 13). The first school performances, for students from Ontario and Michigan, were held in the Festival Theatre at the end of the 1958 season, another Langham initiative. All of this activity generated higher audience figures but the overall profits were down by the end of the season. Langham started to suffer from a growing sense that the Festival had not lived up to Guthrie's commitments. Members of the company made their disquiet about the fact that the artistic director, two of the designers and the head of the properties department were still not Canadian. The story was picked up by the press and escalated into a national issue. Langham recalls: 'In heavy print it was said that the Stratford productions were not Canadian so much as an extension of British colonialism. And much abuse followed' (1968: 8). While it took him several years in the job to be recognized as the talented director he was, when recognition of his command of the space did come, it was at the cost of his health. At the end of 1958 Langham became very ill and was forced to take the 1959 season to recover.

The season without him was artistically disastrous. Peter Wood, the young British director of *As You Like It*, received scathing reviews; although costumes designed by Heeley were singled out for praise. The first all-Canadian production of *Othello* fared no better. Gascon and McCowan directed, Robert Prévost came from Montreal to design and the show starred Campbell, Rain, Hyland and newcomer to Stratford Kate Reid. Attendance was the worst ever for the season. Even a Royal visit by Queen Elizabeth and Prince Philip for the 2 July production of *As You Like It* did little to increase the show's popularity. The Canada Council sponsored a train to bring students from across the country to the seven school performances, fulfilling another of Langham's aims. But it was not until August of 1959, when Langham presented the board with a report on his experiences and his full plan for the company, that a future direction became apparent. He wanted to expand the Festival to include three plays and felt strongly that the third play should be non-Shakespearean, either another classical text or a Canadian play. He suggested that a core of eight actors be retained to provide some continuity and that the apprenticeship approach he had introduced should be extended to the wardrobe and properties departments. Finally, Langham formalized his desire to provide the heads of all of the departments with long-term contracts and stressed the need for school performances and tours to universities to develop new audiences. After seven seasons, a plan to stabilize the ship and set it on a new and more stable course had been drawn up.

Renewed energy and direction (1960–2)

Langham, looking back at this time, describes his sense of transformation after his illness: 'I returned to Canada with a new assurance' (1968: 10). With time to reflect Langham realized that he had been working against the Festival stage. 'I was still wrestling with the stage in much the same way the acting company was still wrestling with the Shakespearean text, almost as if it were a foe' (1968: 7). The 1960 season followed through on Langham's plan to introduce a third play but on this occasion, it was another Shakespeare. Douglas Seale was brought in to direct *King John*, Campbell took on *A Midsummer Night's Dream* but it was once again Langham's *Romeo and Juliet* that received capacity audiences and rave reviews. According to Pettigrew and Portman, 'after this *Romeo and Juliet* there was no longer any question but that Langham was their leader, and [the company] now transferred to him the kind of allegiance, even reverence, that had been Guthrie's' (1985a: 1:146). However, it was also in 1960 that Guthrie returned to the Festival for the first time to direct *H.M.S. Pinafore* resulting in sold-out performances at the Avon Theatre. This production, which starred members of the Festival's acting company (Eric House and Campbell) and was designed by Brian Jackson, was later televised and taken by Guthrie on tour to New York, Montreal, Panama City and then on to England. This season was the Festival's best yet in terms of ticket sales and attendance by audiences from the United States rose to 23 per cent for the first time (equal to those attending from Toronto) (Pettigrew and Portman

1985a: 1:150). A competition for new Canadian work was introduced, which resulted in studio performances of two plays. While the repertoire did not shift very much on the mainstage in this year, the future intention was signaled by the fact that it was the first year that 'Shakespearean' was dropped from the title, and it became simply the Stratford Festival.

At the season's end Langham set off to direct once more at Stratford-upon-Avon and the Old Vic, but not before announcing the 1961 season, which was to be extended by two weeks, including an extra week of school performances. When he returned in April to start directing *Coriolanus* and *Love's Labours Lost* he brought with him Paul Scofield and his wife Joy Parker, who would take on the role of visiting stars but also role models and inspiration for the Canadian company. Scofield excelled as *Coriolanus* and the company rallied around him and Langham in Moiseiwitsch's Napoleonic design. Cushman suggests that Scofield's 'charm, charisma, ringing heroic delivery and sense of unyielding mission' made him ideally suited to the role (2002: 48). The Australian actress Zoe Caldwell was cast as Rosaline in *Love's Labour's Lost* in what was to become a success of mythic proportions: 'Langham gave it one of his best productions, and its democratic spread of responsibility (sixteen major roles and not a star in any of them) occasioned the best demonstration yet of the company's strength' (Cushman 2002: 46). Moiseiwitsch's designs transported the action, with the help of John Cook's music, into a delicately balanced social dance, punctuated by a dark centre which was represented by Scofield's spidery Don Armado. The third play on the Festival stage this year, *Henry VIII*, was directed by McCowan and designed as an opulent pageant by Jackson, with Campbell in the leading role. At the Avon Theatre the first Canadian play was staged, Donald Lamont Jack's *The Canvas Barricado*, directed by McCowan, and Guthrie's second lavish musical, *The Pirates of Penzance*, played to capacity crowds. Even though audiences resolutely stayed away from the Canadian play, because of the success of

Guthrie's production, the Music Festival made a profit for the first time.

In 1962 it was time for the Festival stage and auditorium to be redesigned to incorporate everything that had been learnt about the space. Langham had strong feelings about how he wanted the stage to work; 'The two side stairway entrances proved ineffectual for strong or dignified entrances. They seemed to have a "backstairs" aura, and tended to propel characters down a narrow flight of stairs right into a pillar' (Stratford Festival 1962). As a result, the side entrances were moved further apart and aligned with the vomitoria to create a flow of action across the diagonal that Langham found so important: 'Shakespeare's plays frequently require a clash of opposing forces or characters, a situation effectively exploited on the stage if there is a direct diagonal from opposing corners leading to the inevitable conflict in the centre' (Stratford Festival 1962). Langham worked with Moiseiwitsch, Fairfield and designer Brian Jackson to redesign the stage: we 'widened [the central] entrance, to lessen the number of pillars (as well as to change their size), raised the balcony, and placed the whole of this area on an isolated island or rostrum' (Stratford Festival 1962). By creating another level to the stage, the area underneath the balcony became a space for private or intimate action. The interaction between the stage, text, actors, directors and designers at the Festival was always being tested, and these adjustments to the theatre reflected the spirit of experimentation established (Figure 7).

Unfortunately, the new stage was unveiled in a disastrous production of *Macbeth* which opened the 1962 season, with Plummer in the lead. Sydney Johnson suggests the relationship between Macbeth and Lady Macbeth was more maternal than sexual; Plummer had 'the indetermination of a youthful Hamlet – and one really mad – being firmly pushed into the path of murder by a domineering matriarch of granite character' (1962a). Englishman Peter Coe had been engaged to not only direct this production, but the hope was that he would prove a worthy successor to Langham by the end of the season.

FIGURE 7 *Festival Theatre Stage, 1962. Photograph by Peter Smith. Courtesy of the Stratford Festival.*

However, four days after *Macbeth* opened, Langham agreed to return to head the Festival the following year. McCowan's production of *The Tempest* was also not well received (see Chapter 9). Once again, it was up to Langham to save the season, which he did with popular productions of *Taming of the Shrew* and *Cyrano de Bergerac*. His *Shrew* was the first play to be repeated at the Festival and it placed Langham's direction in direct comparison to Guthrie's earlier show. According to Pettigrew and Portman 'Langham directed his *Shrew* as a comedy, not a farce, with [John] Colicos's Petrucio and Kate Reid's Shrew establishing a relationship of a quality not unlike that between Benedick and Beatrice' (1985a: 1:163). The audience were firm supporters of the artistic director by this point and his production of *Cyrano*, which starred Plummer, sold out. The Gilbert and Sullivan tradition carried on at the

Avon Theatre with *The Gondoliers* but Guthrie was replaced by Leon Major as the director. Langham's desire for a tour to eleven universities was fulfilled in this year but with a sampling of Shakespeare's speeches rather than a full production.

Langham's renewed commitment (1963–5)

Langham's intention to leave the Festival on a high note after the success of the 1960–2 seasons was thwarted by the disagreement over finding someone to replace him. He was convinced by the board to stay on for a further period but was wary of repeating himself: 'I eventually persuaded myself to regard this matter not as one of staying, but as one of coming to a completely new job' (Langham 1968: 11). His desire was to transform the Festival by creating more politically aware theatre, moving away from pure entertainment: 'I had two main intentions during this phase; first, to achieve an operating continuity, involving the performance of contemporary plays, winter tours and eventually a winter home in Montreal. Second, and more important, to try to relate our work on the stage more vividly to the world around us' (1968: 11). The pull between the expensively produced musicals, which reliably drew in large appreciative audiences, and politically aware productions of Shakespeare, which challenged audiences, would be a battle faced by each subsequent artistic director.

One of the first actions of this new phase of the Festival was the purchase of the Avon Theatre, but it required huge renovations which could not be undertaken for another year. *The Mikado* was staged there in the summer of 1963, directed by Norman Campbell, and building work began in January 1964. The Festival Theatre in 1963 was true to Langham's intention to make the audience think as well as feel since it saw three of Shakespeare's least known plays performed: *Troilus and Cressida, Comedy of Errors* and *Timon of Athens*. This gamble did not entirely pay off. The season opened with Langham's *Troilus and Cressida*, beautifully designed by Heeley, but audience attendance was the lowest in the history of the Festival. Reviews faulted the play rather than the production, but this did not help the box-office returns. The hit of the season was Gascon's *Comedy of Errors*, which was performed with costumes by Prévost and Mark Negin, suggesting performers of the Commedia dell'arte. Performed as farce, it was condemned by critics but adored by audiences. *Timon of Athens* was meant to be directed by Peter Coe, but he withdrew a week before rehearsals began, and Langham was forced to take on the production himself. This modern-dress production, with music by Duke Ellington, divided critics with its pre-revolutionary Cuban setting and seemingly incongruous use of air-raid sirens and barbed wire, juxtaposed by couture-fuelled decadence (Hunter 2001: 175–6). Langham's production of *Cyrano* was repeated in this season, with Colicos in the lead, providing a saleable, if somewhat predictable, final piece in a season which included no imported stars for the first time.

In 1964 the company was invited to tour its productions to the Chichester Theatre for the 400th anniversary of Shakespeare's birth. The stage of the British theatre was inspired by the Festival Theatre in Ontario but had been produced on a much smaller scale and with a fraction of the budget. Advice had been provided by the Stratford Festival, and wood was donated for the stage, but there was no balcony for the audience, or onstage, and the stage itself was much wider than in Stratford. On his arrival in Chichester Langham adjusted the stage to accommodate his remounted productions of *Love's Labour's Lost* and *Timon of Athens*. A newly staged version of Molière's *Le Bourgeois Gentilhomme*, directed by Gascon, was the final production of this three-week residency. Sybil Thorndike led 400 actors from London to see the dress rehearsal of *Love's Labour's Lost*, the first Shakespeare play to be performed on the Chichester stage. Ronald Bryden in the *New Statesman* records: 'The production is conceived in height as well as breadth, designed to tumble fluidly from back to forestage, shooting the whole play forward into the audience like the sculpted frieze on a clipper's prow. [. . .] their integration is flawless, and they play their instrument like a Stradivarius' (1964). In this account Bryden sums up the key aspects of Langham's approach: the fluid movement of the actors, their work as an ensemble and their mastery of the space. The positive reception that the company received finally secured the Festival's international reputation, although it also helped to spread the idea that the Festival was most noted for movement and spectacle. George Seddon writes in *The Observer*, 'Three pretty second-rate plays were given a great boost by being turned into lavish, free-flowing cultural spectacles' (1964). But Hunter suggests that Langham's *Timon* surprised the British critics, with its modern setting and radical interpretation (2001: 177). While the attendance of the Queen Mother and London reviews gave the Festival a decided boost, the financial burden of the tour, combined with the fact that the Avon Theatre renovations proved more extensive and expensive than anticipated, meant that the main season of 1964 again began with a sense of depletion.

Langham decided to celebrate the 400th anniversary in Stratford by staging all eight history plays at the Festival between 1964 and 1967, giving Canadian audiences their first opportunity to witness them performed live in chronological order. The season opened with *Richard II*, starring William Hutt in the lead, directed by Stuart Burge in a production that featured stillness, in contrast to the fluid movement on stage of the company's Chichester residence. Hutt's King Richard was entirely unsympathetic, and Leo Ciceri presented a Bolingbroke who was at sea in the changing political events around him. While opening night was not well received (the play lasted over four hours), as the season progressed this production provided a stable base on which to build the rest of the history sequence. Tackling all eight plays over four seasons was designed to enable Langham to accomplish his aim of developing a company of actors, directors and designers who could carry on following his departure. But it was Langham's own production of *King Lear*, starring Colicos, that was the triumph of the season. It was his first attempt at staging one of Shakespeare's great tragedies on the Festival stage and it succeeded admirably, providing sold-out performances. The season also featured two non-Shakespearean plays on the Festival stage: Gascon's *Bourgeois Gentilhomme* and *The Country Wife*. At the Avon Theatre the final Gilbert and Sullivan production (until the 1980s), *The Yeoman of the Guard*, directed by William Ball, and Gascon's *The Marriage of Figaro* both received a sympathetic response. This season took a step towards Langham's aim to broaden the repertoire, but audiences proved resistant to too much change and largely stayed away from the non-Shakespearean drama.

The work involved in the celebration year took its toll, and in 1965 Langham took a sabbatical, handing the reigns to Douglas Campbell, who had been working with Guthrie at the Minneapolis Theatre since it opened in 1963. The American Guthrie Theatre was larger than Chichester but smaller than Stratford. It featured an asymmetrical stage and auditorium, which were once again the work of Guthrie and Moiseiwitsch. As at Chichester, there was no balcony on stage or in the auditorium, and the audience arc surrounding the stage was 200-degrees, more manageable than Stratford's 220-degree sweep. When Campbell arrived in Stratford the programme was largely already fixed, since the key Shakespeare productions were to be the two parts of *Henry IV*. Burge returned to direct both plays, the second of which was titled *Falstaff*, to attract audiences. The continuity of casting paid off, with Ciceri playing King Henry IV, following on from *Richard II* the previous year, and Douglas Rain playing Hal again after the 1958 production of the play. However, Tony van Bridge as Falstaff was singled out by many reviewers as the key to the productions' success. Jackson claims van Bridge delivered 'a performance of superb versatility that comes from a part that has been conceived as a complete unity' (qtd in Pettigrew and Portman 1985a: 1:182–3). The company was finally becoming the ensemble that Langham had been working towards, and audiences and local critics were entirely invested in the development project, growing in their understanding of Shakespeare's work with each season.

In 1965 the first Chekhov play was attempted on the Festival stage. John Hirsch, from the Manitoba Theatre Centre, came to direct a version of *The Cherry Orchard*, (translated by Guthrie and Leonid Kipnis), with considerable success. With designs by Jackson the stage was able to convey the feelings of isolation and confinement that are so essential to the play. According to Pettigrew and Portman; '[Hirsch] proved, as Guthrie was doing at Minneapolis and Olivier had done with *Uncle Vanya* at Chichester, that the proper Chekhovian intimacy could, in fact, be captured on the thrust stage' (1985a: 1:183). The artistic interaction of these three theatres seemed to work to increase the impact and influence of them all. However, each theatre was only as successful as its weakest play, and in this season it turned out to be Campbell's *Julius Caesar*, which did not stand up to comparisons with Langham's earlier version. But critical and audience reception often differ, and the play remained popular with audiences. The revival of Gascon's *The Marriage of Figaro* and the North American première of Brecht and Weill's *Rise and Fall of the City of Mahogonny* were performed in the Avon Theatre in that year, although not quite to full houses. But despite mixed reviews and questions about the choice of plays the 1965 season set new records for both revenue and attendance.

Denouement (1966–7)

When Langham returned to head up the last two seasons of his tenure he was preparing for the Centennial celebrations of the country's founding in 1967, as well as moving forward with his planned development schedule. In anticipation of a national tour Langham chose to tackle *Henry V* for a second time. Ironically, this time it was his earlier production which stood as the watermark he was compared against unfavourably.

Langham points out how the shifting political climate for the play altered his interpretation; in 1956 there 'seemed to be a good future, a hope for the relationship between French and English cultures and the production was a genuine expression of hopefulness' (Langham 1982: 419–20). However, audiences who came expecting a romantic nationalist interpretation of the play were faced in 1966 with a dark vision of the present and future. In this second production the Chorus was interpreted 'not as telling the truth, but as the medium, the ministry of information putting out propaganda that contradicted completely the truth that we were showing on stage' (Langham 1982: 420). This dark Brechtian interpretation came directly out of the productions of the two plays which had preceded it, in which Rain as Hal was calculating and cold. Interestingly, Gascon, now an established director at the Festival, played the King of France. For those who saw it in the context of the history cycle it was considered a triumph, but for those looking for a repetition of the 1956 vision of optimism it was a disappointment. This production was filmed for television broadcast by CTV, creating another new precedent. Hirsch's production of *Henry VI* (the first half of John Barton's *War of the Roses* created for the RSC) was received more generously since it was the North American première of the play and audiences had little to compare it with. Unfortunately, attendance was so low and the cost of the elaborate costumes was so high that plans to perform the second half of Barton's work (*Edward IV*) in the 1967 season were shelved. But this production was not without importance: Martha Henry and Frances Hyland, who had joined the company playing ingenues, here performed the stronger characters of Joan of Arc and Queen Margaret, respectively.

In terms of audience response, the success of the season was English director David William's *Twelfth Night*. This production did not go over budget, did extremely well at the box office and was applauded critically, the three key criteria of the board. Special mention in the reviews was reserved for Henry as Viola and Ciceri's Malvolio. The fact that William became a future artistic director (1990–3) and the show also featured another artistic director in the making, a young Richard Monette as Sebastian, illustrates how important these early productions were in establishing the bedrock for the future of the Festival, as well as the board's priorities. The Avon Theatre in 1966 was host to Gascon's productions of Mozart's *Don Giovanni* and Strindberg's *The Dance of Death*. Gascon also starred in the Strindberg play, opposite Denise Pelletier, with great success. The third production at the Avon, *The Last of the Tsars*, directed by Langham, was his only attempt at mounting a play on this stage. This season of plays, which highlighted European masters, was seen by cultural critics as further proof of Langham's lack of support for Canadian work. The cost of renovations for the Avon Theatre, increased administrative costs, and the redemption of the bonds set up to pay for the Festival Theatre all came due in this season. Disappointing ticket sales for the history plays, combined with a rising sense of Canadian nationalism, which resulted in a great deal of bad press for the Festival (some of it aimed directly at Langham), meant that William's production of *Twelfth Night* and Langham's new production of *The Government Inspecto*r were selected to go on the largest Canadian tour in the Festival's history, rather than his production of *Henry V* as originally planned.

For his last season as artistic director Langham convinced Plummer to return to play the lead in *Antony and Cleopatra*, opposite Zoe Caldwell. This production then went on to represent the Festival at Expo'67 in Montreal, Plummer's hometown, at the end of the summer. To finish the history cycle Hirsh was trusted with the production of *Richard III*, with the British star Alan Bates imported to play the king. Bates also took on Master Ford in the *Merry Wives of Windsor*, which William directed. Once again, the production of *Richard III* suffered by comparison with the opening production, given that Hirsh's version was dark and psychologically real rather than comic. Critics and reviewers found that the final scene, during which Richard threw his sword to Richmond to finish him off, took away any sense of triumph at the end of the play. *Merry Wives* was seen as a passable production but not up to the standard of William's *Twelfth Night*. Langham's production of Gogol's *The Government Inspector* was critically praised but it drew smaller crowds to the Festival Theatre than expected. Meanwhile the Avon Theatre hosted three productions: William's production of *Albert Herring*, Gascon's *Cosi Fan Tutti* and most importantly, Hirsh's production of a new Canadian play by James Reaney, *Colours in the Dark*. These three productions drew only moderate audiences, which meant a deficit for the Festival in this year. This may have been one of the reasons that in September of 1967, a new general manager was appointed. Langham had taken on the responsibilities of this post, but it was clear that the combined role was too much for one person. Artistic and business leadership were divided, and William T. Wylie came from the Manitoba Theatre Centre (MTC) to take up this post.

Antony and Cleopatra was meant to be Langham's last triumph when it ended the summer season and then transferred to Expo'67. While the show was sold out before it opened, it received scathing reviews during its Stratford run, many critics sensing that Plummer had little interest in the part. Langham's production of *The Government Inspector* was chosen as the second play to be presented in Montreal. Both shows did well at the box office there, and the cosmopolitan audience attending Expo'67 responded rather better to his interpretative choices. It was not quite the ending he had hoped for, but his departure marked the end of a strong period of growth for the Festival, moving it towards stability and sustainability. After leaving Stratford Langham took on freelance directing for a period and then became the artistic director of the Guthrie Theatre in 1970, bringing to that company a similar approach to the stage and to the ensemble. Gascon, the first Canadian artistic director, was given the responsibility of taking the Festival forward.

Achieving 'maturity' and stability

4

Canadian expansion and British reinvention – Jean Gascon, John Hirsch and Robin Phillips (1968–80)

The appointment of Jean Gascon as artistic director, with John Hirsch as his associate in the first two years, resulted in a move away from Shakespeare to a more diverse repertoire. Gascon's vision embraced a European approach to classical theatre and culture more generally. He also challenged his audiences with the first performances of some of Shakespeare's lesser-known plays, *Pericles* and *Cymbeline*, which proved to be his best work. But Gascon's reign divided critics, audiences and even the board. The seasons he planned were seen as uneven, unfocused and eventually old-fashioned. So, when the board brought the British director Robin Phillips in as his successor, there was a sense of a new beginning. The beauty and stillness of Phillips's work provided what Kennedy calls a period of 'neo-pictorialism' (1993: 288). But Phillips's leadership soon raised issues of concern for cultural critics who questioned, once again, the dominance of foreign influences. During the increasingly nationalist 1970s the seemingly elitist Festival was pitted against the developing grassroots alternative theatre movements, which aimed to create a native theatre for ordinary Canadians. Phillips and the Festival came under increasing pressure to justify themselves in nationalist terms. This pressure was exacerbated when, at the end of his tenure, the board tried to hire another British director, John Dexter, to take his place, resulting in the most unpleasant period in the Festival's history.

The alternative theatre movement

With Expo '67 the eyes of the world were on Canada for the first time, but this attention fuelled two different forms of nationalism. In English Canada the aim was to develop a cultural identity for the nation. However, in Quebec, the nationalism on the rise related to the province and its desire for independence. The political unrest of the early 1960s, known as the Quiet Revolution, came out of a resurgence of separatist feeling, which manifested itself in two ways. In 1970 the Front de Liberation du Québec (FLQ) employed terrorist action to further the cause of an independent francophone nation. In 1976 the separatist party, the Parti Québécois, won a majority victory in the provincial election, and René Lévesque became Premier of the Province with his policy for 'souverainete-association' and his slogan 'maîtres chez nous'. In theatrical terms when Michel Tremblay wrote *Les Belles Soeurs* in 1968, it broke overnight the restrictive silence which many French Canadians had felt in the theatre. With the production of this play written in *joual*, the street language of Montreal, Quebec had a voice which was unlike any other nation. After generations of hearing and seeing the world through the eyes of strangers, suddenly there was a playwright who reflected life as it was outside the theatre doors. Similarly, Robert Gurik's satirical political allegory *Hamlet, prince du Québec* (1968) (see Chapter 8), which replaced the play's characters with real people in Canadian politics, provided a new approach to Shakespeare's work. Leanore Lieblein writes, 'In Gurik's hands, Shakespeare became not romantic but political, and the production of his play showed not that Quebec artists could do Shakespeare but that they could undo it' (2002: 180). The work of these playwrights was designed to further the ends of a political movement; 'the Québécois voice with which Shakespeare was made to speak represented a vision of a homogeneous Quebec for which national sovereignty was a shared objective' (Lieblein 2002: 181). In Quebec Shakespeare adaptation became part of a well-defined political movement.

The surge of separatist nationalism in Quebec was met with a combination of dismay and distrust by the rest of Canada. Ironically, as soon as the country began a process of self-definition, it came into conflict. In both communities the home-grown theatre that developed in the late 1960s and early 1970s was designed to present an alternative to the highly conventional and conservative mainstream civic theatre, which largely emulated the Festival's methods and success. Between 1965 and 1975 many new companies emerged as part of the *jeune théâtre* movement in Quebec and the alternative theatre in English Canada to produce locally created work, largely funded by government grants aimed at improving employment possibilities for young people. In English Canada, according to Alan Filewod, the alternative theatre movement 'manifested a belief that theatre can be part of the process of cultural change' (1987: 78). So, while both movements wanted to challenge the creation of theatre as high art, Quebec's intellectual, politically coherent approach was contrasted by the more populist and anti-intellectual approach employed by the English Canadian companies, that combined 'intimate realism with a delight in broad gesture', replacing 'the traditional British-trained diction with recognizable Canadian accents' (Filewod 1987: 187). Both traditions were focused on developing a local language for Canadian audiences, however, their approach to the international community reveals a great deal about their ethos and purpose. Robert Wallace argues that the Quebec government used the arts to promote the province, 'to sell Quebec to other countries and, not coincidentally, to consolidate Montreal's image as a major cultural competitor' (1990: 37). Whereas Toronto's not-for-profit theatres tended to tour their work across the country rather than looking to the wider world for recognition. The result, Wallace suggests, was a Toronto theatre scene that was more Canadian but 'much more insular than that of Montreal' (1990: 38–9). So, while in Quebec, as Leiblein points out, theatre artists 'assumed the possibility of a Québécois voice, one that could speak for a language, a culture, and indeed a nation' (2002: 182–3) that was 'worthy even of *le grand Will*' (2002: 182), the English Canadian alternative theatre turned inward to defend itself against seemingly oppressive colonial influences from abroad.

The Gascon/Hirsch years (1968–9)

The appointment of two Canadians as the artistic leaders, one from Quebec and the other from Manitoba, was meant to draw together the strengths of the country's two theatrical traditions. Gascon had the advantage of a classical education in the Jesuit tradition from his childhood in Montreal and the experience of acting with some of the best French actors of his day during his years training and performing in France. When he returned to Montreal in 1951 and co-founded Le Théâtre du Nouveau Monde (TNM), the aim was to do exactly what the Stratford Festival set out to achieve: train a new generation of actors using the models of the classical European theatre. Hunter writes that the TNM 'was vigorous, inventive, boldly experimental but firmly rooted in the traditions of the French classical theatre' (2001: 71–2). Under Gascon's influence the atmosphere at the Festival shifted: 'Where Guthrie and Langham were autocratic and Spartan, Gascon was expansive, generous, and extravagant' (Hunter 2001: 72). But this style contrasted dramatically with that of his associate artistic director. John Hirsch was a Hungarian Jew who was the only member of his family to escape the Second World War. He arrived in Manitoba as a teenager and studied and trained in his adopted home of Winnipeg, where he would help to establish and run the Manitoba Theatre Centre (MTC). Like the man himself, his work was intense, dark and politically motivated. Gascon and Hirsch were not temperamentally compatible, and the result was Hirsch's departure after just two years.

The plan initially was to have a triumvirate at the head of the Festival to spread the workload, with Wylie, the general manager who had also come from the MTC, making the third in the group. In theory Gascon was to report to the board on artistic matters, while Wylie spoke to matters of business. In practice, Wylie was the one who communicated with the board, since Gascon was somewhat disorganized, often making decisions at the last minute. Despite some turbulent moments, Gascon's tenure was significant in two important ways: first, he expanded the repertoire (ballet, puppetry and opera were added to the developing line-up, as well as original Canadian plays); and second, he established the Avon Theatre as a space for serious drama. Coming from Quebec, but trained in France, Gascon had something his predecessors lacked in that he was himself a fine actor with experience of the Festival stage. He worked sympathetically with his fellow company members and under his direction the Festival spread its wings both artistically and physically, touring extensively for the first time. In addition to regular appearances in Ottawa, Montreal, Minneapolis and Chicago the Festival toured to Russia and Europe in 1973 and to Australia the following year. However, Gascon's firm belief in the importance of international influences set him on a collision course with the growing nationalist movements in the country. His lack of engagement with the popular alternative theatres meant that he was seen as part of an older generation which relied on imitative theatrical styles. For an accomplished theatre artist who brought Beckett, Molière and Strindberg to the Festival for the first time, this seems an unfair assessment. However, Gascon's focus on touring and performing European classics meant that he was placed firmly in the 'internationalist' camp which both kinds of nationalists opposed.

In 1968 Gascon entrusted Hirsch with two of the productions on the Festival stage, *A Midsummer Night's Dream* and *The Three Musketeers* in an adaptation by Peter Raby. The Shakespeare play had a pre-season tour to Montreal, Ottawa and Ann Arbor, Michigan, where reviews of its Jan Kott-influenced production did not inspire confidence. By contrast the adaptation of Dumas's work 'filled the Festival stage, and indeed the whole house, with gorgeous swashbuckling excess' (Cushman 2002: 70). The third play on the Festival stage, *Romeo and Juliet* directed by Campbell, starred a French-Canadian Juliet, Louise Marleau and an American Romeo, Christopher Walken, but the play was not cast as a fully bilingual production. While Langham had considered this in 1960 it was not until 1989, when Robert Lepage collaborated with Gordon McCall of the Shakespeare on the Saskatchewan company, that such a production took place (see Carson 2021). Unfortunately, in 1968, the casting meant that Juliet was simply incomprehensible, and critics found Walken too polite. The final production, Gascon's *Tartuffe* starring Hutt in the title role, was the first Molière play to be staged in the main space. Kerr's *New York Times* review was titled simply 'Stratford *Tartuffe* Greater Than Superb' (1968) establishing Gascon and the company's reputation outside the country as interpreters of French classical drama for the first time. Two plays were mounted in the Avon Theatre: Gascon's production of Chekhov's *The Seagull* and Beckett's *Waiting for Godot* directed by Hutt. While Gascon's production was considered overly sombre, Hutt's *Godot* garnered great praise and was sold out. It was an assured beginning indicating the new orientation of the Festival towards European work.

The 1969 season was extended to twenty weeks, with extra weeks of school shows and previews added in May. Before the season opened *The Three Musketeers* was recorded for television by the CBC and Hirsch's *Hamlet* and Gascon's *The Alchemist* toured to the United States and Montreal. While Hirsch's *Hamlet* when it opened in Stratford was nearly sold out, it received unflattering reviews. Kenneth Welsh, the young Canadian actor playing the lead, was seen as full of energy but unprepared for the role (see Chapter 8). Gascon's stab at Ben Jonson's play was seen as too slow and somehow his style of direction did not match the play, but the revival of his production of *Tartuffe* was a great success. The final production at the Festival Theatre, *Measure for Measure*, was staged by the British television director David Giles. Critics were impressed by Hutt's performance as the Duke, but otherwise the reviews were mixed. The Avon Theatre featured a disastrous new music comedy called *The Satyricon*, directed by Hirsch, and Gascon's production of Peter Luke's *Hadrian VII*, starring Hume Cronyn in the title role. While the quality of the season was variable, the schools' performance passed the 500,000 mark for attendance. The Festival had staged these performances at a loss, but students had attended from 4,500 schools in Canada and the United States, meaning that it had been a very wise move in terms of audience development, particularly in the face of the statistic published in a 1969 survey that showed only 4 per cent of Canadians had ever seen a live performance of music, ballet or theatre (Pettigrew and Portman 1985b: 2:11). But Gascon's focus on taking the Festival's work outside the country resulted in the departure of both Hirsh, who wanted a more focused political approach to performance, and Tom Patterson, who felt that the Stratford community and the board were being left behind by this new regime.

Gascon carries on 1970–3

Undeterred and left to run the company on his own in 1970, Gascon expanded the touring schedule. The season's main productions *The Merchant of Venice* and *The School for Scandal* travelled to the University of Illinois in Chicago, then to Montreal and Ottawa. A second tour of Peter Hay's *As You Like It* in 1972 went to schools in the Ottawa area. There were also studio productions at the National Arts

Centre of one-act plays. All of this activity was designed to fulfil Langham's desire for the company to be occupied in the winter months, but it stretched the resources of the Festival and Gascon became increasingly exhausted. To shore up his season Gascon invited back the key designers of earlier periods – Moiseiwitsch, Leslie Hurry, Jackson and Heeley. He also welcomed actors back who had not performed at the Festival for some time, but perhaps most importantly, he invited Langham back to direct *The School for Scandal*. This production won over audiences and critics alike. Unfortunately Gascon's *Merchant* was not as well received by the critics who found it overwrought, ponderous and slow. Peter Gill was invited to come from Britain to stage *Hedda Gabler* on the Festival stage, but the production failed to capture the feelings of claustrophobia in the play. Somewhat surprisingly, Gascon's second Shakespeare play on the Festival stage was a hit, the North American première of *Cymbeline*. The play was given a Stonehenge setting by Moiseiwitsch, in a production that revelled in the play's storytelling elements. The text's mixing of styles led Gascon and Moiseiwitsch to combine costumes from several historical periods, raising some questions from the critics. The Avon stage was used only for drama in this season, with three plays that audiences did not respond well to, leaving the sense that Gascon had lost his way. There was no overlap between the actors or the directors working in the Avon and the Festival Theatres, and with seven directors and seven designers employed in this season, Langham's sense of an ensemble was being eroded. After the summer season *Cymbeline* and *Tartuffe* travelled to the National Arts Centre, but there were rumblings about the cost of these productions and it was clear that this relationship would not last. The Festival published statistics in this year reporting that 72 per cent of its revenue came from box-office sales (19 per cent from government grants and 9 per cent from gifts), a larger percentage than in any European theatre, forcing Gascon to increasingly rely on producing a popular repertoire (Pettigrew and Portman 1985b: 2:21).

In his final three seasons at the Festival Gascon pared back the pre-season tour schedule. In 1971 and 1972, the tour visited only the Guthrie Theatre in Minneapolis and the National Arts Centre in Ottawa. On both occasions the productions mounted were directed by Hutt (*Much Ado About Nothing*, 1971 and *As You Like It*, 1972) and Gascon (John Webster's *The Duchess of Malfi*, 1971 and Musset's *Lorenzaccio, 1972*). These tours gave the company a chance to test the productions before they arrived in Stratford, but attendance and reception were mixed. They were costly both financially and in terms of the energy and resources of the company so that this pre-season work was abandoned after 1972. But this two-year experiment had the benefit of expanding audiences for the work of the company and advancing Gascon's vision of broadening the repertoire to other plays from the period. The main Festival season in 1971 saw the addition of Peter Gill's *Macbeth*, directed as a political allegory, and David William's production of Ben Jonson's *Volpone*, which shifted the action to the nineteenth century. This season very much adhered to Langham's notion that the company could benefit from moving beyond Shakespeare to test the abilities of the actors, and the audiences could benefit from work which engaged with the world outside them. However, at the Avon Theatre in this season Gascon directed two French farces, *An Italian Straw Hat* and Feydeau's *Le Dindon*, produced in English under the title *There's One in Every Marriage*. These productions, and the Feydeau, in particular, received enthusiastic reviews, and sold-out audiences, and a tour to New York City, where it also received rave reviews. But perhaps the most important event in 1971 was the opening of the Third Stage, in what had been the Festival Concert Hall. This new 250-seat theatre was designed to be the company's experimental space for new work, further expanding the activities of the Festival and moving its focus decidedly away from Shakespeare.

In 1972 the two plays directed by Gascon and Hutt were joined on the Festival stage by Michael Bawtree's production of Goldsmith's *She Stoops to Conquor* and David William's production of *King Lear* with Hutt in the lead. Both productions were hugely popular with audiences and critics alike. Whittaker calls Hutt's Lear 'a thundering, good king, ruling over a kingdom of powerful figures' in 'William's scholarly and precise production' (1972). By the end of this season it was clear that Gascon and Hutt shared a relationship that was instinctive and respectful; they were both tremendous actors as well as directors. But while Hutt was happy directing Shakespeare, Gascon's celebrated productions continued to be non-Shakesperean plays. In contrast to the master and pupil relationship that might have described the interaction between Langham and the young Christopher Plummer, or the conflicted relationship between Gascon and Hirsch, the Gascon-Hutt partnership was built on experience of the dynamics of the Festival stage and the artistic tension created when the emotional Gallic temperament of French Canada and the cool calculation of English Canadian technique were combined. This was truly a Canadian coming together of talents, with material that suited both them and their audiences. However, the entirely Canadian season at the Third Stage and the Canadian play at the Avon *La Guerre, Yes Sir!* did not leave a lasting impression. A survey conducted by the Ontario Ministry of Industry and Tourism in 1972 may hold the answer. By this point audiences from the United States had risen to 44 per cent of the total attending, responsible for 56 per cent of all tickets sold (Pettigrew and Portman 1985b: 2:32). The impact of this shift in audience demographics may well explain many of the artistic decisions that followed.

The 1973 season saw the first major international tour for the Festival to Europe and Russia. The production of *King Lear*, starring Hutt, and a new production of *The Taming of the Shrew* directed by Gascon were the two plays featured. Hutt received a nine-minute ovation for his Lear in Leningrad (St Petersburg). When they returned to Stratford for the summer season Gascon's *Shrew* was joined by a revival of *She Stoops to Conquer* and a disastrous production of *Othello* directed by William, who had insisted on casting an Israeli actor in the lead who spoke virtually no English. 'Othello turned out to be more a travesty than a tragedy, evoking more laughter than tears' (Stanton 1973). The unexpected success on the Festival stage was Gascon's production of *Pericles* in which he once again relished the storytelling elements of the play, seeing Gower as the writer, director and designer of the action on stage. 'Gascon's sumptuous production [. . .] reveals the play's theatrical magic, its captivating variety of mood and effect, and its abundant power to both move and entertain an audience' (Jackson 1973). Hutt directed two Russian plays on the Avon stage this season and again the Third Stage focused on Canadian work. But by the end of this season Gascon had already informed the board that 1974 would be his last year in charge.

As a result, the final year of Gascon's reign was his busiest of all. It started with a tour to Australia of Molière's *The Imaginary Invalid*, with Hutt in the lead. This production then opened the season and was joined by a revival of Gascon's *Pericles*, a new production of *Love's Labour's Lost* directed by Michael Bawtree and *King John*, directed by Englishman Peter Dews. In the Avon Theatre, Gascon played it safe by producing just one play, which he directed, Offenbach's *La Vie Parisienne*. Another Canadian season at the Third Stage established it as the home for new operatic work under Bawtree. But the daring Shakespeare programming on the main stage, combined with a teachers' strike, resulted in a drop in attendance at school performances for the first time. Summing up his tenure Hunter writes: 'No other director of the Festival has demonstrated as great a range or as wide a scope or has created a working environment so dominated by an unabashed love of the actor's art' (2001: 75). But Gascon, like Langham before him, was drawn in several directions at once, trying to both ensure the survival of the Festival and continue artistic experimentation. Gascon was much loved by the acting company, but his relationship with local audiences and the alternative theatre community was uneasy. His approach to the repertoire and touring was successful in broadening the work of the company, but this work was evidence for some critics that during this period the Festival was 'entrenching itself as the Canadian home of high culture' (Knowles 2004: 37). The job of the next leader would be to try to reconnect the Festival with the cultural environment that was growing up around it.

The repertory theatres funded by the Canada Council that had been set up across the country leading up to the Centennial celebrations emulated the Stratford Festival's success in attracting audiences and catering to middle-class urban tastes. But, as Knowles points out, 'much of the struggle at the time was between contesting views of nationalism, economics, and cultural production, views that were rooted in questions of class' (2004: 39). Both language traditions focused on creating new work, but in Quebec in the late 1970s a new trend of creative translations of Shakespeare's work also emerged. Michel Garneau coined the term 'tradaptation' (Lieblein 2002: 182) for his work, which, according to Lieblein, 'did not dethrone Shakespeare by explicitly rewriting his plays' but rather 'chose to enthrone Québécois by, ironically, making it the voice of Shakespeare' (2002: 182). His translation of *Macbeth* was designed in opposition to both the English Canadian tradition of Shakespeare and the French translations of his work most often performed in Quebec. 'Garneau's [*Macbeth*] signalled its distance from what Shakespeare in Western culture (institutionalized in Canada in the Stratford Festival) had become by using a language that was specifically not associated with High Culture' (Leiblein 2002: 182). The Festival during the Gascon and Hirsch/Hutt period tried to bring together the strengths of the country's two theatre traditions through training actors to perform in, and audiences to watch, classical theatre, despite the recognition of an increasingly large American audience. However, by the end of the 1970s, the Festival was seen by a new generation of theatre makers as the embodiment of conservative, colonially inspired approaches to theatre in general and to Shakespeare's work specifically. Ironically, the board turned to an Englishman to address this situation.

Robin Phillips (1975–7)

On his arrival the extraordinary challenge that Phillips faced was carrying on the work already taking place while also bringing the Festival into conversation with the increasingly antagonistic alternative theatre movement. Phillips, who began his career as an actor but quickly moved into directing both television and theatre, worked at the Chichester Theatre and then became the artistic director at the Greenwich Theatre. He was invited to visit the Stratford Festival in 1973 and impressed the board's search committee with his astute assessment of the limitations of the current offering, which he found too conventional. While he loved the Festival Theatre space, he was wary of the board's future direction and initially declined the offer to become artistic director. The board surprised and enraged many when it pursued Phillips, passing over both Hirsch and Hutt, because it was felt that the Festival needed a new direction and Phillips was the man for the job. While Hutt was gracious in the face of this decision, Hirsch worked with others to present a manifesto to the board questioning its mandate and approach. Phillips was faced with a barrage of hate mail and bad press and was subjected to a very unsympathetic interview in the inaugural issue of *Canadian Theatre Review* (CTR) in 1974. Unsurprisingly, Phillips found his reception disheartening, but he was convinced by board President John Killer to stay and publish his plans for the Festival. Phillips spent 1974 (Gascon's final season) touring Canada and studying the structures at Stratford. He accepted the call by the other theatres he visited to make the Festival honour its role as Canada's unofficial national theatre, setting up a board of associate directors drawn from across the country.

Phillips's first initiative was to establish a touring Young Company to help connect the Festival to the theatre world around it. He chose two of Shakespeare's earliest plays, *Two Gentlemen of Verona* and *The Comedy of Errors*, to highlight the sense of a new beginning. Phillips wanted to return to first principles and a renewed focus on the text. When these two productions came to Stratford they would form the first Shakespeare productions to feature at the Avon Theatre. Jackson considered the updated *Two Gentleman* 'full of the juice of youth' (1975: 25). *The Comedy of Errors* was given a North American pioneer setting in the late 1800s, in which a Conestoga wagon dominated the stage; 'The wagon was everything and no one thing perhaps a symbol of migration, whether over seas or prairies, and final settlement' (Jackson 1975: 28). The Phillips reign was to be one of expansion and renewal, and he began by making significant changes to all three theatres. The Third Stage was modified to extend the thrust stage and increase the capacity to 300. The Avon Theatre was redecorated, and the stage was extended over the orchestra pit, signifying his desire to re-establish this theatre as a home for drama. The largest changes were reserved for the Festival Theatre, where the stage balcony became retractable and adjustments were made to the entrances and exits. The other key change Phillips made on his arrival was to appoint Daphne Dare as the Head of Design. Dare came from Britain but with a commitment to train young Canadian designers. From the start Phillips was admired by the acting company who were excited by his vision and passion for their future. Understanding the importance of recognizing the existing company Phillips wrote a letter to Hutt asking him to collaborate and giving Hutt the responsibility to open the 1975 season with a production of Shaw's *Saint Joan*. Unfortunately, the production reinforced the notion that the Festival's current acting approach was stuffy and outdated.

Canadian nationalists were not pleased to hear that the first Shakespeare play to be directed as part of this new regime would be by the Royal Shakespeare Company's David Jones. However, Jones's *Twelfth Night* was the hit of the season. Beautifully designed by Susan Benson, this production was to introduce to the Festival audience one of its new stars, Brian Bedford as Malvolio, played as 'an unlovely and unlovable prig of a man with a monumental capacity for self-approval'

(Jackson 1975: 30). Born in Britain Bedford had moved to the United States to make his mark as an actor. He was to startle audiences with his versatility when he next appeared on the Festival stage as Angelo in Phillips's first Stratford production, *Measure for Measure*. This politically relevant production, set in Vienna just before the First World War, 'established the world of Freud and Wittgenstein by costumes indicating repressed sexuality and by dominating realist set pieces' (Kennedy 1993: 289). The production was 'hard, spare and uncompromising' (Pettigrew and Portman 1985b: 2:63). The stillness and quiet that Hutt brought to the character of the Duke won over audiences; 'He played the Duke as Authority, implacable, apparently capricious, frequently impersonal, inscrutable and secret, not obliged to offer answers or explanations, morally self-sufficient' (Jackson 1975: 32) (Figure 8). The production took audiences accustomed to experiencing spectacle and movement by surprise. Urjo Kareda writes in the *Toronto Star*: 'People caught their breath to hear murmured conversations [. . .] The accumulation of tension hovered over the action with electrifying intensity' (qtd in Pettigrew and Portman 1985b: 2:64). Martha Henry as Isabella ended the play with an expression of agony as the stage darkened (Jackson 1975: 32). Phillips encouraged his actors to look within to discover the meaning of the lines in personal terms and filled the stage with realistic detail. As Kennedy points out, this pictorial approach had the impact of 'effectively denying the Elizabethanist condition of the stage' (1993: 289). From the first moment of this production, it became clear that a different atmosphere was in place at the Festival.

At the Avon Theatre, Phillips was to begin several new trends; expanding the repertoire to include modern plays and casting performers in similar roles in classic and modern drama to extend their techniques. Alongside the exuberant Young Company productions in the Avon, Phillips directed Brecht's play, *Trumpets and Drums* in the Festival Theatre. In another first, Arthur Miller's *The Crucible*, directed by John Wood, starred Henry in the role of Mary Proctor, producing resonances

FIGURE 8 *William Hutt as Duke (in disguise) and Martha Henry as Isabella in* Measure for Measure *(Stratford Festival, 1975). Photograph by Robert C. Ragsdale. Directed by Robin Phillips. Designed by Daphne Dare. Lighting design by Gil Wechsler. Courtesy of the Stratford Festival.*

for audiences watching this actress move from Isabella to Mary, two women facing persecution across the centuries. The Third Stage expanded these possibilities with future artistic director Richard Monette taking a key role in *Kennedy's Children*, directed by Bill Glasco, (a member of the Toronto alternative theatre) and playing Algernon in Phillips's production of *The Importance of Being Earnest* which ended the season. This final play gave Hutt the unusual opportunity of switching between the roles of the Duke and Lady Bracknell, with enormous success. The season was a triumph in that it exceeded previous levels of attendance and box-office sales. Phillips was also successful in another way, not only had he brought Glasco in from Toronto to direct, he also convinced Urjo Kareda to leave his job as *Toronto Star* theatre critic to become the first literary manager at the Festival, a shrewd and insightful move.

The 1976 season began with the Young Company taking on two of Shakespeare's most mature plays, *Hamlet* and *The Tempest*. Phillips wanted to test the company and give its rising stars opportunities that would increase their potential. As a result, he cast two quite different actors in the title role of Hamlet. British-born Nicholas Pennell and Canadian Richard Monette alternated the role, with two different actresses playing Gertrude. These actors then played Ariel and Caliban respectively, with Hutt as Prospero, in *The Tempest* (see Chapters 8 and 9). The two productions toured briefly before taking up residence over the summer at the Avon Theatre. The final production on this stage was a revival of *The Importance of Being Earnest* with Hutt reprising his role as Lady Bracknell, this time giving audiences the opportunity to see him alternate between Wilde's great dame and Shakespeare's great magician. On the Festival stage Phillips directed *The Way of the World* and *Antony and Cleopatra*, introducing his next star, Maggie Smith, in both productions. *Antony and Cleopatra* divided opinion; some critics were annoyed by Phillips's decision to see the play as a middle-aged love affair, others were angry at the removal of the onstage balcony, but Smith drew consistently positive responses. In fact, Clive Barnes writes in *The New York Times*: 'Miss Smith's Cleopatra was the best I have ever seen [. . .] It has such immediacy and spirit, there is a kind of wistful grandeur, yet above all a womanliness that most Cleopatras disregard' (1976b). Phillips was making his mark on the Festival and its theatres by moving them away from what audiences had come to expect. But not all of his initiatives worked. The season also boasted the internationally acclaimed acting couple of Hume Cronyn and Jessica Tandy. Cronyn played Shylock in a production of *The Merchant of Venice* directed by Glasco, in this director's first and last production on the Festival stage. The show was not well received by critics, apart from Cronyn's performance, fuelling the contrasting arguments that Canadian directors could not cope with the stage's particular demands and that Glasco had been set up to fail. Visiting actors faced similar problems to directors in terms of integrating with the established company, but Smith made her commitment to the Festival tangible by moving her family to the town and taking on small roles, as well as large ones, including Mistress Overdone in the revival of *Measure for Measure*. Tandy, as the second female star of the season, played both Hippolyta and Titania in Phillips's production of *A Midsummer Night's Dream* (with Cronyn as Bottom) and the title role in *Eve*, the first new Canadian play to garner success on the Avon stage. The season was in many ways a triumph, but Phillips was exhausted by the workload and discouraged by the continued negative response of the Canadian critics.

Phillips was a pragmatic man of the theatre but as a leader was seen by some of the actors as autocratic, secretive and even manipulative. He liked to control every aspect of the Festival's operations so when Bruce Swerdfager resigned his post as general manager, following a heart attack, he was not replaced and Phillips absorbed the role. Phillips invited Hirsch to direct *Three Sisters* which starred Smith, Henry and Marti Maraden, and this production was considered one of the great successes of the season. Gina Mallet writes, 'it overshadowed all that has gone before' (qtd in Pettigrew and Portman 1985b 2:100). Hirsch continued to criticize Phillips both privately in rehearsals and publicly, suggesting that Phillips was directing so many plays because he was given an additional fee for each one. Not only was this not true but it was in order to save the Festival money that Phillips had taken on what was an unsustainable workload. In terms of income the 1976 season was a tremendous success, reporting an increase in revenue of over C$1 million, but costs had also shot up, largely due to inflation. Phillips was cutting costs by directing himself but he also decided at the end of the year to end the music programme and the film festival was cancelled in this year. The great success of Hirsch's *Three Sisters* led some to suggest that this director was not asked to return out of jealousy. Given

Hirsch's public criticism of him it would be natural for Phillips to feel a sense of frustration, but he carried on, inviting Smith and Henry to join him in directing third-year students who arrived from the National Theatre School in September of that year to be trained in the methods of the company.

The following season, which celebrated the Festival's twenty-fifth anniversary in 1977 (at the same time as the Queen's Silver Jubilee), was layered with complexity. The company in this year included eighty-three members, fifty-two of whom were born in Canada, twenty-six of whom were landed immigrants with only three being imported stars and yet still the nationalists grumbled. Kate Reid, a formidable Canadian star, withdrew at the last minute and so British actress Margaret Tyzack was brought in to play three key roles: the Countess in *All's Well That Ends Well*, Queen Margaret in *Richard III* and Mrs Alving in *Ghosts*. Actors Equity (ACTRA) complained until it was pointed out that Tyzack was needed because a Canadian star made herself unavailable. The return to the Festival's original two plays was a conscious effort to create continuity with *All's Well* welcoming back Moiseiwitsch as designer. But critics found David Johns's production to be lugubrious and stilted. By contrast, *Richard III* starring Bedford in the title role, directed by Phillips, was a huge success. It contrasted Guthrie's original production in every way, with the balcony removed Richard entered the black expansive stage alone. This was a bottled spider of a Richard who lacked charisma, yet his interactions with the women of the play were electrifying. Tyzack's curses as Margaret were amplified electronically to increase their menace and resonance. Smith was affecting as the tragic Elizabeth and Henry's Lady Anne was devastating and sexual at the same time. Bedford as Richard was quiet and still, the pageant, when it came for the coronation and the battles, made it clear that these environments were not his natural home. Entirely alone in his struggle this Richard impaled himself at the end of the play. The critical response was resolutely positive comparing the production favourably with Guthrie's. Cushman's review in *The Observer* was particularly effusive: '*Richard III* ranks with the finest Shakespeare I have ever seen. [. . .] Mr Bedford's opening soliloquy is full not of actorish glee, but, as the lines suggest, of corroding resentment. He enters through the audience and, with his hump to us, surveys the set: one man against the world' (1977). This may well have been what Phillips himself felt in this season when a radio recording of this production was prevented by ACTRA due to the presence of 'foreign' stars in the production.

But despite mounting obstacles placed in his way in the name of nationalism Phillips managed a season of well-received Shakespeare productions. While the opening of the Festival misfired somewhat with William's uninspiring *Romeo and Juliet*, starring Monette and Maraden, there were also great successes. *A Midsummer Night's Dream* was revived with Smith taking on the roles originally played by Tandy. Jack Tinker of the *Daily Mail* paid this production the compliment of comparing it favourably with Peter Brook's celebrated RSC version. Tinker also highlighted the importance of the doubling of the roles: 'She [Smith] plays the dual role of Hippolyta and Titania as twin manifestations of the first Elizabeth. [. . .] It sends echoes through the text which linger in the senses' (1977). Smith shone in the other Phillips production which was a hit at the end of the season, *As You Like It*. The production won over audiences and critics alike with its beautiful late eighteenth-century setting, which replaced the balcony on stage with an enormous, gnarled tree. It was a production that would be revived the following year but remain in the imaginations of audience members for many years to come. Unfortunately the other late-opening production, Marigold Charlesworth's *Much Ado About Nothing*, was widely criticized as mannered and old-fashioned; Mallet called it 'embalmed Shakespeare' (1977). Given that Phillips had consciously hired Charlesworth to combat what he saw as male chauvinism in the Canadian theatre, and she was the first Canadian woman to direct on the Festival stage, it was extremely unfortunate that the production was so badly received. Despite her experience directing at the National Arts Centre Charlesworth's show was unsuccessful, largely, according to Pettigrew and Portman, due to conflict with the company (1985b: 2:119).

The twenty-fifth anniversary season ended with Phillips mapping out his vision for the future of the Festival, including his plan to establish a new space which would house experimental theatre, training programmes and film and television broadcast studios:

> A quarter century ago, Stratford, with an act of daring and imagination, created the theatre of the future. But the world changes swiftly, and that future must constantly be redefined: Stage One will be prepared to meet the new future of technology.
>
> At just the time when the feasibility of touring is becoming prohibitively costly, technology is providing more and more advanced means of reaching new audiences: films, TV, video cassettes. We want to link our resources of talent with the potential of the communications media. (Stratford Festival 1977)

The board supported these ideas when a new contract was negotiated with Phillips the year before but no mention was made of the cost of this venture. It would take until the Festival's fiftieth anniversary to establish the Studio Theatre for experimental work on the space behind the Avon, which was originally designated for Stage One. Similarly, the plans to film productions and to create training programmes for theatre makers that Phillips outlined as part of this bold new plan developed much later. At this moment, Phillips's vision exceeded what was financially possible.

The second three years (1978–80)

To try to combat his increasing workload and the problem of attracting visiting directors to the Festival Phillips began to co-direct productions in 1978. This season was incredibly ambitious with six Shakespeare plays being mounted, one-third of the eighteen productions, which ran between June and October that year. Some members of the board were unhappy about the rate of expansion, feeling that they were losing control. They were also concerned when Phillips drew the Festival for the first time into a dispute about how government funding was allocated. The Secretary of State, John Roberts, had announced a C$1.1 million grant to create a company to perform and tour in English and French, based at the National Arts Centre and directed by Gascon. Phillips spoke publicly, and on behalf of Canadian theatre, denouncing the plan. This made nearly everyone uncomfortable but for varying reasons (see Pettigrew and Portman 1985b: 2:128–9). Engaging with national arts funding policy also added to Phillips's workload, stretching him even more thinly.

The 1978 season featured a Restoration *Merry Wives of Windsor* directed by Peter Moss (the Canadian actor-director who had assisted Phillips on *Richard III* in 1977) and a *Macbeth* directed by Phillips that divided critics, although Smith's performance garnered praise: 'Maggie Smith's Lady Macbeth was a study in severity and intensity. Dark haired, dressed all in black, she concentrated with a chilling intensity, on dominating her husband' (Berry 1979: 173). Moss and Phillips also worked together on *A Winter's Tale* set in Tsarist Russia with Bedford starring as Leontes. Berry suggests that the '*New York Times* spoke for many in finding the ending "serene but utterly cold"' (1979: 170) largely because Hermione did not embrace her husband but instead focused her attention on Perdita; 'This was the core reunion, mother with child' (1979: 169). The hit of the season was the revival of Phillips's *As You Like It*, which Portman called a 'production of unforgettable beauty' (1977). But the workload became overwhelming, and Phillips fell ill and returned to England for an operation in the middle of the season. He was forced to hand over the directing of *Private Lives* to his co-director, Keith Batten. Bedford and Smith received rave reviews, but a great deal of critical attention was shifted to the drama taking place offstage.

While he was recovering in England Phillips submitted his resignation to the board. Negotiations to woo him to return began immediately, and eventually he agreed to take a sabbatical from directing in 1979 and finish his tenure in 1980. The final two plays of the 1978 season, *Julius Caesar* directed by John Wood and *Titus Andronicus* directed by Bedford, were lost somewhat in the press excitement focused on the leadership crisis. Hutt was praised as Titus, but the play was unknown to audiences, who largely stayed away. The season also included productions of *Candide, The Devils, Uncle Vanya* (in a new adaptation by John Murrell) and two new works, as well as three Canadian plays at the Third Stage, which was reopened. The 1978 season was perplexing in that it achieved record attendance and box-office revenue but resulted in a loss of C$200,000. The effects of inflation, and Phillips's lack of focus on the finances of the Festival for the first time, started a trend which was to last for the final two years of his tenure.

In 1979 Phillips agreed to oversee the programme and take on a vastly reduced directing load. He remounted *The Importance of Being Earnest* and directed Peter Ustinov in *King Lear*. But when Langham, who had initially agreed to return to open the Festival, became unavailable Phillips and Kareda stepped in to direct *Love's Labour's Lost*. In the end Phillips only took six weeks of rest before returning to Stratford to supervise the season he had curated. A key innovation in the programming in this year was the inclusion of five female directors. Phillips wanted to contribute to the development of new theatrical talent and it seemed to him that women were not being given the opportunity to take on large directing assignments. Moss was employed again to direct *Henry IV Parts 1 and 2* and a new play *Ned and Jack* with Kareda. The Henry plays featured gritty comic characters in Eastcheap and both Lewis Gordon, as Falstaff, and Stephen Russell, as Hotspur, received good reviews. But the houses were only half full, a disaster financially when 75 per cent attendance was regularly budgeted. *Richard II*, directed by Zoe Caldwell at the Avon Theatre, featured three pairs of actors alternating as the King and Bolingbroke in a Japanese-inspired, sterile white production. The concept was instigated by Phillips and Dare but Caldwell adopted it willingly. The critical response was as chilly as the production; John Barber in the *Daily Telegraph* called it 'icebox Shakespeare' (1979). Pamela Hawthorn's *Taming of the Shrew* at the Third Stage was considered workmanlike. Frances Hyland received rather better reviews for her *Othello* staring Alan Scarfe as the Moor and Domini Blythe as Desdemona. But it was Nicholas Pennell as Iago who drew the greatest attention and praise. An adaptation of Lorca's *Yerma* set in Southern Ontario and directed by Pam Brighton was considered a mixed success, which attracted moderate audiences. The season relied on Phillips's final show to recover both audiences and box-office revenue. With Ustinov in the lead *King Lear* sold out before it opened. The mid-Victorian setting struck some critics as too pedestrian, but others enjoyed Ustinov's truly funny Lear. Hutt, as the Fool, also brought a poignant humour to the play. But this success was not enough to counteract what was seen as a lacklustre season. At the end of the summer Phillips was forced to admit that the Festival was in a dire financial position. Inflation had reduced the government funding received from 19 per cent in 1970 to 11 per cent in 1979. Despite not increasing the administrative staff over this period and reusing costumes each season, the Festival was facing a loss of C$ 647,000. Despite a record-breaking box-office return of C$ 4.7 million in 1979, the Festival could not balance its books (Pettigrew and Portman 1985b: 2:169–70).

The 1980 season of sixteen productions looked to have a healthy outward-looking approach. Phillips stressed the need to focus on the Festival's potential for internationalism, and plans were in place to take four productions to London. But two of the season's key Shakespeare productions were revivals, Bedford's *Titus Andronicus* and Phillips's *King Lea*r with Ustinov in the lead. The other Shakespeare offerings this season included two new productions by Phillips, *Twelfth Night* with Bedford again as Malvolio and Hutt as Feste and *Much Ado About Nothing* with Bedford and Smith as Benedick and Beatrice. These reliable hits with international stars were contrasted by the Canadian-led productions of *Henry V* directed by Moss, with Monette and Jack Wetherall alternating in the lead, and a condensed version of *Henry VI Parts 1-3* directed by Pam Brighton, featuring no stars. To complement the Shakespeare offering and test the mettle of the company, the season featured John Gay's *The Beggar's Opera*, Goldoni's *The Servant of Two Masters*, and O'Neill's *Long Day's Journey into Night* at the Avon Theatre. Chekhov's *The Seagull*, was performed on the Festival stage in an adaptation by John Murrell, which reunited the same team that had mounted *Uncle Vanya* in 1978, with Phillips and Kareda directing and starring Smith, Bedford, Roberta Maxwell, Hutt, Wetherall, and Galloway. The final season of Phillips's reign had everything that should have resulted in a resounding success, but nothing on stage could match the looming crisis off stage.

Financial ruin still seemed a real possibility, and the board was slow to take seriously the fact that Phillips was committed to leaving the Festival at the end of the season. The huge success of a production like *Much Ado*, which sold nearly a million dollars in ticket sales, meant that there was disbelief that the Festival could fail. However, the fact that the history plays did not draw audiences, combined with increasing costs due to rampant inflation, meant that the company was in a real crisis. Phillips was drawn into devising possible solutions for the future, including a splitting of the role of artistic director into three, giving the board hope that he could be convinced to stay on in some capacity. The situation was so perilous that the President of the Board, Robert V. Hicks, submitted a document to the Ontario Arts Council in February 1980 entitled 'Challenge For the Eighties – Artistic Achievement or Financial Collapse' in which he spelt out in detail what he saw as the only way forward – further government subsidy. He pointed out that ticket prices had risen by nearly 50 per cent over the 1970s and there was no more room for additional increases (Pettigrew and Portman 1985b: 2:192). The task of both generating sufficient income to carry on and developing a uniquely Canadian theatre became overwhelming for Phillips.

Taking on the role of general manager, as well as artistic director, made him exhausted as well as autocratic. The deficit caused by staging the history plays and the collapse of the London tour of *King Lear* led to a financial and artistic crisis at the end of his tenure.

Phillips's reign was marked by enormous expansion and development, but it was also a time of competing visions of what the Festival should be trying to do. From 1975 to 1977 he was establishing himself and confronting the Canadian nationalists from a position of enthusiasm but with limited knowledge. During this period he expanded the number of productions and lengthened the season, using the Avon Theatre for Shakespeare for the first time. The visiting stars he brought in, Bedford and Smith, spoke to his sense that the company needed to be international. However, he also started the Young Company tour, brought in Canadian directors and reopened the Third Stage to focus on Canadian drama. All this activity meant that the second period from 1978 to 1980 led to increased exhaustion and discouragement. Struggling to address the Festival's mounting costs he took on the direction of more and more plays, but he also instigated co-direction as a key way of developing new directing talent. Despite his efforts to become involved in Canadian arts policy (he joined the Professional Association of Canadian Theatre (PACT)), the Festival continued to be seen as inward-looking and a colonial imposition by some vocal critics. The steady increase of American audience members put pressure on the Festival to produce shows which foregrounded entertainment over developing Canadian work. The reliance of the town of Stratford on the financial success of the Festival also weighed heavily on Phillips's shoulders. However, the seasons that featured Bedford and Smith, surrounded by a solid company of Canadian actors, in sparkling productions that used the thrust stage to create meaning and intimacy established a reputation for the Festival and determined my experience of what Shakespearean performance should look like as a young audience member.

5

A challenging time of change – John Hirsch and John Neville (1981–9)

A difficult transition

The end of the Phillips reign left the company in disarray artistically, financially and some would even say spiritually, in that there was a sense of loss of purpose and direction. The battle to justify a subsidized theatre which was performing the work of non-Canadian writers, featuring non-Canadian artists, would carry on. The fight to keep the Festival on course financially and to tackle the accumulated budget deficit was also ongoing. But perhaps the most challenging task for the two artistic directors who followed Phillips in the 1980s was to try to create a style of performance that was as easily recognizable as those who had gone before. Hutt gives an overview of the styles created by the four artistic directors who had led the Festival up to this point:

> With Tyrone Guthrie, the heartbeat of a production was loud, obvious, robust and healthy; with Langham, rhythmic, predictable and safe; with Gascon, it ran fast – you suspected high blood pressure; with Robin Phillips, the

heartbeat was thunderingly silent: it's the audience's hearts you hear beating. (qtd in Campbell 1982: 320)

The activities of the board in its attempts to replace Phillips have been debated at length (Pettigrew and Portman 1985b: 2:187–227; Knelman 1982), although much of what went on behind closed doors remains uncertain. What is clear is that initially Hirsch was overlooked. An approach was made to John Neville, who had been working in Canada for several years by this point. While Neville visited the Festival to speak with the committee about some sort of collaboration with Phillips, ultimately, given his dislike of large institutional theatres and Phillips's clear desire to move on, he decided not to take the post at this time. The involvement of Hicks, in petitioning the Ontario Arts Council for additional funding, shows that there was serious engagement by the board but opinion was split on whether or not the Festival should be aiming to expand further, to include a Toronto residency in the winter season, as Phillips suggested. Gary Taylor makes the point that 'the mid-1980s represented a decisive turning point, a crisis of decline after two decades of expansion' caused by the need to perform the same plays over and over dulling 'the public's appetite for their trademark product' (1999: 349). The fear in Stratford was that expansion of the Festival would take the emphasis, and the economic power, of the company to the urban centre where actors would be more readily available. Clearly new audiences needed to be reached but the question remained how best to cultivate them.

When the board was unable to appoint a successor Phillips became involved in setting up a two-tiered committee to run the Festival. The first tier was to consist of three co-artistic directors: Brian Bedford, Len Cariou and Martha Henry. The second tier involved five resident directors: Pam Brighton, William Hutt, Urjo Kareda, Peter Moss and Peter Roberts (the Festival's production manager) with both groups taking guidance from Phillips. While in theory this was a nice solution, in practice it was never going to be manageable, and the board never drew up the necessary contracts to make it a reality. As a result, by October of 1980, all but Henry, Brighton, Kareda and Moss had resigned. This 'Gang of Four', as they came to be known, put together a programme for the 1981 season, seemingly with the approval of the board. But the newly appointed English executive director, Peter Stevens, insisted that their plans were not economically viable and suggested that the board approach John Dexter, an internationally renowned English director. The 'Gang of Four' were not told of the decision for ten days, during which time they continued to plan their season. For Canadian Actors' Equity, who had long wished for such a battle, the proposed appointment was an opportunity. In the end the matter was contested all the way to the Houses of Parliament, and Dexter was denied a work permit. The Festival was nearing the opening of the 1981 season without an artistic director or a programme in place. The search committee had to scramble to find a replacement and finally settled on the one person who should have had the job in the first place, Hirsch. All of this activity took place in the context of the first referendum on Quebec's independence. While the result in 1980 was a decisive vote to stay in the country (60 per cent in favour of remaining), the issue gained attention and political credibility, which would grow over the decade, making the country, as well as the Festival, appear increasingly unstable.

John Hirsch (1981–5)

Hirsch had a strong vision for the mission of the Festival and his remit. He believed the Festival should be subsidized by the government to produce great art, which would be an invaluable contribution to the country both culturally and in terms of education. Hirsch wanted to introduce the company, and the Festival audience, to new interpretations of Shakespeare: 'if you are going to run a Shakespeare festival, you have to have a variety of very good directors representing different viewpoints to keep it alive and to present a large enough vision for the place' (1988: 47). During his tenure Hirsch invited several innovative directors to the Festival, remarking that although 'I didn't necessarily agree with all of their approaches, I thought the festival is a place where all those visions should be expressed' (Hirsch 1988: 47). Hirsch felt that the Festival had no business doing new work and should return to the principles set down by Guthrie, training audiences to appreciate the great works of the Western canon. He was prepared to include modern classics in this definition and so moved the Festival towards producing British (Shaw, Rattigan) and American (Williams and Miller) plays from the twentieth century. Similarly, he wanted an acting company that was dedicated to learning the skills of classical acting and was willing to return season after season, working as an ensemble, moving away from Phillips's dependence on stars. 'When you're dealing with a company where there are a number of young people who are straining to learn their craft, it is criminal not to provide them with the best coaches and support system available' (Hirsch 1988: 51). Unfortunately, two of the Festival's most dedicated classical actors left during Hirsch's regime: Hutt and Henry, who were both appalled by the treatment of the 'Gang of Four'. However, other actors, directors and designers were brought back to enrich the ongoing development of new audiences.

Hirsch's vision of the work going on before he arrived perhaps indicates why the board hesitated to appoint him in the first instance: 'A uniformity existed previously in terms of the look of shows, and of their texture, that I thought needed to be mixed with different tastes, different attitudes'; suggesting that previous Shakespeare productions had been 'too tame, too bloodless and too monochrome' (1988: 47). His approach in the rehearsal room was very different from his predecessor's as well; he could be confrontational, challenging actors 'at the first sign of laziness, conventionality or phoniness' (Hunter 2001: 155). However, given how late it was in the season Hirsch agreed to take on the job on the condition that he was not to direct any of the productions in the first year. The programme he put forward for the 1981 season harkened back to his own time as associate artistic director. He engaged Gascon to direct two plays, Molière's *The Misanthrope* on the Festival stage and Dürrenment's *The Visit* on the Avon stage, starring Hutt in his only appearance during the Hirsch regime. Peter Dews, from England (but also from the Gascon days), was engaged to direct *Comedy of Errors* and *The Taming of the Shrew*. Bedford was persuaded to stay on for the season and he starred in *The Misanthrope* and directed a new production of *Coriolanus* with Len Cariou in the title role. Cariou, a Canadian star with some success on Broadway, had been proposed for the first tier of artistic directors but, like Bedford, was passionate about the future of the Festival and stayed on despite the actions of the board. Two eighteenth-century comedies filled out the season, Sheridan's *The Rivals*, also directed by Bedford, and O'Keefe's *Wild Oats*, directed by Derek Goldby. Working with producer Muriel Sherrin, Hirsch increased both ticket prices and actors' salaries. One of the key tasks that faced Hirsch was rebuilding the administrative branch of the organization, which had been eroded by Phillips. He insisted on the appointment of a general manager and a more sophisticated approach to marketing, aiming to make classical drama something that the general public wanted to see. Unfortunately, the season ran over budget and underperformed at the box office. With half the number of productions (eight in 1981 compared with sixteen in 1980) but with the same-sized company, the year ended in a net loss of over C$1 million. The season was not an artistic triumph, but given that he was battling with an institution in disarray, keeping the Festival afloat was Hirsch's key accomplishment in this year.

In his first production as artistic director Hirsch chose to stage *The Tempest* in 1982, working with designer Heeley and Cariou as Prospero. While this production featured some extraordinarily theatrical moments, it was seen as too full of showmanship by critics (see Chapter 9). Hirsch's experience as the sole survivor of a Hungarian Jewish family influenced his outlook and his direction of Shakespeare throughout his tenure. Hirsch's second Shakespeare, *As You Like It* in 1983 reflected his own experience of power with the 'usurper's Palace as a jackbooted HQ' (Cushman 2002: 136). He saw the play as a vision of tyranny, but this bleak vision on stage stood in stark contrast to the expectations of the audience for a comedy. When his *A Midsummer Night's Dream* of 1984 began with the Amazon battle at the beginning of the play, critics questioned the justification for this decision. Nicolas Pennell and Patricia Conolly moved from the roles of Theseus and Hippolyta to Oberon and Titania, (as in Phillips's previous production), but this time the characters became increasingly angry with one another. Heeley's beautiful designs, in a Kott-inspired production, left audiences bemused. Hirsch's childhood as an orphan featured in several of his productions by including a bewildered child on stage, such as the changeling child in his *A Midsummer Night's Dream*. This device was most effectively used in his production of *King Lear* in 1985, when, at the end of the play, a child was left stranded and alone between the advancing armies of France and England (Cushman 2002: 139). While Hirsch was interested in 'the political, the social and above all the humanistic aspects of the pieces' he also insists that: 'my vision was very personal, connected with my own life, my own past, my own experience of history and the world' (1988: 46). Campbell took on the role of Lear with Pennell as the Fool. While Campbell was able to rage against the impressive storm produced on stage, his acting was seen as mannered, and his blustering old king did not win over audience members who fondly remembered Ustinov and Hutt from Phillips's 1979 production.

The work of Hirsch's visiting directors who came to tackle Shakespeare was also considered uneven. Des McAnuff staged a disappointing *Macbeth* in 1983 with Pennell and Maxwell in the leading roles on the Festival stage. Mark Lamos's *The Merchant of Venice* in 1984 was notable for the moment when Monette's Antonio placed a crucifix around the neck of Neville's Shylock, highlighting the work of two actors who would go on to take on the post of artistic director in the future. Dew's last

Stratford production was a *Romeo and Juliet* in 1984, with Colm Feore as Romeo and Seanna McKenna as Juliet. True to Hirsch's aims, both actors had been taken from the ranks of the company and both would go on to become major stars of the Festival in future years. The star-studded partnership of Bedford and Smith, under Phillips, was replaced by homegrown stars in the making, working together with the audience to create something new. Hirsch worked with David Giles to direct *Twelfth Night* in 1985, starring McKenna as Viola and Foere as Orsino. This pair also performed together in David William's *She Stoops to Conquer*, in the same year, creating resonances across these plays.

Perhaps the most outlandish production staged to enliven the work on the thrust stage was by the radical British Shakespearean duo of Michael Bogdanov and Chris Dyer with their leather-clad *Measure for Measure* in 1985, with Scarfe as the Duke and Pennell as Angelo. The production garnered mixed reactions, particularly in response to the half-hour pre-show engagement during which audience members were asked to join Lucio and his friends on stage. The star of *Measure for Measure* was undoubtedly Richard McMillan as Lucio, an actor who had become a Stratford staple in the Gilbert and Sullivan seasons, who was a master of audience interaction. The loyal Festival audience was unnerved by the disruption of the usual audience–actor relationship, but it was this production which first opened my eyes to the possibility of derailing the passivity of Stratford audiences with a political interpretation of the play. My youthful enthusiasm for turning a questioning political gaze on the audience was not shared by many. However, the cross-casting, with Pennell playing the roles of Angelo and Malvolio in the same season, gave the audience the opportunity to see two contrasting Puritan parts (Bedford had taken on these two roles in Phillips's first season in 1975). So again, Hirsch was courting comparison while also dispelling the sense that there was insufficient talent within the company to provide both leadership and new stars.

Hirsch directed other work from the classical canon including *Mary Stuart* in 1982, which allowed for a wonderful coming together of artistic talent; 'How often do you get Ming Cho Lee, Tany Moiseiwitsch and Beverley Emmons working together on a production?' (Hirsch 1988: 48). But when he worked with Moiseiwitsch on a new production of *Tartuffe* in 1983 and 1984 with Bedford in the leading role (taking over from Hutt), the result was a direct and unfavourable comparison with his predecessors. Turning to tested directors, Langham returned to stage *Arms and the Man* in a Heeley-designed production on the Festival stage (which reinstated the stage balcony) and Bedford proved to be a talented director of comedy with Noël Coward's *Blithe Spirit* both in 1982. William directed *Separate Tables* in 1984 featuring Neville in a production that transferred, along with *Blithe Spirit*, to the Royal Alexandra Theatre in Toronto establishing, on a very small scale, the metropolitan base that Phillips had been so keen on. Working in the other direction, bringing young talent from Toronto to the Festival, Guy Sprung directed *Translations* in 1982 at the Third Stage and *Death of a Salesman* in 1983. English director Leon Rubin tackled *Waiting for Godot* in 1984, starring Bedford and Edward Atienza and Ronald Eyre came in to direct *The Government Inspector* in 1985 with a design by Moiseiwitsch. Hirsch established a reputation for sensitively directing the work of Tennessee Williams at the Festival with *Streetcar Named Desire* in 1984, and *The Glass Menagerie* in 1985, the latter starring Scott Wentworth and Susan Coyne, who would both go on to become key actors in the company. Hirsch's 1985 productions of *King Lear* and *Twelfth Night* went on an extensive North American tour, another return to the practices of the Gascon era, and while these productions did not garner outstanding reviews or audience accolades, they were very much part of Hirsch's model for shoring up the future of the company. Hirsch was returning to the Festival's origins but with his own political vision.

The other key initiative that Hirsch developed was the increased use of the Third Stage for experimental work and the re-establishment of the Young Company, which he turned over to Langham's direction in 1983. One of the benefits of this venue was that it was leased rather than owned by the Festival, so the stage had to be dismantled and could be redesigned each year. While Langham's *Much Ado About Nothing* was disappointing, he directed another wonderful *Love's Labour's Lost*, starring Neville, that was so admired it was revived on the Festival stage in 1984 (starring three generations of Campbells, Douglas, Benedict and Torquil). In his second year in charge of the Young Company Langham directed *Henry IV Part 1* in 1984 and Rubin directed *The Two Gentlemen of Verona*, in which senior members of the company acted as mentors. In 1985, Neville took over the Young Company when it had been announced that he would be Hirsch's successor. Neville decided to take a break from Shakespeare for that year and asked William to stage *Antigone* and Edwin Stevenson from Victoria, British Columbia, to direct *The Beaux Strategem*, starring Lucy Peacock, another actor who would become a Stratford star. He reduced the senior members of the main company to just Needles and Conolly, making the focus the training of young actors. Despite all of this activity audience numbers were declining. While from 1953 to 1962 box-office returns averaged 87 per cent, in 1985 this dropped to only 65 per cent. Taylor attributes this to an audience tired of Shakespeare, but the increasing ticket prices also had an impact (1999: 349).

To address this downturn in revenue Hirsch revived Gilbert and Sullivan musicals in the Avon Theatre. In 1981 *H.M.S. Pinafore* was directed by Leon Major with moderate success. But the next year, when Brian Macdonald was brought in to direct *The Mikado*, it was wildly successful and was taken to London, then restaged in Stratford the following two years. In 1983 *The Mikado* was performed alongside *The Gondoliers*, which was replaced in 1984 by *Iolanthe*. The final Gilbert and Sullivan, *The Pirates of Penzance*, was staged by Macdonald in 1985. Susan Benson designed all of these productions with elaborately innovative stage machinery. This combined with beautiful choreography made the shows extremely popular. *The Mikado* toured extensively and went to Broadway, where it was nominated for two Tony Awards, and was later revived at the Festival in 1993.

Overall Hirsch's regime of five years produced a selection of Shakespeare plays, but he avoided scheduling the more difficult and less well-known ones. In terms of actor training, Hirsch was extremely good at spotting new talent and developing Canadian actors' skills and confidence. The Young Company was also very productive in bringing a sense of history and continuity to the Festival in that it brought back Langham and provided a stepping stone for the incoming artistic director Neville. One final initiative established by Hirsch in 1982, which has had a lasting impact, was the establishment of the first writers lecture series, featuring Robertson Davies, Northrop Frye, Hugh McLennan and Arthur Miller. This began a long association between the Festival and great writers which continues today. Summing up his approach, Hirsch says, 'I have always maintained that this Festival, which is Canadian at heart and in spirit, should not neglect an international and cosmopolitan character' (1981: 7). However, as Cushman highlights, his mixed approach had a cost; 'The eras of Guthrie, Langham and Phillips were defined by the shows that they themselves directed. With Hirsch this stopped' (2002: 153). A definitive style of performance had become one of the markers of the Festival's success. However, for me, as an audience member, the availability of experimental political work was a highlight of the Hirsch regime.

John Neville (1986–9)

The consolidation of the repertoire and the company was to continue up to the end of the decade under the British-born artistic director Neville. Although he was seen by some as being similar to the other English directors who preceded him, his background and work up to the point when he joined the

Festival set him apart. Neville was born into a working-class family in North London and gained his early experience in acting through a youth club. He was offered a scholarship to RADA but was called up to the Royal Navy before he could take up his position there. When the war ended, he was a member of the first post-war graduating class. He performed at the Open Air Theatre in Regent's Park and at the Birmingham Repertory Theatre. Neville was a committed socialist and was wary of large institutional theatres. He gained attention as an actor at the Old Vic in the 1950s but soon moved into directing and eventually became the artistic director of the Nottingham Playhouse. He was first invited to direct in Canada in Ottawa in 1971. From there he went on to become the artistic director at the Citadel Theatre in Edmonton and the Neptune Theatre in Halifax. Hirsch and Neville disliked each other personally, however, both wanted to avoid the rancorous transition of Hirsch's early years. While Neville was keen to stage the work of Brecht alongside Shakespeare, Hirsch had left him with a considerable deficit (one of the key reasons for his departure). To balance the books Neville introduced musical theatre on the Festival Stage for the first time. *The Boys from Syracuse* and *Kiss me Kate* replaced the Gilbert and Sullivan musicals and the number of Shakespeare plays increased. Neville invited Phillips back to run the Young Company at the Third Stage establishing what was to become one of the most exciting times at the Festival for young actors. According to Cimolino Neville was 'very much an actor/manager [who] . . . had a sense of building a company and a sense of a communion with the actor' (Ouzounian 2002: 375). As a talented actor himself Neville was able to re-establish some of the loyalty and devotion from the company which had been eroded somewhat during the Hirsch years. He also worked to build connections with the local community, including new education work, to create a sense of place and local involvement which had been neglected by Hirsch.

In his first season Neville was bold in his Shakespeare programming, scheduling the three least commonly performed late romances *Pericles, The Winter's Tale* and *Cymbeline* in 1986. In an effort to involve Canadian directors in the season he hired Richard Ouzounian, who directed a Turkish-inspired *Pericles* starring Geraint Wyn Davies in the lead, with blues singer Renée Rogers as Gower. Jane Wilson argues it was 'a seductive ploy', with Rogers providing 'a dynamic figure with her striking appearance and multi-octave range' (1986). *The Winter's Tale* featured Feore as Leontes and Goldie Semple as Hermione, who presented a passionate pair of lovers under the direction of William in 'an enchanting fairy story' (Pennington 1986). *Cymbeline* marked Phillips's return to the Festival after six years, and he surprised everyone by bringing Henry in as his assistant and setting the play in Britain just before the Second World War. Rather than an otherworldly storybook setting, Daphne Dare's design helped to ground the play in a realistic twentieth-century Britain, with the Romans appearing as Fascists. Eric Donkin's Cymbeline evoked George V, while Robert Crew saw Susan Wright's 'malicious Queen [as] a glorious mixture of Queen Mary and Snow White's wicked stepmother' (1986b). While there were anachronisms caused by this choice of setting, Crew suggests that it gave the production 'a surprising clarity of focus' (1986b) which worked to make the action more accessible for the audience. Portman concludes 'for lovers of true theatricality at its most uninhibited and entertaining, the rewards are many [. . .] it's been a long time since a director has used the famous Festival Theatre stage with such authority' (1986). Cross-casting the three plays also provided illuminating comparisons. Semple played both lost wives, Thaisa and Hermoine, Feore played the Machiavellian Iachimo alongside his jealous Leontes and Susan Wright was formidable both as the Queen and as Paulina. Pennington concludes there was 'good reason to hope that this could be the summer of Stratford's content' (1986).

The Avon Theatre had a separate company in 1986 and featured a spectacular production of *Henry VIII* directed by Brian Rintoul. This production welcomed Hutt back after four seasons to play 'a silkily epicene Cardinal Wolsey, a machiavel in canonical scarlet' with Leon Pownall taking on the role of the King, presenting 'lively masculine force with some burly sexiness to it' (DeVine 1986). The setting provided a luxurious three-dimensional Holbein-inspired picture frame production, where the characters seemed aware of their own vulnerability. Elizabeth Shepherd as Katharine of Aragon was not meek and pious but simmering with fury. This portrayal was enhanced by the fact that she was also cast as Gertrude in Neville's production of *Hamlet* in the same theatre. In this production she was a sympathetic soul caught in an impossible situation. Her son, played by Brent Carver, was overly sensitive, and Peacock, in her first role on the mainstage, was driven to distraction as Ophelia (see Chapter 8). Neville's planning for the Avon Theatre included two companion pieces for the Shakespeare work, Robert Bolt's *A Man for All Seasons* for *Henry VIII* and Tom Stoppard's *Rosencrantz and Guildenstern Are Dead* for *Hamlet*. The latter pairing made more sense and created greater resonances since the entire cast of the two plays was replicated, apart from the roles of Rosencrantz and Guildenstern, which were reversed. John Wood had the actors parody their performances in the Neville production, which they did exuberantly. In the *Henry VIII* and *Man for All Seasons* pairing there were fewer characters in common but those that did overlap resulted in some creative casting. Pownall was the King in both plays, and Michael Fawkes was Thomas Cromwell. But David Gardner took on Cardinal Wolsey, and Hutt moved from Wolsey to play Thomas More in Walter Lerning's production of Bolt's play. 'The result is a sensitive and mesmerizing portrayal of Sir Thomas More in a production notable for its wit and understated eloquence' (Mietkiewicz 1986). The two plays for the Young Company also provided some wonderful parallels, *Macbeth* and Brecht's *The Resistible Rise of Arturo Ui*, with Maurice Godin performing both the Porter and Arturo and Kim Coates playing Macbeth and Roma. Artistically it was a wonderful first season but as Taylor notes; 'In 1986 – the year of the critically acclaimed season of romances – overall box office dropped again, to sixty-two percent' (1999: 349). It was clear that Shakespeare and creative casting would not save the Festival.

In 1987 Neville brought Brecht back to the Festival stage with his production of *Mother Courage* starring Susan Wright. The stage balcony was removed once again to accommodate the cart, which creates the symbolic central image in the play. The action moved forward in time through costume changes to make the ideas more universal in an obvious but useful way. The other plays scheduled for this season all adhered to the theme of war. William's production of *Troilus and Cressida* in the Avon Theatre was given a mixture of twentieth-century war settings, which was designed to support the outrageous boisterous actions of the characters (Thersites had his head shoved down a latrine) but the effect was to drain the characters of any sympathy. In the same theatre Robert Beard directed Stephen MacDonald's play about poets Owen and Sassoon, *Not About Heroes*, which theoretically justified William's approach. The two plays on the Festival stage in this year involved soldiers outside of their battle environment, *Much Ado About Nothing* and *Othello*. Moss directed an Edwardian *Much Ado*, which added some suffragette suffering to Tandy Cronyn's Beatrice and her claims of unfair treatment, and Monette played her moody Benedick. Hutt, as Leonato, delighted his audience singing Barbershop songs with Atienza's Don Pedro. This amiable production was contrasted by Neville's somewhat disastrous *Othello*. African-American actor Howard Rollins played the Moor but was not right for the role. The bright spot was the pairing once again of Feore and Semple as a couple, this time as Iago and Emilia.

Following on from his successful *Cymbeline* Phillips directed four productions in 1987, three of them for the Young Company. His one Festival Theatre production, *The School for Scandal*, was seen as taking liberties with the text, trying to make it a more serious examination of corrupt society than was warranted. So, it was his work at the Third Stage, with a stage built to his exact specifications, that drew all the attention. His *Romeo and Juliet* was set in a North American military college where social rivalries were rife, and the men understandably carried weapons. Albert Shultz was exuberant and rash as Romeo and Susan Coyne was earnest and heartfelt as Juliet. The balcony scene allowed the audience to see the action from her point of view. The second Young Company production, *As You Like It*, was one of only a handful of plays that set the action in Southern Ontario. Nancy Palk took on the role of Rosalind with Nigel Hamer as Orlando, learning from her the lessons of a rural community, cut off from big city conventions. The final play to fit into the overall theme of the season, with its First World War setting, was R.C. Sherriff's *Journey's End* starring Shultz as Stanhope, the young officer trying to quell the fears of his men in the face of battle. The actors all spoke with their own accents, transporting the play to a Canadian regiment fighting in a war they did not understand or believe in. These three productions catered to the audience expectation of the now conventional First World War setting, but added resonances that were specifically Canadian.

The Young Company was kept together for the following year, with a few additions. As a result, Phillips was able to work on cross-casting over two years, developing both the actors' and the audiences' appreciation of two plays he had directed before with great success. *Twelfth Night* in 1988 saw Nancy Palk move from Rosalind to Viola, Coyne as Olivia had a bit of her earlier Juliet, and Shultz was able to shift from Touchstone to Feste, improving his comic timing and flair. For *King Lear* Hutt was brought in to play the leading role, which he did with subtlety in the intimate space of the stage created. The Company, again in Edwardian dress, were indeed a family by this point and the interactions of characters took on new meaning in light of the other productions they had performed in together. Shultz took on Edgar and Coyne was Regan, interesting extensions of the fools and the romantic leads they had played previously. The impact of this production was profound on the actors, the audiences and on another young critic in the making. Margaret Jane Kidnie credits this show with igniting in her a passion for Shakespeare; 'I didn't really have any expectations, but the show blew me away. I don't think I'd have become a Shakespearean if I hadn't gone along to the Festival in the late 1980s' (2020). As the final production for the company Phillips directed a double bill of Sophocles's *Oedipus* and Sheridan's *The Critic*, a combination made popular by Olivier. This wonderful season, and the experience it provided for the Young Company, resulted in six of these actors going on to found Soulpepper Theatre in Toronto in 1998 (see Chapter 7).

But another production was to have a more immediate impact on the future of the Festival; Monette's first attempt at staging Shakespeare on the Festival Stage, *The Taming of the Shrew*, in 1988 with Feore and Semple paired once again. The two created a romantic couple who suffered together through the taming process. It was an ebullient production set in 1950s Italy, which used almost as many inventive stage machines and sight gags as the musicals. To celebrate the Festival's thirty-fifth season in 1988 both *Richard III* and *All's Well That Ends Well* were staged once again. Unfortunately, Feore gave what critics considered an underwhelming performance as Richard in Rintoul's production. Moss's *Gone With the Wind* inspired production of *All's Well*, set in the American Civil War, was considered an anachronistic and unsatisfying presentation of the play by critics. Peacock as Helena was admirably upbeat, but the setting made a nonsense of the social hierarchies in the play. Oddly the picture-book setting which would have helped make sense of the action of *All's Well* was given instead to a production of *Two Gentlemen of Verona* staged at the Avon Theatre with Beard directing and Brian Jackson returning to design. The non-Shakespeare plays in this year were T. S. Eliot's *Murder in the Cathedral* and *The Three Musketeers,* which made a triumphant return to the Festival stage. Pennell united these two productions with his two opposing clerics, Thomas Beckett and Cardinal Richelieu.

Neville's final season in 1989 highlighted the work of two other former members of the Festival company, Bedford as Shylock in a production of *The Merchant of Venice* which

Langham directed. This Victorian production, designed by Heeley, was influenced by Langham's staging of the play in Washington with Bedford, and demonstrated the command that both men had over the Festival stage. Shylock in this production may even be seen to reflect some influences from Hirsch in that Bedford shouted the 'Hath not a Jew eyes' (3.1.50) speech into the face of a young boy who had been tormenting him. But Langham skirted around the idea of Jewish persecution and the play's anti-Semitism by cutting Shylock's forced conversion. The First World War was once again the setting for Wood's *Henry V*, starring Wyn Davies as Henry, and William Needles as the Chorus, a role he had played in the 1956 production. However, a similar wartime setting, which in theory established a moment when British and Canadian history converged, proved problematic for Ouzounian's *A Midsummer Night's Dream*.

Somewhat surprisingly a double bill of *Titus Andronicus* directed by Jeannette Lambermont in Kabuki style and Monette's *The Comedy of Errors* also graced the Festival stage in 1989. While Pennell as Titus was insufficiently weighty to carry off the leading role, the cutting of the play also made it a challenge for audiences to follow. Monette further confused audiences by casting the same actor as each of the twins, in a production of *Comedy* that was full of fun but not of heart. Better suited to his directing talents perhaps was Vanbrugh's *The Relapse* which starred Bedford in the leading role. While both productions were elaborately decorated confections, Bedford's skill as an actor, supported by an excellent company, was able to find more depth in the Restoration comedy. The remaining production on the Festival stage was Dekker's *The Shoemaker's Holiday* directed by William, (who had by this point been announced as Neville's successor). Debra Hanson's period set and costumes helped to prove that the Festival could tackle Shakespeare's contemporaries, although this production made connections with more modern work through cross-casting. James Blendick's performance as the Shoemaker was complemented by the same actor's performance as Big

Daddy in Williams's *Cat on a Hot Tin Roof*. Semple and Geordie Johnson shifted from their roles in *The Relapse* to Maggie and Brick, respectively. Bernard Hopkins both starred in *Three Sisters*, directed by Neville, and oversaw the Young Company in this year. But the two productions by the Young Company did not match the success of the Phillips years, with an underpowered *Love's Labour's Lost* directed by Hopkins and *The Changeling* directed by Kelly Handerek.

Neville's four-year regime was one of increased stability, both financially and artistically. He completed his assigned task of righting the ship admirably but was not keen to carry on in this demanding role. While his Shakespeare productions did not excite in the way that those of Langham and Phillips had in the past, the return of these two directors demonstrated the maturity of the organization. The work of the Young Company, in particular, was to have a lasting impact on the future of the Festival. But Neville's greatest achievement and influence was in balancing the books by bringing musicals to the centre of the programme on the Festival stage. Campbell's *The Boys from Syracuse* in 1986 featured actors from the main company in the leading roles, at Neville's insistence. This was followed in 1987 by *Cabaret*, directed by Macdonald, who had so successfully brought new life to the Gilbert and Sullivan seasons. Audiences who witnessed Brent Carver's delicate *Hamlet* on the Avon stage in 1986 enjoyed his Master of Ceremonies on the Festival stage the following year. Gascon returned to direct *My Fair Lady* in 1988, (starring Neville as Henry Higgins), but he died shortly before the production opened. Despite these tragic circumstances, Peacock as Eliza, with Campbell as her father Alfred Doolitte, charmed audiences. In the same year a second musical was staged at the Avon Theatre, *Irma La Douce*, directed and choreographed by Jeff Hyslop. The final musical of Neville's tenure, *Kiss Me Kate* in 1989, was directed and choreographed by Donald Saddler, bringing together Shakespeare adaptation with musical theatre in a fitting finale. While Shakespeare was somewhat displaced by musical theatre during Neville's reign, he proved that it was possible to run the Festival in a way that both challenged his audiences and remained in the black financially. Together Hirsch and Neville inspired a new generation of Canadian acting talent, as well as fledgling critics.

6

From festival to corporation – David William and Richard Monette (1990–2002)

The political moment

The 1990s saw the fallout of the wrangling for independence by Quebec in the form of repeated attempts to construct a constitutional accord which the province felt it could sign into law. Although Canada's constitution was signed by Queen Elizabeth and Prime Minister Trudeau on 17 April 1982, negotiations around the adoption of this new constitution ended without Quebec's approval. The failure of further negotiations in the Meech Lake Accord of 1987, which was rejected by the other provinces, and the Charlottetown Accord of 1992, which was rejected by the electorate of the country in a nationwide referendum (54 per cent of Canadians voted against it) led to a second referendum to determine the country's future. The incredibly narrow outcome of the 1995 vote on Quebec sovereignty (51 per cent to stay and 49 per cent to leave) rocked the confidence of the country both culturally and economically. Many businesses and individuals that conducted their work entirely in English moved out of the province. Relations between Quebec and the rest of the country became fraught, and the province remains a 'stateless nation' with separatist aspirations to this day. For the Festival this meant that it was keener than ever to maintain the cultural influences which made it unique, but economic dependence on American visitors remained a central concern. The productions staged during this period were viewed by Canadian audiences either as an escape from the political strife of the nation or as a reflection of it, often regardless of the political intensions of the directors. Perhaps for the first time since 1956, in the 1990s audiences responded to the vision of Canada presented onstage through Shakespeare from two quite different nationalist viewpoints.

David William (1990–3)

When William took up the post of artistic director, he had been directing work at the Festival for over twenty years. His first production on the Festival stage was *Twelfth Night* in 1966, followed by *The Merry Wives of Windsor* (1967), *King Lear* (1972), *Othello* (1973) and *Romeo and Juliet* (1977). He also directed work at the Avon Theatre, including *Albert Herring* (1967), *Separate Tables* starring John Neville (1984) and *She Stoops to Conquer* (1985). William was in many ways the most conventionally English artistic director the Festival had ever had. He attended Oxford where he read English and worked as an actor and director at the Old Vic for several years before he came to Canada. While all of this would have made his appointment incredibly unpopular a decade earlier, by 1990 the debate around nationalism had become decidedly more complicated. William's official status at the time of his appointment was as a landed immigrant, and, as such, he qualified as a new Canadian, even if he had all the markers of a great imperialist. William was a safe pair of hands in troubled economic and social times who had demonstrated his commitment to the company. In his four seasons in charge, he established Canadian plays in the Avon as well as in what was to become in 1991 the Tom Patterson Theatre (formerly the Third Stage). He encouraged Canadian directors, particularly those who came from the company (Monette, Henry, Maraden and Hopkins), and arranged for the return of Molière to the Festival Theatre. However, his academic approach to the plays left audiences cold and his tendency to ignore the financial side of production meant that the Festival accumulated a deficit of approximately C$1 million each year he was in post, despite the fact that each season featured incredibly successful musicals directed by Macdonald. William's strength was that he knew the stages and the company, having directed under every artistic director before him apart from Guthrie. During his time in charge, he nurtured the Festival's most talented actors and directors, reinforcing the company's identity and making it ready for the first Festival-trained artistic director, Richard Monette.

William directed only three mainstage productions of Shakespeare during his tenure. In 1990, he co-directed *Macbeth* with Robert Beard, with Bedford and Semple in the leading roles. The show opened with a bloody battle and included scenes some found gratuitous, such as the onstage rape and murder of a pregnant Lady Macduff. His *Hamlet*, with Feore in the lead, was considered lacklustre in 1991 (see Chapter 8). The production of *The Tempest* he directed in 1992, starring Alan Scarfe as Prospero, featured a spectacular storm but little else to recommend it (see Chapter 9). William's other work during his reign included Congreve's *Love for Love* (1990), Wilde's *The Importance of Being Earnest* (1993) and Euripides's *The Baccahe* (1993), which was staged in the renamed Tom Patterson Theatre, with Feore in the lead. Other members of the company were given the opportunity to direct on the main stages, with Hopkins taking on *The Merry Wives of Windsor* (1990) at the Festival Theatre and *Twelfth Night* (1991) at the Avon. Hopkins was also seen on stage as Dull in Maraden's first mainstage production, *Love's Labour's Lost* (1992), in another Edwardian setting. Maraden cast Feore as

Berowne, with Alison Sealy-Smith, the first Black actress in the role, as his Rosaline, challenging somewhat Taylor's notion that 'racial stereotypes at work here are even more blatant than those that have historically governed black casting in the RSC' (1999: 342). However, the inclusion of Black actors in the company was sporadic, based on the availability and the inclination of individuals, rather than a planned programme of inclusion (see Chapter 8).

Familiarity was an essential part of this period in the Festival, which again involved inviting back well-known names. Langham directed his second production of *Timon of Athens* in 1991, in which he revived Duke Ellington's score and retained the modern setting. Bedford took on the leading role, in the Patterson Theatre, creating an intimacy that was enhanced for audience members aware of his portrayal of Noël Coward characters, which he mirrored in the benevolent Timon of the first half of the play. This familiarity with his former work was also key to Bedford's performance in Langham's *Measure for Measure* in 1992, given that the actor shifted from the role of Angelo to the Duke. In 1993 Phillips returned to the Festival to direct *King John* at the Patterson Theatre in a production which 'used the stage to create an internally coherent, historically precise, and theatrically stylized world of the Europe' (Knowles 1994: 223) just before the First World War. Notable for the strength of its female leads, Janet Wright as Queen Elinor and Semple as Constance, this production helped to establish the Patterson Theatre as a space for the display of female power in the history plays. Stephen Ouimette, cast as the Bastard, used the intimacy of the space to comment on the action to the audience, establishing another tradition and an actor at the Festival who was to go on to many more roles as a comic commentator. As Knowles puts it this 'Bastard's natural affiliations were with Eleanor and Hubert, and he, more than anyone else, made the audience aware of the cost of politics' (1994: 225). This was to be Phillips's last full production at Stratford and it made a fitting end, given his dedication to the development of new spaces and members of the company, particularly women.

In the years leading up to his reign as artistic director Monette was one of the busiest resident directors under William. In his 1990 production of *As You Like It,* in which William played Jacques, the action was set in New France (modern-day Quebec) just before the British invasion. C. E. McGee writes:

> Monette's *As You Like It* made use of both the physical and the human geography of Canada. A huge metallic tree with brightly lit red, orange, and golden leaves dominated the stage. At the outset of the production, aboriginals, voyageurs, peasants, and gentry entered singing the Québécois folk song, 'Un Canadien errant,' and at the end, the ensemble celebrated happily with step dancing to the music of fiddles and spoons. (2002: 146)

While McGee suggests that the setting gave the impression that the production was aiming for a nostalgic 'vision of prelapsarian Canada' (2002: 148), Monette was not keen to define his intentions. Reviews of the production saw the setting as primarily a form of spectacle. McGee draws together three key responses: 'John Laycock ("Showbiz, not politics [assuming they are separate] is Monette's true sourcebook"); Stewart Brown ("Too much should not be read into this Quebec setting . . . "); Audrey Ashley ("The maple syrup is [. . .] laid on with a trowel. Never mind. It's all done, I presume, in a spirit of fun")' (2002: 148). But the politics of the day had an influence on how this production was received by audiences, creating 'a context that politicized the reception of it' (McGee 2002: 150). This production is one of only a few staged at Stratford set in a discernibly Canadian environment, and so it is hardly surprising that audiences, keen to see a vision of unity, took pleasure in the idea of the country's pastoral past. The links between the constitutional debate raging in the country and this rose-tinted rural setting of the story were tenuous, but audiences were happy to embrace the play's positive ending as significant.

Monette was able to repeat this sense of creating a production with particularly Canadian resonances with his

Romeo and Juliet in 1992, (captured on film and broadcast on the CBC), because it starred as Juliet the country's sweetheart, Megan Follows, best known for her portrayal as Anne in the television adaptation of *Anne of Green Gables*. As her Romeo was future director, general manager and artistic director, Antoni Cimolino. While it was generally agreed by critics that the show belonged to Feore as Mercutio, this production, set in the 1920s, established Monette's ability to tackle the tragedies on the big stage. Monette rounded out his direction of tragedies under William with *Antony and Cleopatra* set in the nineteenth century, with the Romans being dressed as an occupying army in Egypt. The cross-casting of this show with Phillips's *King John* proved important for audiences. As Knowles notes; 'The casting of Semple as both Constance and Cleopatra, for example, highlighted the plays' parallel uses of messenger scenes in which strong women receive the news of their personal betrayal by powerful men for political reasons' (1994: 217). Again, the ensemble and the loyal audience were rewarded for their dedication to the Festival's production processes.

William had a knack for reviving the Festival's past by breathing new life into old favourites. Hutt returned to star in Molière's *The Imaginary Invalid* in 1993, twenty years after he first tackled the role and following a break of five years with the company. Henry made her return to the Festival as a director with a production of Ibsen's *The Enemy of the People* in the Avon Theatre. (She had been working as a director since leaving the Festival in 1980 and had been appointed as the artistic director of the Grand Theatre in London, Ontario.) American classics by O'Neill (*Ah! Wilderness*, 1990) and Wilder (*Our Town*, 1991) directed by Vivian Matalon and more recent plays (*Love Letters*, 1991) directed by William filled out the repertoire and provided an incentive for the American audiences to make the trip across the border. Other more recent works including David Storey's *Home*, directed by Maraden in 1990, and Joe Orton's *Entertaining Mr Sloane*, directed by William in 1992, provided additional breadth. The Young Company did not fare particularly well during William's regime, staging only one play a year. In 1990 Hopkins and Pat Galloway directed *The Knight of the Burning Pestle* rather unsuccessfully but still this production was revived in 1991. In 1992 Maraden took over the company and staged *The Two Gentlemen of Verona* (1992) and Corneille's *The Illusion* (1993).

Canadian plays were performed more during William's time at the helm than in any other director's regime since Phillips. Elliot Hayes, the Festival's dramaturg, wrote *Homeward Bound*, which Maraden successfully directed in 1991, and his adaptation of *Treasure Island* was given a spectacular staging in the same year on the main stage, directed by William. Hayes's adaptation of Robertson Davies's *World of Wonders* in 1992 managed to entice Richard Rose of Toronto's Necessary Angel Theatre to direct his first full production at Stratford. Most importantly the work of Quebec playwright Michel Tremblay made its debut on the Stratford stage with productions of *Forever Yours Marie-Lou* in 1990 directed by former company actor Lorne Kennedy (featuring Maraden), and *Les Belles Soeurs*, which Maraden directed in 1991. *Bonjour là Bonjour* was then staged in the Patterson Theatre in 1992, directed by Albert Millaire, creating the first trilogy of Canadian plays to be staged as modern classics. The irony of William's reign was the fact that while he was committed to producing Canadian classics, his biggest success was with work that was strongly linked to the Quebec separatist movement. The coming together of the English and French traditions at Stratford had made this theatre quite different from anything that had developed south of the border, but this cultural mixture was in jeopardy politically.

Richard Monette (1994–2002)

Monette fulfilled the board's and the cultural critics' desires when he took on the role he had been trained to fill for his entire career, but he was faced with unrest nationally and an enormous deficit locally. He shared with his predecessor the fact that he was an accomplished actor before becoming a director but, unlike William, he had gained most of his directing experience at the Festival. Monette began his professional career starring as Hamlet at the Crest Theatre in Toronto at the age of nineteen. He then joined the Festival as an actor for three seasons in 1965. Next came a period in England where he performed with the New Shakespeare Company in Regent's Park and was one of the original cast members of *Oh! Calcutta!* He returned to Canada and to the Festival in 1972 but left again when his portrayal of the central character in Tremblay's *Hosanna* gained national acclaim and he travelled to New York. When he came back to the Festival in 1978 he had his first opportunity to direct a short Beckett play but continued to perform as an actor. It was not until his hugely successful production of *The Shrew* in 1988 that Monette became a regular director at the Festival.

When he took on the post of artistic director Monette was very aware of the history of the job; he had been a vocal opponent of the dismissal of the 'Gang of Four', although he remained loyal to the Festival. Following on from William, he worked carefully to bring back established actors and directors to create a season in 1994 that could attract audiences and would eventually balance the books. In this first season he brought together Molière, Langham, and Bedford to create a double bill of lesser-known plays entitled *Husbands and Cuckolds* (*The Imaginary Cuckold* and *The School for Husbands*). This gamble on the Festival stage paid off, with Bedford in both leading roles. In contrast to the expansive comedy on the thrust stage, the intimate space of the Patterson Theatre realized its greatest triumph with Diana Leblanc's staging of O'Neill's *Long Day's Journey Into Night*. First staged at the Festival in 1980, this return of a classic American play starred Henry and Hutt as the senior Tyrones and Peter Donaldson and Tom McCamus as their sons. This production was so successful it was revived and filmed the following year. The third triumphant production of his opening season also looked into the Festival's back catalogue, bringing *Cyrano de Bergerac* to the stage for the first time since Langham had directed Plummer in the leading role in 1962–3. Monette had planned for this to be Phillips's final return, but when this director had to cancel he was replaced by Derek Goldby at short notice. Feore took on the central role, confirming him as the natural successor to Plummer and one of the Festival's biggest home-grown stars.

Monette directed two Shakespeare productions for his opening season, *Hamlet* in the Patterson Theatre starring Ouimette (see Chapter 8) and *Twelfth Night* on the Festival stage. The latter featured Ouimette as Sir Andrew Aguecheek, William, back to play Malvolio, and Bedford taking on the role of Feste. The production went against the expectations of both audiences and critics who found it to be too dark an interpretation, playing as it did against Monette's reputation for frivolity. However, the assumption that he fared better when directing the comedies was played out in two later productions which relied on actors who were reprising their roles. The first, *Merry Wives of Windsor*, which was co-directed with Cimolino in 1995, saw Hutt taking on Falstaff for a second time in a Victorian setting. The second, *A Midsummer Night's Dream* in 1999, featured Bedford as Bottom again, this time with the Ancient Greek characters unusually set in ancient Greece. Perhaps the most successful use of acting talent, working across the plays they performed in, was the pairing of Henry and Bedford as Beatrice and Benedick as the somewhat older than usual warring lovers, in Monette's 1998 production of *Much Ado About Nothing*. This production, which was once again set at the end of the First World War, featured Hutt's Leanato, getting quietly drunk in a 1920s Italian palazzo. It transferred to New York with his production of *The Miser*, starring Hutt as Harpagon and Henry as Frosine, establishing quite firmly that the Festival was by this point critically attuned to Broadway rather than London's West End or Stratford-upon-Avon. Two of the most loved productions mounted by Monette at the end of the twentieth century were those which featured Hutt in the leading roles he had played twice before, King Lear and

Prospero (see Chapter 9). These two productions rewarded loyal audience members with the layering of this performance onto Hutt's previous work, giving audiences the opportunity to map their own life experiences onto the journeys taken by these characters and this actor.

In addition to his own work Monette was careful in his invitations to visiting directors. Wood was given the opportunity to direct *Richard III* in 1997, in celebration of the Festival's forty-fifth anniversary. Ouimette took on the title role at the Patterson Theatre, playing it as 'a misfit usurper with a lacerating sense of humour' (Cushman 2002: 196). Lambermont took on *As You Like It* in 2000, with Peacock playing Rosalind for a second time. But the director who perhaps had the biggest impact was Rose, who wanted to provide a political context for his productions. His *Comedy of Errors* for the Young Company in 1994 (revived in 1995) featured a police state. In 1996 he gave two actresses (Kristina Nicoll and Jane Spidell) the chance to alternate in the role of Rosalind, and another two (Tamara Bernier and Caroline Gillis) the opportunity to take on Celia in his *As You Like It*. Rose's mainstage production of *The Taming of the Shrew* in 1997 moved Monette's production of 1988 a decade forward, placing the action in 1960s New York (or New Padua) but it was equally cartoonish in its characterization. According to McGee: 'the production represented the United States of America as the land of bilk and money. The very last image was that of Katherina and Petruchio, side by side on a bed on the upper stage, throwing into the air the cash won through his wagers and her dutiful performance' (2002: 151). Ironically, American critics found the production particularly Canadian in its vilification of American values (McGee 2002: 151). But significantly, Rose managed to produce the play in a way that engaged both Stratford audiences and visitors from the South.

The relative success of this production meant that Rose was entrusted with three more mainstage productions. The most Canadian of these was his version of *The Two Gentlemen of*

Verona set in a turn of the twentieth century North American high school. Taylor describes how; 'the opening scene imaginatively and economically established the play's social world: a championship-hockey-team photo shoot, followed by Graham Abbey's jock-Valentine and David Jansen's nerd-Proteus circling each other on the ice' (1999: 340). The play was set once again just before the First World War, but this time the director tried to critique the sentimental image of harmonious Canadian-British relationships established by former Stratford productions. McGee suggests that the characters moved 'effortlessly from their privileged position in the colonies into the world of the leisured class of England' (2002: 154) but this Proteus, instead 'of being a cunning traitor [. . .] was a nerd who had to be hoodwinked into maturity' (2002: 153). The production was designed to look at the role of Canada within the British empire and the implications of that role for 'colonial innocents abroad' (McGee 2002: 153), young men required to fight for a foreign nation. In many ways this production took to the Festival stage Phillips's concept and setting from the Young Company's *Journey's End* (1987) and *King Lear* (1988), illustrating an increasing sense of disquiet with the British Imperial project. Rose initially staged a thought-provoking ending, with Valentine and Proteus being led off to war in opposite directions. But preview audiences found this outcome problematic. Actor David Jansen recalls 'audiences wouldn't allow it. They fought against it' (quoted in McGee 2002: 155). So somewhat ironically, when Monette tried to depoliticize his 1990 *As You Like It*, audiences found resonance in it anyway, but when Rose tried to impose a political message on his *Two Gents*, audiences rebelled.

Rose's final two productions were unromantic presentations of two of Shakespeare's Roman plays at the Patterson Theatre, *Coriolanus* in 1997 and *Titus Andronicus* in 2000. Tom McCamus's Coriolanus, a 'pure thin-lipped war-loving, crowd-despising psychotic' (Cushman 2002: 197), was matched in rancour by Henry as Volumnia. Rose's *Titus* was set in between the wars in Italy with James Blendick 'as an honest and believable Titus who lacked the character's terrible logical insanity' (Cushman 2002: 197). These productions helped to create what Knowles calls 'a "third-stage" audience that, in theory at least, is more adventuresome than that frequenting the other theaters, more willing to take risks on new work' (1994: 223) confirming the Festival's smallest space as the place to stage politically charged Shakespeare.

Monette gave several actresses in the company support to become established directors, particularly of the history plays. Henry directed *Richard II* on the Patterson stage with Geordie Johnson in the leading role in 1999. His 'fair-haired Richard, though lacking in anger and irony, was fluent and excitingly fast, accepting his defeat and enjoying it' (Cushman 2002: 199). John Dolan's Bolingbroke was decidedly older than usual, and the entire cast was costumed in medieval dress apart from Richard, who wore a modern white singlet and trousers, providing a split view generationally of this historic battle for power. (This production was the first play in the history cycle which would culminate in Henry's *Richard III* in 2002.) Maraden was another actress-director who thrived under Monette, with productions of *Macbeth* in 1995, starring Wentworth and McKenna, and *The Merchant of Venice* in 1996, set in pre-Fascist Italy, which showcased Douglas Rain in one of his best performances as Shylock. Leblanc, who after her success on the small stage with O'Neill's domestic tragedy, was asked to tackle Shakespeare's most domestic epic, *Romeo and Juliet*, on the main stage in 1997. Unusually, but successfully, the production was set in the Caribbean in the nineteenth century, allowing a Black actor, Roy Lewis, to take on the role of Capulet. This was followed by one of the Festival's most successful stagings of *Macbeth*, featuring the real-life couple of Rod Beattie and Henry in the leading roles. The play, as staged in the Patterson Theatre, was intimate rather than epic, with the sounds of thunder and knocking rousing the audience as well as the characters to a heightened state of tension.

However, productions which relied on the company's history and stalwarts did not always bring enthusiasm or excitement.

In 1997 Campbell remounted Guthrie's 1954 production of *Oedipus Rex*, with three of the original cast members in leading roles; William Needles again as the Old Shepherd, Roland Hewgill taking on Creon and Douglas Rain performing Tiresias, in a nostalgic tribute to the original Festival company. Benedict Campbell, the director's son, took over the role from his father in costumes that recreated Moiseiwitsch's designs. It was a worthy but unmoving exercise. Campbell's 1998 production of *Julius Caesar* was even less well received. Taylor reports the opinion of reviewer David Murray that it was 'by a long way the worst *Caesar* I've seen' (qtd in 1999: 341–2). Bedford's 1994 *Othello* (which was originally to be staged by Phillips) was set in Washington around 1945, providing a viable setting for the play's racism, but Ron O'Neal as Othello was seen as out of his depth. By contrast Bedford staged Beckett's *Waiting for Godot* with considerable success in 1996 starring the comic duo who continue to dominate the Stratford stages today, McCamus and Ouimette (it was revived in 1998). But Bedford was most successful with his production of *The Winter's Tale* in 1998 at the Patterson Theatre. In fact, Taylor calls it 'the best production of the play I have ever seen' (1999: 336). Wayne Best took on the role of Leontes which Bedford had made his own. The sheep-shearing became a 1960s hippie happening, in 'someplace resembling rural Ontario [. . . where] a very vigorous display of agricultural male strength and dexterity – created a genuine sense of a party' (Taylor 1999: 337) with Johnson as a playful Autolycus. A more rewarding Greek play was finally staged in 2000 with *Medea*, directed by Miles Potter, at the Patterson Theatre. McKenna presented a leading lady who was both modern and ancient at once, lacerating her Jason, played by Wentworth, at every turn, creating a powerful intimate performance that shifted between periods with ease and affect. Throughout this period the classical plays performed on the Patterson Theatre's intimate thrust stage continued to receive the best reviews.

In terms of new work, Monette was cautious. Rose directed Jean Marc Dalpé's *In the Ring* in 1994 and David Young's

Glenn, about Glenn Gould, as played by four different actors in 1999, both produced in the Patterson Theatre. Timothy Findley, a member of the original acting company, had his play *The Stillborn Lover* directed in 1995 by Moss with Hutt and Henry in the leading roles. But it was Findley's second play at the Festival which was to bring him his greatest success in 2000. *Elizabeth Rex* imagines the night before the execution of the Earl of Essex, when by some extraordinary chance the Queen encounters Shakespeare's company of actors. Directed by Henry, with Diane D'Aquila in the leading role, it is a production which has a special place in the hearts of audience members who attended. It was later filmed by the CBC and remains an important contribution to Canadian drama, providing evidence that the Festival could inspire important new work. Monette was faulted more than any other artistic director for making the offerings of the Festival more 'popular' which some critics suggested meant his seasons lacked depth. The fact that he was able to balance the books seemed evidence that he was appealing to the lowest common denominator. Gary Taylor documents the calls in the Toronto press for Monette's resignation (see Ray Conlogue 1998 and Kate Taylor 1998) in which 'his financial success was taken as evidence that he had abandoned the Bard for the box office' (1999: 346). But the problems faced by the Festival were due primarily to changing audience tastes and demographics.

However, considering what were seen as the 'popular' choices reveals a clever approach to dealing with repeat visitors. Monette was very aware that he was now catering to the children and grandchildren of the Festival's loyal audience and so turning to family-friendly shows was essential. Staging adaptations of classic novels for a family audience was seen as evidence that the Festival was selling out, yet *Alice Through the Looking Glass* (1994, 1996), *Little Women* (1997) and *Pride and Prejudice* (1997) all dealt with serious themes. Macdonald returned to stage Gilbert and Sullivan musicals for a second time with *The Pirates of Penzance* (1994) and *The Gondoliers* (1995), but this time including topical political references in the libretto, which increased their popularity. Even *The Boy Friend* (1995) and *The Music Man* (1996) can be seen to provide an opportunity for young audience members to think as well as feel. After Macdonald's departure Monette directed *Camelot* in 1997. But in 1998 Susan H. Schulman came from New York to direct *Man of La Mancha*, creating a show which, somewhat ironically, Taylor describes as 'the only production that actually used the Festival Stage effectively' (1999: 345). A Canadian musical was staged in 1999, *Dracula*, by its author-director Ouzounian, but this was an aberration. *West Side Story*, directed by Kelly Robinson, was the real hit of 1999, followed by *Fiddler on the Roof*, with Schulman back in charge, in 2000. As Neville had discovered, putting these shows on the Festival stage guaranteed the future of the Festival both financially and in terms of audience development, allowing for greater risks to be taken at the Avon, but particularly at the Patterson Theatre.

The idea of an apprenticeship model, which Guthrie established both to test potential incoming artistic directors and nurture young actors, was very much in evidence at the Festival and, although Monette abolished the Young Company, he replaced it with the Birmingham Conservatory, a classical actor training scheme which paid actors to learn their craft in the months preceding the Festival. These actors then often moved into key roles in the main acting company as in Cimolino's *Twelfth Night* in 2001 on the Festival Stage, which featured two Conservatory graduates in the leading roles of Olivia and Viola. But the company was given its greatest sense of cohesion in the performance of the history plays, with *Richard II* (1999) starting the sequence, followed by *Henry IV Parts 1 and 2* (Part 2 renamed *Falstaff*) in 2001, with Campbell as Falstaff, his son Benedict playing King Henry and Graham Abbey as Hal, directed by actor-director Wentworth in the Patterson Theatre. *Henry V* was staged in the same season at the Avon directed by Lambermont, again with Abbey in the lead. This production gestured to all wars, with the English in First World War uniforms, but the French in medieval dress. As at the RSC, this history cycle created some continuity through casting but allowed the individual directors to interpret the plays independently.

These four productions set the scene for the fiftieth anniversary year of 2002 with the final history plays, *Henry VI* performed in two parts (titled *Revenge in France* and *Revolt in England*), directed by Rubin at the Patterson Theatre, and *Richard III*, directed by Henry, at the Avon starring McCamus. Knowles provides an in-depth analysis of the latter production highlighting the complex layers of reception it received, 'the building was alive with echoes – different echoes for different audiences' (2005: 303). He notes the audience who might have seen Guinness in the role fifty years earlier; the audience who had seen the production of the play starring Henry as Lady Anne, alongside Bedford as Richard and Smith as Queen Elizabeth, directed by Phillips for the twenty-fifth anniversary in 1977; or the more recent production with Ouimette in 1997. But even for audience members who were visiting the Festival for the first time in 2002 there was the potential for a complex relationship with the other actor playing Richard at the Patterson Theatre, Haysam Kadri, or the other character played by McCamus in the same season, MacHeath in Brecht's *Threepenny Opera*, directed by Ouimette. Knowles concludes that 'The overriding context through which all productions at Stratford must be read is "the company"' (2005: 304) which he defines at the start of the twenty-first century as the acting, administrative and production staff, on the one hand, and 'the company in its corporate sense' (2005: 304) with a budget of C$41 million in 2002, on the other. But Knowles points out the various ways that this *Richard III* went against the overarching celebrations of the Festival's legacy in interesting ways; 'Louis Applebaum's heroic fanfare, used elsewhere to celebrate the Festival's achievements, played here to celebrate and accompany the demonized Richard's ascent to the throne' (2005: 310). The history plays in this season were meant to acknowledge the Festival's history, but for Henry and others, that history was not unproblematic. In fact, the naturalistic method acting of both Henry and McCamus went against the epic style of the play. A connection was created instead with the director and actor's other famous partnership, as mother and son in *Long Day's Journey Into Night*, which audience members may have seen on film as well as in the theatre. McCamus's Richard suffered (naturalistically) from cerebral palsy and his contorted body, on occasion, was seemingly out of his control, as when he fell in his approach to the throne during his coronation and when his hand refused to stab Richmond. This production, harkening back to Phillips's and Monette's lyrical productions of *As You Like It* (1977 and 1990) featured a large onstage tree, but this time with a difference; 'Richard was first seen perched in a gnarled upstage tree, and was finally returned to that tree at the end of the action, stripped and strung up by Richmond's soldiers where, according to Henry, McCamus discovered (sentimentally) that the weight of his body after death would finally let him straighten' (Knowles 2005: 315). To Knowles McCamus's Richard 'was a remarkable embodiment of discursively fractured subjectivity, housed in a body, a nation, a Festival, a "company," and a production at odds with itself' (2005: 317). The Festival's fiftieth birthday celebrations were not entirely positive or coherent.

The other productions staged in honour of this anniversary in 2002 showed a similar fight between the old and the new. Plummer's triumphant return to the Festival Theatre was the highlight of a production of *King Lear* directed by Jonathan Miller, and Monette's production of *My Fair Lady* was offered starring Feore, Wyn Davies and Monette himself alternatively taking on the role of Higgins. *All's Well That Ends Well,* which was also directed by Monette on the Festival stage, rounded out the inevitable return to these two plays, with Hutt as the King of France. This production was so steeped in Festival history that it projected an image of Guinness and Worth in the leading roles in 1953 behind the actors. To complete the performance of the entire canon, *The Two Noble Kinsmen* had its first performance at the Patterson Theatre, directed by

David Latham. It is hard to imagine a more self-referential and reverential season, and yet there was also a new commitment to the production of small-scale experimental work with the opening of a fourth theatre, the Studio, on the land behind the Avon Theatre, which was first identified by Robin Phillips as the location for his proposed, but never created, Studio One. Monette had achieved financial stability, growing the company into a multi-million-dollar organization, but one question remained: How was the Festival to maintain its local audience, and its sense of history, while expanding the scope of its work to appeal to, and influence, the international world of Shakespeare in performance, as Guthrie originally planned? As a Shakespeare scholar based in Britain during this decade my annual return to the Festival was tinged with nostalgia, but also a sense of frustration at the narrow scope of the productions I witnessed. As the Festival turned increasingly to an American audience during this period it seemed to lose its connection with the broader European tradition of performance and to what Shakespeare could mean politically to audiences locally.

Moving towards a new model

7

The Stratford Festival in the twenty-first century – Monette, McAnuff and Cimolino (2003–22)

The history of the Stratford Festival up to the beginning of the twenty-first century can be seen to be relatively coherent, in that the Festival's self-conception and its critical reception both oscillated between the seemingly opposing poles of an imposed colonial model and the desire to create something uniquely Canadian. But the beginning of the twenty-first century presented the Festival with a series of challenges that altered both of these perspectives. First was the disruption of the continuity of the company through the steady loss of its founding members. Second was the fact that Monette had built the Festival into a multi-million dollar organization which relied heavily on government funding, corporate sponsors and American audiences to sustain it. Third, was the impact on the free movement of tourists from America to Stratford caused first by the outbreak of the SARS virus in Southern Ontario in 2003, then by conflicts in Afghanistan and Iraq and finally by the Covid crisis of 2020. The new millennium also brought with it a shift in critical attention, both in the press and in scholarly debate, from a focus on nationalism to questions about the Festival's approach to representation, particularly of race, gender and ethnicity. The vision of the Festival as unique, as it had been within Canadian theatre, was replaced by international, intercultural perspectives which placed the Festival within the context of a tourist-oriented circuit of similar endeavours. Knowles identifies this as 'the founding of a multinational theatrical corporation' within the context of 'corporate colonialism in a post-national world' (2004: 47). The Festival's processes and reception were further complicated, but also enhanced, by the introduction of cinema broadcast of productions, which created a new outlet for Stratford's performances for an international audience unable to travel to Canada, as well as critical accounts of that work (Kidnie 2018; Bennett 2022). Over the past twenty years the Festival has tried to grapple with the issues raised by these critics but also by changing demographics. While Robert Ormsby notes 'what is commonly called the "Stratford Experience" includes a complex series of relationships that defies any simple label of globalization' (2017: 573), Erin Julian and Kim Solga pointedly ask the question 'what does diversity presently mean at Stratford' (2021: 193)? The established methods of the twentieth century needed to change in the twenty-first century to represent the lived experience of Canadians in person and an international audience online.

Changes in delivery methods were already underway when the Festival was forced to pivot to an online model during the pandemic lockdown of 2020. Productions created for the Stratford Festival on Film programme could easily be streamed for a virtual audience. However, finding ways of interacting with varied audiences and recovering the costs of performance proved more challenging. The influence of one man during the period from 2003 to 2022 is significant and makes linking the last three artistic directorships together both useful and necessary. Antoni Cimolino was a close collaborator with Richard Monette, co-directing with him initially then directing several key productions on his own before assuming the role of general manager in 1999. Significantly, when the time came for Monette to step down in 2007 due to ill health, Cimolino took on the position of general director, a role which was elevated above the artistic directors for the first time, making it clear that a business model was at the heart of the Festival. The organization had become so large that it needed a huge administrative infrastructure to sustain it. As Ormsby notes: 'the economically important and historically determined global relationships at Stratford were with multinational corporate sponsors' (2017: 30). Cimolino, as general director, oversaw these relationships, while a triumvirate was appointed to manage the artistic side of the Festival. In 2008 Des McAnuff shared the reigns of artistic power with Marti Maraden and Don Shipley, but this arrangement lasted only one year. McAnuff carried on alone until 2012. When he moved on to pursue other opportunities Cimolino became the artistic director in 2013. During this time critical responses increasingly examined the Festival's corporate, as well as its artistic, practices. As Ormsby suggests the Festival had entered 'its multinationalist era where home, whiteness, and the common humanity of Shakespeare had to be located according to new points of orientation' (2017: 581). The past two decades have renewed and intensified the challenges the Festival has always faced, balancing the need for innovation which draws on outside influences, with maintaining a sense of continuity through building on past successes and audience loyalty, but the advent of an international online audience resulted in new forms of interaction and scrutiny.

Monette's second stint (2003–7)

Monette, despite enormous criticism during his final five years at the helm, skilfully catered to a popular audience while also creating opportunities for new Canadian work. Alongside the increasing number of American plays produced (*Cat on a Hot Tin Roof* (2005), *The Glass Menagerie* (2006), *To Kill a*

Mockingbird and *Of Mice and Men* (2007)) important new Canadian plays were staged (*The Swanne* trilogy (2002–4), *Harlem Duet* (2006) and *Shakespeare's Will* (2007)). Monette slowly reduced the proportion of Shakespeare plays in the total repertoire and distributed those productions strategically in different venues, while also supporting the development of new writing which critically engaged with Shakespeare's work and his historical period. The 2003 season, for example, boasted sixteen productions on four stages. The Festival Theatre was host to four productions, three of which were by Shakespeare (*The Taming of the Shrew* dir. Potter, *Pericles* dir. Rubin and *Love's Labour's Lost* dir. Cimolino), accompanied by one musical (*The King and I* dir. Schulman). Of the remaining twelve productions only two were Shakespeare's work and these were performed in the Patterson Theatre (*Antony and Cleopatra* dir. Henry and *Troilus and Cressida* dir. Monette). In 2004 again three Shakespeare plays were performed on the Festival stage (*Midsummer Night's Dream* dir. Rubin, *Macbeth* dir. Wood and *King Henry VIII* dir. Monette), alongside *Guys and Dolls* directed by Kelly Robinson. The Patterson Theatre in this year was taken over by productions of Shakespeare's lesser-performed plays (*Timon of Athens* dir. Ouimette, *Cymbeline* dir. Latham and *King John* dir. Cimolino). This programming belies the consistent criticism of Monette that he tended to 'program vulgar fare without artistic merit' (Parolin 2009: 202). Peter Parolin argues that Monette's beliefs, 'the universally redemptive power of classical theatre (especially Shakespeare) and the importance of experiential plenitude in a festival setting' (2009: 200) were by this point dated. In many ways Monette returned to Guthrie's original aims, but at the beginning of the twenty-first century his desire to combine universality with commercial success led Kate Taylor to say of the Festival, 'far too much of its energies go toward producing commercial entertainment – or disguising Shakespeare as such' (1998: C1). The Festival was again faulted for being self-aggrandizing and inward-looking.

This complaint could be seen as justified when in 2005 Monette looked to the Festival's and his own past, in a very self-referential way, to provide Hutt with a fitting farewell on the thrust stage, remounting his 1999 production of *The Tempest* (see Chapter 9). But changes were also underway; Cimolino directed *As You Like It* in 2005 on the Festival stage, with Dion Johnstone, the first Black actor to play Orlando, shifting the company from occasionally casting Black actors to consciously making them key members of the company. In the Patterson Theatre there was just one Shakespeare in this year, *Measure for Measure* directed by Rubin. The 2006 season saw three Shakespeare plays on the Festival stage with Cimolino's *Coriolanus*, Ouimette's *Much Ado About Nothing* and Rubin's *Twelfth Night*, showing a reliance on tried and tested directing talent. Monette directed a production of *Henry IV Part 1* in the Patterson Theatre but it was the only Shakespeare there. In Monette's final season (2007) he directed only *An Ideal Husband* on the Festival stage, turning the Shakespeare productions over to Bedford, who directed and starred in *King Lear*, and to Rose, who directed *The Merchant of Venice*. Monette's only Shakespeare production in this season was *The Comedy of Errors* at the Avon Theatre.

Monette's extremely popular but commercial productions gained little scholarly attention, apart from Parolin's detailed study of his directorship. However, Ormsby and Kidnie highlight the work of the British director, Leon Rubin, in terms of his intercultural approach, during this period. Rubin was engaged to stage six Shakespeare productions between 2002 and 2006, and three of these, a South American *A Midsummer Night's Dream* (2004), a nineteenth-century Indian *Twelfth Night* (2006) and *The Adventures of Pericles* (2003) which 'evoked various points between "Arabia" and Japan', could be considered 'consciously intercultural' (Ormsby 2017: 568). Kidnie focuses her attention on *Pericles,* in which the multiracial casting presented an 'imprecisely executed treatment of race and culture' and 'did little to challenge assumptions that the "real" Shakespearean body is white' (2004: 318–19). Ormsby, on the other hand, felt that 'the production's casting returned theatre-goers to the multicultural Canadian/North American present of 2003' (2017: 580), noting that the 'non-white actors in *Pericles* were not marginalized but took on principle roles' (2017: 580–1). Both critics find it significant that the original Festival stage was obscured by a spectacular and exotic design. Ormsby writes; 'The relentless scenic metamorphosis necessary to keep pace with *Pericles*' episodic structure made the stage an emblem of mobility and, arguably, rootlessness, those signature features of globalization' (2017: 574). The aim of this production, and Rubin's other intercultural endeavours, was to provide new entry points to what had been, up to this point, a very white Western approach. But Kennedy's question seems appropriate here: 'Does a spectator shift cultural ground by watching interculturalism at work?' (2017: 443). Moving to include more diverse casting and staging approaches demonstrates a shift in the work on the Festival stage in this period but there continued to be a reliance on established company members as both actors and directors, with just a few additions, such as Johnstone.

A more significant shift in practice can be seen in the 2006 staging of the important Canadian adaptation of *Othello* by Djanet Sears, *Harlem Duet*, which depicts three different mixed-race couples that take the events of Shakespeare's play as their starting point. Produced in the Studio Theatre, the experimental space established in 2002, this production provides an example of the kind of work the Festival was also encouraging. Knowles writes; '*Harlem Duet* is both very much a product of its historical place and moment and at the same time *productive* of its moment and of subsequent moments as a marker of, and site for the negotiation of social change around specific issues' (2004: 162). When I met Kidnie at a performance of this play we both celebrated Johnstone's notion that '*Harlem Duet* was huge for this company. All of a sudden, a whole audience of black people came to Stratford' (qtd, in Parolin 2009: 207). Another important Shakespeare spinoff was performed in the Studio Theatre in 2007, *Shakespeare's*

Will by Vern Thiessen, (dir Potter) a one-woman show starring McKenna, which looks at the life of Anne Shakespeare, left in Stratford-upon-Avon to raise the children. This second play relates to a tradition of new work at the Festival under Monette which 'was explicitly engaged in revisionist history' (Kuling 2017: 72). Peter Kuling in 'Counterfactual history at the Stratford Festival: Timothy Findley's *Elizabeth Rex* and Peter Hinton's *The Swanne*' makes the point that these two playwrights were rewriting the past with a purpose: 'These new speculative histories at Stratford reflect Ewan Fernie's vision of an emergent, globalized Shakespeare in the wake of cultural materialism that cultivates "racial and social minorities as special interest markets"' (Kuling 2017: 73). In *Elizabeth Rex* (2000) Ned, an actor in Shakespeare's company is dying of syphilis, given to him by an ex-lover. Queen Elizabeth and the player exchange sympathies and advice regarding their respective forbidden and fateful love affairs. Kuling suggests that in Hinton's *The Swanne* trilogy, which references different periods of British royal history, '[p]layful anachronism and counterfactual history' are used 'to generate unconventional and provocative performances of Canadian, queer, gendered and racialized identities' (Kuling 2017: 75). Hinton directed his three plays in the Studio Theatre between 2002 and 2004, each of which focuses on a different Royal figure, George III, Princess Charlotte and Queen Victoria, while making allusions to Shakespeare's plays. Monette continued to programme lavish popular productions which attracted tourist audiences in the Festival and Avon stages, but more challenging work, which looked at Canadian identity in the twenty-first century, was being staged in the Patterson and Studio spaces.

Monette's final years were extraordinarily productive but under this workload and the constant barrage of bad press, his health began to fail. Like Phillips, the artistic director he most admired, Monette took on too much responsibility. The Festival was a difficult master and proved ultimately overwhelming. Monette stepped down at the end of 2007 and passed away in September 2008 at the age of sixty-four.

Marti Maraden, Des McAnuff and Don Shipley (2008)

The triumvirate installed to take the Festival forward was designed to divide the workload which had crippled their predecessor. Each of the directors appointed had a different background and area of expertise. According to Campbell Robertson, writing in *The New York Times*, Maraden was appointed for her knowledge of Canadian theatre, McAnuff for his success in producing new musicals and Shipley for his 'Rolodex of names from Europe' (Robertson 2008). Robertson highlights Monette's legacy; not only had the Festival's budget doubled during his leadership but he was responsible for introducing the Birmingham Conservatory for classical theatre, building the Studio Theatre and increasing the Festival's reserves so that 'a $1 million rainy-day fund became a $55 million endowment' (2008). In 2007 just 4 per cent of the budget came from government funding, with three-quarters of the monies spent coming directly from the box office (US$33 million), relying on one-third of the audience coming from the United States (Robertson 2008). It is little wonder then that the board wanted a group that could confidently cover all of the work that Monette had instigated.

Of the three directors appointed Maraden had the longest association with the Festival. Born in the United States, Maraden immigrated to Canada in the 1960s, with her husband. They soon became active in theatre in Vancouver and were then accepted into the Stratford Festival company where they performed in the 1970s. Marti Maraden's most notable roles, Ophelia, Miranda (see Chapters 8 and 9) and Regan opposite Ustinov's Lear, gave her the basis for her directing career which followed, first at the Shaw Festival during the 1980s and then as the artistic director of English Theatre at the National Arts Centre from 1997 to 2016. She returned to direct at Stratford regularly and so seemed an ideal candidate to co-direct the Festival with McAnuff and Shipley. During the one season of her tenure, she directed *All's Well That Ends Well* on the Festival stage and *The Trojan Women* at the Patterson Theatre.

McAnuff was also born in the United States but moved to Canada as a child and was raised in Southern Ontario. He studied theatre at Ryerson University and then became very involved in the burgeoning alternative theatre in Toronto in the early 1970s. He directed and wrote plays for Factory Theatre Lab, Toronto Free Theatre and Theatre Passe Muraille. But he developed an uneasy relationship with the theatre critics of that city and moved to New York in 1976. In 1982, he moved to San Diego and then spent eighteen years at La Jolla Playhouse where he had great success with the development of the musical *Big River*. Further success in directing Shakespeare and musical theatre (*Tommy, Jersey Boys*) led to international acclaim. He returned to Canada occasionally, largely directing other musical productions. However, no musicals were scheduled on the Festival stage in 2008. Instead, according to Parolin, 'McAnuff's productions of *Romeo and Juliet* and *Caesar and Cleopatra*, both at the Festival Theatre, asserted Stratford as a place for aggressive stage design, breathtaking special effects and accelerated pacing' (2009: 222). His multiracial casting of *Romeo and Juliet* and the return to Stratford of Christopher Plummer in the Shaw play, (which was the first to be filmed for cinema release), helped to establish McAnuff's intercultural and internationalist priorities for the company. Adrian Noble's production of *Hamlet* (see Chapter 8) shows that British directors were again encouraged at the Festival to provide inspiration, and Hinton's *The Taming of the Shrew* demonstrates that Canadian talent was still being nurtured. The musicals in this season (*The Music Man* and *Cabaret*) were both performed at the Avon Theatre. At the Patterson Theatre Langham directed his final production of *Love's Labour's Lost*, with members of the Birmingham Conservatory, simultaneously illustrating a commitment to the past and the future of the company.

It is difficult to determine the role of Don Shipley in the triumvirate, since he directed no plays during this season. As the former artistic director of the Dublin International Theatre Festival, the Grand Theatre in London, Ontario, and the Belfry Theatre in Victoria, British Columbia, he had a wealth of experience. Parolin quotes Shipley saying that he was very keen to find 'international voices that could invigorate the company' (qtd 2009: 214). When both Maraden and Shipley resigned, before the 2008 season had even opened, it caused considerable controversy. Michael Posner reports: 'Maraden says her resignation as co-artistic director 12 days ago was the result of creative interference and an agenda imposed by general director Antoni Cimolino' (2008). Maraden is quoted at length, expressing her view that she was led to believe she would have autonomy in the role but ultimately Cimolino's 'increasing involvement in artistic decision-making [. . .] made it impossible for me to continue' (qtd in Posner 2008). McAnuff's comments conclude the article saying of his co-directors; 'We didn't know each other and trust did not build up' (qtd in Posner 2008). Unlike the 'Gang of Four', who had previously worked together, this triumvirate was constructed of relative strangers, designed to divide the responsibilities and cripplingly pressure experienced by Langham, Phillips and Monette. The 2008 season went ahead as planned, although Shipley was replaced as the director of a double bill of Beckett and O'Neill plays. At the end of the 2008 season a year-long study of the Festival Theatre stage was instigated 'to determine what needs to be done to keep it in peak condition as a state-of-the-art performance facility' (McAnuff qtd. Parolin 2009: 220). Clearly this was to be a period of reassessment as well as renewal.

Des McAnuff (2009–12)

The success of the American-focused McAnuff over the Canadian-based Maraden and the European-focused Shipley had a profound impact on the Festival. In his first solo season McAnuff returned to *Macbeth*, the only Shakespeare play he had previously directed in the Festival Theatre in 1983. The 2009 Festival also saw the return of two established and spectacular audience favourites, *Cyrano de Bergerac* (dir. Donna Feore) for the fourth time and *A Midsummer Night's Dream* for its eleventh production (dir. David Grindley). Repetition was again necessary to balance the needs of a loyal returning audience and first-time visitors, but McAnuff tackled this problem in a new way. In the Avon Theatre in 2009 *Julius Caesar* (dir. James Macdonald) had its seventh production, but for the first time it was paired with *A Funny Thing Happened on the Way to the Forum*, the first musical McAnuff would direct at the Festival. At the Patterson Theatre Henry directed the Festival's third production of *Three Sisters*, the play she had performed in with such great success alongside Maraden and Smith. Cimolino returned to directing, even while juggling the job of general director, and this season took on *Bartholomew Fair* at the Patterson Theatre for its first appearance at the Festival. The Studio continued to produce Canadian plays in this season. So, while only three Shakespeare plays were produced, there was again some innovative programming in the smaller spaces.

In 2010 the number of Shakespeare plays increased again to four, with McAnuff taking on two of them, in the Festival Theatre: *As You Like It* and *The Tempest*. The latter starred Plummer (see cover image and Chapter 9) in a production which was filmed by Bravo! for cinema and television broadcast, expanding the audience for the Festival's work exponentially. *The Winter's Tale*, the Festival's fifth production, was directed by Maraden at the Patterson Theatre and *The Two Gentlemen of Verona*, in its eighth retelling, was directed by Dean Gabourie at the Studio Theatre. This season reduced the number of productions offered to twelve, something which was repeated in 2011, in another season in which just four Shakespeare plays were staged, only two of which were on the Festival Stage: *The Merry Wives of Windsor* (dir. Frank Galati) and McAnuff's *Twelfth*

Night. *Richard III* at the Patterson Theatre starred McKenna as Richard and Henry as Queen Margaret, challenging the former casting of the history plays in a production directed by Potter. Also, at the Patterson Theatre *Titus Andronicus* had its fifth outing (dir. Darko Tresnjak), while Thiessen's *Shakespeare's Will* (dir. Potter) was remounted at the Studio Theatre.

In his final season in 2012 McAnuff directed *Henry V* alongside Christopher Newton's *Much Ado About Nothing* on the Festival stage, while *Cymbeline* was directed by Cimolino at the Patterson Theatre. New plays *The Best Brothers* by Daniel McIvor and *Hirsch*, a play developed about the childhood of the former artistic director, directed by Paul Thompson, featured at the Studio Theatre. Ironically, it was Hirsch who saw no place for new plays at the Festival, while McAnuff was a strong defender of new Canadian work. Throughout his time as artistic director McAnuff divided critics. There were those who felt his flamboyant productions were too filled with spectacle, which buried the text in extravagant performance, a familiar refrain which returned to haunt him, as it had Guthrie and Monette. There is no doubt that McAnuff was a showman with an internationalist approach. But he also nurtured important new work and attracted wider audiences to the theatre, both with the first cinema broadcasts of Stratford performances and by bringing back Christopher Plummer. In his Director's message in 2010 McAnuff writes, 'The Stratford Shakespeare Festival is that rare place where tradition meets innovation, where the classical intersects with the contemporary' (*Tempest* programme 2010). In a tribute to the Festival's legacy the Michael Langham Workshop for Classical Direction and the Playwrights Retreat were established, both of which continue today.

Antoni Cimolino (2013–22)

Cimolino's ascendancy at the Festival was swift but it took a different path from his predecessors. After studying for a BFA at the University of Windsor he acted in Toronto before joining the Stratford Festival in 1988. Working increasingly closely with Monette, he was given both management and directing assignments in 1994. From 1995 to 1996 he was named an artistic associate, and then in 1997–8 he was associate producer, planning and special projects. In 1999 he became the general manager, in 2001 the executive director, and then the general director in 2007. This experience meant that when he became the artistic director in 2013, he was uniquely qualified to manage the administrative side of the organization. But he also knew the toll of taking on the artistic and administrative burdens simultaneously and worked throughout his directorship with executive director Anita Gaffney (daughter of the original contractor who built the auditorium in 1953). Cimolino curated a 2013 season which again involved twelve plays, with two Shakespeare productions on the Festival stage, *Romeo and Juliet* (dir. Tim Carroll) and his own *The Merchant of Venice*. The Avon Theatre hosted the musical, *Tommy* with McAnuff back to direct, and an additional Shakespeare play, *Othello* directed by Chris Abraham, while the Patterson saw Henry's *Measure for Measure*. The Studio boasted a world première of a new Canadian play by Judith Thompson, *The Thrill*, directed by Gabourie and Leblanc's production of *Taking Shakespeare* by John Murrell, about a Professor and a student discussing the plays, starring Henry as Prof. Cimolino also introduced the Meighen Forum in his inaugural year, a series of events which reflect on the ideas raised in the plays, linking them to current debates, that has become an increasingly important element of the Festival's offering. This was an assured beginning which illustrated that Cimolino knew how to mix the familiar with the new, guest directors with established Stratford stars.

The 2014 season followed the same pattern, with Cimolino's *King Lear* and Abraham's *A Midsummer Night's Dream* on the Festival stage, with the two other Shakespeare plays performed on the Patterson stage, *King John* (dir. Carroll) and *Antony and Cleopatra* (dir. Giffen), alongside *Mother Courage and Her Children* (dir. Henry). Three of these productions (*King Lear*,

King John and *Antony and Cleopatra*) became the first to be filmed by the Festival and screened in cinemas across Canada before their release on the CBC, on DVD (and subsequently online). Kidnie notes the 'choice to document performance is often strategic, affording cultural and intellectual prestige to companies that might otherwise be overlooked within the canon of theatre history' (2018: 138). But these films were not the only way that the Festival was 'writing itself into international theatrical and academic discourses' (Kidnie 2018: 138). This year also boasted a surprising Shakespeare adaptation, *A Midsummer Night's Dream: a chamber play* directed by Peter Sellars at the Stratford Masonic Concert Hall which Kidnie examines, suggesting it provided important resonances for Abraham's mainstage production of the same play (2016). In 2015 the Festival stage was host to Cimolino's *Hamlet* (see Chapter 8), Abraham's *The Taming of the Shrew* and John Caird's *Love's Labour's Lost*. The fourth play, *Pericles* directed by Wentworth, was at the Patterson Theatre. All four productions were filmed in this year proving Kidnie's point that the 'Festival has reinvented itself, in effect, as a multimedia production company' (2018: 139). The Studio Theatre featured a world première of a play about Katherine Parr entitled *The Last Wife*, by Kate Hennig, (dir. Alan Dilworth) the first of a new historical trilogy and *Possible Worlds* by John Mighton (dir. Mitchell Cushman).

In 2016 Cimolino directed *Macbeth* for the mainstage, which was again filmed, and Jillian Kelly staged *As You Like It*. To celebrate the 400th anniversary of Shakespeare's death the *Henry IV* plays, combined with *Henry V*, were staged at the Patterson Theatre in two parts, *Breath of Kings: Rebellion* and *Breath of Kings: Redemption*, both directed by Weyni Mengesha (see Buccola 2019). By the 2017 season there was a decided sense of déja vu as the Festival staged its twelfth *Twelfth Night*, directed by Henry, and its eleventh *Romeo and Juliet* directed by Wentworth, although the mixed-race cast for the latter play drew some attention when distributed on film. Even the lesser-known play this season, *Timon of Athens,* at the Patterson Theatre, was in its fourth production. However, Ouimette's second production of *Timon* (the first to be filmed) was a surprise hit. Ouimette is the only director to have staged this play apart from Langham, who also staged it twice, once in 1963 and once in 1991. While Langham's 1960s production found an international audience when it toured to Chichester in 1964, the 2017 production, starring Joseph Ziegler, reached a wider audience through cinema broadcast. Like the RSC, the Stratford Festival is well-positioned, and I would argue has a responsibility to stage Shakespeare's work that cannot find an audience elsewhere. This unlikely play was not only a hit in the 2017 season, but it established the Festival's international stature, twice.

The Studio Theatre again featured new work by Canadian playwrights, including *The Virgin Trial*, a play by Hennig about the trial of Princess Elizabeth (dir. Dilworth). The other two plays, *The Komagata Maru Incident* (dir. Kiera Loughran) and *The Breathing Hole* (dir. Reneltta Arluk), tackled elements of Canadian history and identity. The first, a play by Sharon Pollock, deals with the role of Canada in British colonial migration during the First World War, and the second addresses the traditions of the Innuit people. The Festival used the Studio Theatre to experiment with what Julian and Solga call the 'challenge of practicing (and not just representing) diversity' (2021: 192) on stage, although they report that Loughran found herself 'having to carry the heavy weight of representing her entire culture on her shoulders' (2021: 204) and members of her cast found aspects of her approach troubling (Stratford Festival 2020b).

For the 2018 season Cimolino tackled *The Tempest* for the first time, with Henry as Prospero on the mainstage (see Chapter 9). This production was in stark contrast to the staging of *Coriolanus*, by Robert Lepage, which filled the proscenium arch stage of the Avon Theatre that season with screens and technology. Despite his international reputation for his groundbreaking Shakespeare productions, this was Lepage's first production for the Stratford Festival. *Coriolanus* and *The Tempest*, were cross-cast and filmed for cinema broadcast, allowing audiences to watch the same actors playing contrasting roles in very different productions (Ouimette as Trinculo and Junius Brutus, McCamus as Stephano and Menenius). In some ways, these contrasting shows recalled the excitement caused by Langham's production of *Henry V*, when audiences revelled in the opportunity to watch the country's two theatre traditions on display. But Lepage's young Black male leads (André Sills as Coriolanus and Sebastian and Michael Blake as Cominius and Caliban) also highlighted the frustration felt by younger members of the company in the face of a tradition that was not always inclusive (see Chapter 9 and Stratford Festival 2020a). The third Shakespeare play on the Festival stage in this year was Wentworth's *Julius Caesar*, with McKenna in the title role, again tackling the Festival's history of promoting men (although interestingly this production was not filmed). The Patterson Theatre was closed in this year in preparation for its transformation, so the Studio Theatre was pressed into action to fill the need for productions that would be recognizable to the loyal audience. *Long Day's Journey Into Night* (dir. Potter) received its fourth production and *The Comedy of Errors* (dir. Loughran) its eighth. Julian and Solga look in detail at the ethical issues raised in Loughran's production, which tried to address gender fluidity but found that 'the largest obstacle for diversity work at Stratford is its repertory model' (2021: 200) because the actors cast had to be approved by more than one director. The new work produced this season, *Bronte* (dir. Vanessa Porteous) a play by Jordi Mand, which examines the life of the literary sisters, and *Paradise Lost* (dir. Jackie Maxwell) by Erin Shields, adapted from John Milton's poem, harkened back to Britain's rather than Canada's literary history.

The final pre-pandemic season of 2019 did little to challenge the established repertory patterns, although *Othello* had its first director of colour in Nigel Shawn Williams, which was performed alongside Cimolino's *The Merry Wives of Windsor* on the Festival stage. The cross-casting of these plays led to some interesting insights, which again are documented on film. While the production of *Othello* was set in a dark and menacingly ordinary contemporary army environment, the companion piece was a cartoonish 1950s production of *Merry Wives* (Michael Blake played both Othello and Master Page and Gordon S. Miller was Iago and Dr Caius). As in 2018, the contrast with the politically motivated modern setting, inspired by a director from outside the Festival tradition, made Cimolino's production seem tame and nostalgic by comparison. Both plays were performed at the Festival for the eighth time, highlighting how the meaning of these performances (watched live or virtually) could be read differently by those who knew the plays and the Stratford actors well, and those coming to either or both for the first time. The dexterity of Blake and Miller in these two contrasting productions underlines Julian and Solga's point that 'actors who can shift across a range of productions and identity experiences apparently seamlessly – will be preferred over those who may be perceived as "stuck" in the "politics" of their own identities' (2021: 201). The absence of the Patterson Theatre again meant that the only other Shakespeare play was performed in the Studio Theatre, *Henry VIII* (dir. Henry), which was the last of Shakespeare's plays recorded on film at the time of writing. The Studio Theatre also featured *Mother's Daughter* (dir. Dilworth), Hennig's third play about women in power in England, which dealt with the reign of Mary, daughter of Katherine of Aragon. The aim of this historical trilogy was to mirror the approach and success of *The Swanne* trilogy, overseen by Monette, but with a focus this time on the concerns of powerful women.

Just as the new Patterson Theatre was nearing completion the pandemic made it necessary to cancel the 2020 season. The Festival quickly moved to online delivery of screenings of previously filmed productions in 2020, alongside Watch Parties which generated new material, including interviews with the creative and production staff, all of which was made freely available on the Stratfest@home site. In 2021 two canopy spaces were created to accommodate audiences in person on a small scale and performances in these venues were made available online to international audiences. The Festival Theatre Canopy hosted five concerts and a production of *R + J* directed by Ravi Jain. The Patterson Theatre Canopy saw four stage productions, including *A Midsummer Night's Dream* (dir. Peter Pasyk) employing puppets; *I am William* (dir. Esther Jun), a musical by Rébecca Déraspe which suggests that William's sister Margaret might have written the plays; *The Rez Sisters* (dir. Jessica Carmichael), a play by established Indigenous Canadian playwright Tomson Highway; and *Serving Elizabeth* (dir. Kimberley Rampersad), a play by Marcia Johnson about the visit of Princess Elizabeth to Africa in 1952. The Studio Theatre was the only space that was open this year and just one play was staged there, Edward Albee's *Three Tall Women*, directed by Leblanc and starring Henry, Peacock and the young actress who played Miranda to Henry's Prospero in 2018, Mamie Zwettler. This season was a testament to the resilience of the Festival.

Looking back at this season Treasurer of the board David Adams writes in 2022: 'we made the deliberate decision to invest in returning to the stages in 2021 as a means of staying connected with artists and audiences while serving as a sign of hope for the broader community' (2022). But he also points out how the Festival's focus had changed after the pandemic: 'we invested in equity, diversity and inclusion; created digital content; [and] reinvented the professional training programs' (2022). Adams reports a modest surplus for 2021 and acknowledges the need to make new plans in the face of great uncertainty: 'The recovery from the pandemic is a multi-year one [. . .] 2021 saw us take performances outdoors [. . .], while continuing to expand our digital content; and 2022 sees us returning to indoor venues with 10 productions, while developing complementary digital offerings' (Adams 2022). The Stratford Festival has grown in both size and function since 1953, becoming an essential part of the local and national theatre culture and creative economy. It has provided a focal point for training for new generations of Canadian actors, directors, designers and musicians. Starting out as a radical experiment, then quickly becoming an institution, the Stratford Festival has had to be nimble in adjusting to the circumstances that surrounded it. Over the years the influence of Britain has waned, but the Festival has remained a loyal defender of Shakespeare's work. Through its online platform the Festival now finds itself in a position to influence international cultural movements from a new vantage point.

Critical and creative engagement in the twenty-first century: The challenge of representation

The two collections of essays titled *Shakespeare in Canada* (2002 and 2017) make the case that the Stratford Festival is now part of a varied Shakespeare performance tradition in the country. The first with its subtitle 'A World Elsewhere' presents, as Brydon and Makaryk note, 'an apt metaphor for the position of Shakespeare in Canada, a variant of Northrop Frye's now commonplace phrase, "Where is here?" – the question of cultural coordinates' (2002: 3). In quoting both Shakespeare and Frye, the editors demonstrate that the path of discussing Shakespeare and Canada is littered with previous attempts to make this connection, leading to the generation of more questions. Brydon and Makaryk ask: 'Is Britain the locus of tradition and value? New York? Paris? Kyiv? Beijing? Or, is the centre, in fact, really here' (2002: 3–4)? In 2002 drawing together a cultural history that addressed Canada's complex intercultural perspectives seemed almost manageable. But the second collection, published in 2017 with the subtitle 'Remembrances of Ourselves', takes on the more daunting task of positioning Canada within the global response to the anniversary celebrations of 2016. The Shakespeare 400 project at the University of Ottawa was a small but important acknowledgement of Canada's international impact. The collection covers the work of the Festival (Ormsby, Kuling, McGee), its parody in the television series *Slings and Arrows* (Kailin Wright and Don Moore) and Ian Rae's attempt to establish a pre-history of Shakespeare activity in Stratford before the Festival. This collection also considers the lasting and far-reaching influence of Canada's most famous Shakespeare critics Frye, but also Marshall McLuhan.

The international distribution of *Slings and Arrows* (2003–6) provides an account of the Festival which is both critical and adoring, knowing and innocent, which mocks its audiences as well as its participants. In 1998, members of the Stratford Young Company of the late 1980s established Soulpepper Theatre, Toronto's first new classical theatre in a generation, as a rival to the Festival. Trained by Phillips, its members created a politically motivated company with a commitment to developing a new generation of Canadian actors and audiences. (Phillips directed the first two productions for the new company in 1998 and then left, by agreement, a bit like Guthrie.) So, it is both ironic and important that it was these actors who created the hugely successful television series. Wright says; '*Slings and Arrows* parodies television and theatre viewers and ironically (considering the television medium) privileges theatre audiences as more sophisticated' (2017: 88). In the third and final series the narrative rewrites the transformation story of the Festival with the creation of a new thrust stage featuring as the backdrop to the performance of *King Lear*, played by Hutt as Charles Kingman in the title role. The production's director, Geoffrey Tennant played by Paul Gross, turns his back on the fictional New Burbage Festival to avoid its commercial pressures and creates a new thrust stage which 'facilitates a visceral viewing experience' (Wright 2017: 88). By taking the battle for the thrust stage as a surrogate for Canada's cultural contribution internationally, but also for Canadian cultural autonomy, to an international television audience, the creators of *Slings and Arrows* were able to broaden the experience of this transformational endeavour, and appreciation for its key actor, within a fictional setting.

Ormsby takes this point further arguing that 'the Kingman character draws on and solidifies Hutt's reputation as the nation's foremost Anglophone classical actor by making him the emblem of deliverance from American commercialism and celebrity culture' (2010: 10). The fact that both fictionally, and in reality, Hutt was nearing the end of his life (and his performance of Lear had not been recorded before) illustrates how the series drew attention to the work of an actor and a Festival whose reputations, while celebrated in Canada, were largely unknown outside the country. The wonderful irony of this series is the way that it both celebrates and condemns the Festival for its battles with commercialism, conservatism and self-reverential cronyism.

Don Moore considers the role of Nahum in the series, the Nigerian-born security guard/custodian at the theatre whose commentary puts into perspective the seemingly self-indulgent struggles for cultural identity of the Festival (and Canada). Nahum is a theatre director who was forced to flee his country when his production of Ken Saro-Wiwa's *The Wheel* attracted violent attention (Saro-Wiwa was himself murdered by the Nigerian government). Moore argues Nahum's presence places the series in a broader international context but also that the fictional New Burbage Festival does not challenge 'the white privilege, racism, and social immobility seemingly stunting a character like Nahum, even if his spectral ethical function is to critique those very issues' (2017: 108). There is no doubt that the seeming coherence of the history and practices of the Stratford Festival in the twentieth century involve what Jenelle Jenstad calls a 'whitewashing of Canadian demographics' (2003: 49) and that gender, race and nationality have been barriers for advancement for some. Through the examination of the performance histories of *Hamlet* and *The Tempest* which follow, it is possible to recognize both the existence of those barriers and the Festival's attempts to break them down in the twenty-first century, to reveal how the 'stories we tell about Shakespeare [. . .] are always, but never only, about ourselves' (Makaryk and Prince 2017: 7).

8

The search for a Canadian *Hamlet* at the Festival

In describing his 2015 production Cimolino writes, 'what I see in *Hamlet* is a kind of circular exploration of the power of words, and of the responsibility that comes with that power' (2019: 24). As a circular exploration of the Festival's performance and reception history the ten productions of the play examined in this chapter demonstrate the need to, as Jessica Schagerl puts it, 'gaze at Canada through *Hamlet*' (2002: 160). As the country's largest classical theatre the Festival has been seen as responsible for establishing performance standards and creating a uniquely Canadian style of performance. While at the beginning of this history both the standards to be emulated and the cultural expectations of the audience in attendance were easily identifiable, more recently a sense of who the Festival speaks to, and for, has become more problematic. Cimolino insists that it is 'the living theatre we make out of [*Hamlet*] that catches the conscience of us all and forces us to confront that overwhelming question: Who's there?' (2019: 24). However, who is included in that 'us' is unclear. Canada is a land of immigrants, most of whom have come to the country to find a better life for their children. The shifting of power from one generation to the next within the play has consistently provided a debate on stage about the country's, as well as the Festival's, past and possible future directions.

Beginning with Christopher Plummer in 1957 and ending with Amaka Umeh, the first Black woman in the role, in 2022 the history of *Hamlet* provides an opportunity for an examination of the changing priorities of the Festival and of the country. Historically, Canada, a bit like Hamlet, has been a country which has suffered from both too much self-awareness and excessive self-doubt, caught between the actions it sees others undertake and the weight of a history it has not had a hand in. The future, like the end of the play, will require more decisive action and a clearer definition of what the Festival's role is in developing a performance tradition that is inclusive of the country's diverse cultural heritage. Moving forward, actions, rather than 'words, words, words' (*Ham* (F) 2.2.189), will be required to make the Festival a vibrant centre for the future of Canadian classical theatre as well as a symbol of its past.

Hamlet in Canada

Hamlet in Quebec has been used as a biting political allegory. Robert Gurik's 1968 political satire *Hamlet, Prince du Québec* was first performed in French at L'Escale in Montreal and then in English at the London (Ontario) Little Theatre. This play, written just before the founding of the separatist Parti Québécois, became linked to politics in the province from that year onwards. In fact, Gurik's work was still being cited in 2016 as a key reference point for the election of a new leader for that party. Robert Everett-Green describes the play as 'the granddaddy of modern adaptations' in which 'Hamlet became the personification of Quebec, uncertain when and how to act for independence – or as he puts it, "Être ou ne pas êtres libres!"' (2016: R11). While the play was not widely performed, it nevertheless was extremely influential because of its strong political statement. The characters in Gurik's adaptation were aligned with real people and institutions: Hamlet was Quebec, Claudius the English, Gertrude represented the Catholic Church and Polonius was Lester Pearson (the Prime Minister at the time). Horatio was René Lévesque, a member of the Quebec Legislature and founder of the Parti Québécois, who would go on to become Quebec's Premier in 1976 and hold the first referendum on sovereignty in 1980. Laertes was Pierre Elliot Trudeau, the Justice Minister in Pearson's government, and later in 1968 the fifteenth Prime Minister of Canada. Trudeau was known in Quebec as a strong federalist who would go on to impose the War Measures Act in response to violent action taken by Quebec separatists in the 1970s. He also went on to patriate the Canadian Constitution in 1982, which Quebec has yet to sign. Rosencrantz and Guildenstern were the Bilingualism and Biculturalism Commission, which led to the country adopting English and French as the official languages of the country. Key to this discussion is the appearance of the 'Comedians', Gratien Gélinas and Jean Gascon, who were played by young actors imitating these established political activists, but also Stratford stars.

Outside Quebec, rather than a play of national self-determination, *Hamlet* has been seen to reflect the conflicted state of the central character and the absurdity of his personal position, not unlike the position of Canada internationally. The play speaks about how to communicate personal concerns to the world, which in Canada is very much bound up with technology. To combat the geographic challenges of the country a great deal of energy has been expended on creating physical and technological infrastructure to enable trans-Canadian movement and communication. In a volume entitled *Technology and the Canadian Mind*, Arthur Kroker makes this point: 'The Canadian discourse is neither the American way nor the European way, but an oppositional culture trapped midway between economy and history [. . .] At work in the Canadian mind is, in fact, a great and dynamic polarity between technology and culture, between economy and landscape' (Kroker 1984: 7–8). The result of this state of mind is a country that works through its worries about its presence in the world through internal dialogue about the nature of culture and history and the relationship between these worries and present concerns about economy and geography, which are reliant on technology. This element of the Canadian psyche was particularly well displayed in an influential English Canadian adaptation of the play entitled *Hamlet's Room*, which was produced in 1991 at Theatre Plus in Toronto, starring Tom McCamus. In this adaptation a video screen featured for the Mousetrap scene, and many of the lines of the play were dictated to the actor by computer. While never performed at the Festival; it had an impact on it, since McCamus was to take on a key role in Monette's 1994 production of *Hamlet*. Thus, the ten productions documented here illustrate the changing face of the Festival and highlight the intergenerational issues at stake in each decade of Canada's recent theatre history. The anger of each new generation of theatre makers has been displayed onstage, with the Danish court, and sometimes the director, seen as the country's current cultural elite, in other words, the Festival's established order, which must be displaced.

Hamlet, 1957, Michael Langham, Festival Theatre

If the performance of *Hamlet* is seen to demonstrate the state of Canadian theatre, then there has never been a more anxiously anticipated production than Langham's which opened the new permanent building. The weight of expectation was extremely high following the huge success of his bilingual *Henry V* the previous year, but on the whole, reviews of Christopher Plummer saw his performance as uneven and disjointed. Edinborough notes, 'Plummer started off as a gangling youth, insolent to his new stepfather and full of snide remarks about his mother' but he 'moderated into a richer, more manly individual when Horatio accosted him' (1957: 513). Plummer's Hamlet accentuated the play's generational divide. Jack Karr in the *Toronto Daily Star* writes, 'The Hamlet that [Langham] and Christopher Plummer have worked out is a vengeful youth, concerned solely with setting the score with his evil uncle' (1957), played in this production by the British actor Douglas Campbell. Whittaker describes Campbell's Claudius as a 'sophisticated usurper who makes his dealings with God ring with healthy cynicism' (1957); while Edinborough calls Joy Lafleur's Gertrude a 'sinuous, flippant creature' (1957: 513). Hamlet's road to revenge was blocked by a formidable adversary and an unrepentant mother. But Karr suggests that the director 'seldom lets his audience get too emotionally involved with the characters' (1957). The result, in Whittaker's view, was a production with 'moments of sharp clarity, and others that drag us slowly through Hamlet's predicament' (1957). Plummer portrayed an angry young man whose focus was entirely on revenge, making the case perhaps that the Canadian company was not yet ready to rule this stage unaided.

Edinborough comments on the pace of the show: 'Langham swept through the plot pell-mell keeping the audience constantly interested in what was happening but never allowing them to ask why' (1957: 513). However, one directorial decision had a significant impact on the presentation of the younger generation. Langham chose to make Frances Hyland as Ophelia pregnant, giving her the power of producing the court's next heir. The result was startling. Karr writes 'this Ophelia is a gentle and fragile child, bewildered by the violent events around her' (1957). Atkinson writing in *The New York Times* hails Hyland as 'the finest Ophelia of her generation – girlish and sunny in the opening scenes, phantom-like, wandering-witted in the scenes of madness' (1957:3). This production highlighted the potential of a new Canadian star, alongside Plummer's more established leading man, making the destruction of this young couple more devastating. Because he was keenly aware that the theatre building was also the focus of this production, Langham made use of the stage to accentuate the action. Whittaker requested a seat in the new balcony to better appreciate the space. He writes: 'when there was large action, it held a true balletic adventure' (1957). The energetic performance of the young Canadian actors in this newly christened theatre highlighted both the potential and limitations of the younger generation.

In fact, Plummer broke his ankle partway through the run as a direct result of the athletic acting style he developed. Hutt took on the role for several nights and (possibly to Plummer's annoyance) garnered better reviews. Having played the part for the Canadian Players in a production which toured to the United States and Canada the year before, Hutt was better prepared and brought his own approach to the role. A rivalry was established for Canada's best Danish Prince (demonstrating the usefulness of a preparatory winter tour for actor training). When Plummer returned to the stage, he performed with a cane which, according to Hunter, 'gave his performance a special energy born of frustration and a need to rise above his situation.' (2001: 145). This seeming hindrance actually played very well into Plummer's conception of the role. But for Langham and Plummer the complexity of the play and the cultural moment was too much for one production to confront. This production did not produce the great Canadian Hamlet that the critics and audience craved; however, it served as a fitting start for the new theatre and established a distinction between stately British acting and the emergent Canadian style, which depended on movement and passion.

Hamlet, 1969, John Hirsch, Festival Theatre

Dubbed the 'hippie Hamlet' (Cushman 2002: 68) Hirsch, as the first Canadian to direct the play at the Festival Theatre, achieved 93 per cent houses. His aim was to strip away the pretence of grandeur fashionable in British productions in favour of creating a 'democratic' contemporary Dane, but Kenneth Welsh as Hamlet was even less well prepared for the role than Plummer and lacked his star power. Playing opposite Canadian actor Ciceri, who had trained at the Old Vic Theatre

School, as Claudius, this production focused attention on a more localized power struggle. According to Cushman, 'praise for its energy [was] outweighed by dismay at its inability to communicate the text' (2002: 68). The production had toured to Chicago, Ann Arbor and Montreal before the season began, but the critical response was universally poor. Pettigrew and Portman record the view of one critic who felt that Welsh 'threw the verse away, belting out the soliloquies as if anxious to get them over [. . .] his Hamlet was immensely energetic, but also unprincely, unpoetic, uncomplicated and uninteresting' (qtd in 1985b: 2:10). Edinborough calls the production 'diffuse and meaningless' as well as 'mindless, self-indulgent' (1969: 444). This would be Hirsch's last bold experiment working with Gascon, and he would not return to the play when he came back as artistic director. The acting company and the critics were not ready for this contemporary Canadian interpretation.

Hamlet, 1976, Robin Phillips and William Hutt, Avon Theatre

The next production of the play was skilfully designed to balance British and Canadian talent both on and off the stage. Phillips and Hutt worked together to develop the skills of the two young actors featured in the leading role, Pennell (British) and Monette (Canadian) (Figure 9). These two Princes provided contrasting interpretations of the role on a touring reproduction of the Festival Theatre's thrust stage. The part of Gertrude was also alternated between Pat Galloway, who performed with Pennell, and Patricia Bentley-Fisher, who played opposite Monette. The production's brief tour to Kingston, Montreal and Ottawa gained national attention before it opened at the Avon Theatre, alongside *The Tempest* (see Chapter 9) in which the actors were also cast. Although the aim was to highlight the psychological and sexual elements of the play, the key to the contrast between the two actors was credited to their place of birth and training.

FIGURE 9 *Nicholas Pennell as Hamlet and Richard Monette as Hamlet in* Hamlet *(Stratford Festival, 1976). Photograph by Robert C. Ragsdale. Directed by Robin Phillips and William Hutt. Designed by John Pennoyer. Lighting design by Gil Wechsler.*

Roger Bainbridge writes, 'Pennell's theatre experience is rooted in the British Stage tradition, and Monette is a product of Canadian Theatre' (1976). Of their contrasting approaches Portman writes, 'There's an element of danger in Monette's Hamlet – an edginess which makes us view him warily. This is a Hamlet of seething emotions, capable of boiling over at the slightest provocation. [. . .] Pennell offers us a Hamlet whose normal serenity, and inner equilibrium have suffered a violent disturbance' (Portman 1976a). The Gertrudes were as different as their sons according to Doug Bale: 'Bentley-Fisher plays a coarser, duller but kinder and more vulnerable queen while Galloway's Gertrude is a proud calculating chatelaine intent on status and self-image' (1976). Ultimately Monette portrayed Hamlet as 'a hotblooded, passionate but petulant youth' while Pennell presented 'a more sensitive, poetic and sensuous prince' (Canadian Press 1976). The issues of power and sexuality were articulated through two quite different mother–son relationships.

The issue of sexuality was articulated physically through the Princes' treatment of Ophelia. Bale reports that 'Pennell's approach is less intellectual and more keenly intuitive and thanks to his eloquent command of body language it explains Hamlet better [but] Monette is a slighter man, not until an unexpected physical attack on Ophelia at the beginning of Act Three does he seem a man likely to resort to violence' (1976). Maraden played Ophelia to both Hamlets and was considered by Bale to be 'full of spirit, sense, sympathy and sexuality' (1976). While Monette was performing his first leading role at Stratford, both Pennell and Galloway had performed on the mainstage before and had considerable acting experience. Gina Mallet in the *Toronto Star* attributes the difference between these Hamlets to maturity: 'Monette is witty and romantic [. . .] He snaps with sarcastic relish; ill-concealed impatience fuels him [. . .] Pennell is a naturally more introspective actor, and he speaks the blank verse better' (1976b). Hunter says Monette gave 'a visceral performance that came from the gut, his agile mind a captive of his deep pain' (2001: 145) while Myron Galloway writes 'Monette's suspiciously neurotic student prince shows little respect for his elders and doesn't hesitate to be downright insolent with his mother' (1976a). Working with Phillips and Hutt, the focus of this production was on close textual reading. John Fraser suggests that 'Stratford has come up with designs and approaches that provide a startlingly simple texture that forces our concentration directly on the play and players' (1976) and concludes; 'If there is to be a new style for Canadian classical theatre, a truly distinctive new style, would to God that it remain this one' (1976). A distinctive Stratford style was born out of this doubly cast Danish court, which drew together a British focus on the text with a Canadian approach to physical action and emotion.

Hamlet, 1986, John Neville, Avon Theatre

In the second production of the play on the Avon stage, Englishman Neville drew on his former work in Canada to create a production which subtly spoke to the Festival's own troubles with transitions of power. Brent Carver was seen by Hunter to possess 'a heart-breaking vulnerability; he was a man too sensitive for this or any world, swept along in a black current he could not resist' (2001: 145–6). Neville and Carver had already worked together on the play two years earlier, at the Grand Theatre in London, Ontario, where Hutt had played Claudius alongside Henry's Gertrude (both actors left the Festival following the 'Gang of Four' debacle). On this occasion as Bale recounts 'the play opens unusually [. . .] with Hamlet sitting on a bare stage, clasping his knees in an almost fetal position, and rocking back and forth in anguish, croaking a lament for his dead father: "He is dead and gone lady, he is dead and gone"' (1986). Stealing Ophelia's lines helped to establish from the outset that Carver's Hamlet was 'a nakedly young, quiveringly vulnerable prince' (Cushman 2002: 160). This study in mental anguish, performed on a series of narrowing platforms reminiscent of the Festival stage, could be seen as a direct challenge to Stratford's mistreatment of its artists. But this approach left its female characters little room for expression. Elizabeth Shepherd as Gertrude Bale calls 'consistent and comprehensible' while he writes that 'Lucy Peacock's Ophelia fails to reach the heart of that tragic role' (1986). The CP review suggests that 'Claudius, played with great style by James Blendick, is a man of great substance who only resorts to a devious, murderous plot when trapped' (CP 1986). Only Edward Hayman suggests that 'Neville is more interested than most in the political machinations in *Hamlet* and uses them to propel the evening' (1986). He saw

Wentworth's Laertes as 'nice kid victimized by the greed and decadence of his elders' (1986), suggested by offstage music and onstage party clothes. Working for the second time with Carver, Neville gave his leading actor the freedom to dominate this production, which seemed to openly criticize the impact of the mismanagement of the transfer of power within the Festival.

Perhaps to highlight the absurdity of the Festival's power struggles Neville programmed Stoppard's *Rosencrantz and Guildenstern Are Dead*, directed by Wood, to be performed alongside *Hamlet* at the Avon Theatre, with all but the title characters carrying their roles across the two productions. Although the connections between the Shakespeare and Stoppard plays were more through parody than earnest critique, Hayman writes 'The Stoppard play, in which the dynamic duo become victims themselves, is the logical next step' (1986) hinting at Neville's examination of audience complacency. Schagerl suggests that the 'Stoppard play allowed the actors to bring a sense of character grounded in their twentieth century reality' (2002: 163) and provided the particular kind of 'in joke' that Stratford audiences revel in. Crew notes how the description of the raid by the pirates was 'cheekily heralded by music from *The Pirates of Penzance* performed on the same stage last year with Carver as the Pirate King' (1986a). Neville's production saw the first movement towards a political Hamlet, which turned a critical eye on the audience to question its complicit acceptance of the Festival board's destructive behaviour, but reviewers seemed unaware or unwilling to examine this approach too closely.

Hamlet, 1991, David William, Festival Theatre

William waited until his second season as artistic director to tackle *Hamlet*, in a production which brought another Victorian setting to the Festival stage. William was keen to comment on the decadence surrounding Stratford productions at a time when Federal funding to the arts was being cut. However, Feore in the title role was seen as 'thoughtful but curiously bland' (2002: 178) by Cushman. Hayman writes 'his Hamlet is all surfaces and postures [. . .] He's eloquent, flamboyant, graceful, virile, even a bit playful when called for – everything but human' (1991). Relying on a conflated text 'scholarly William' (Hayman 1991) created a production that was nearly four hours in length. Cushman found Leon Pownall as Claudius 'a brilliant but guilt-ridden politician with great reserves of charm, who finds it all too easy to fall back on brutality' (2002: 178). Hayman found Patricia Collins' Gertrude 'properly regal' but 'otherwise predictable' (1991). Feore, following on from Carver, says he was keen to show Hamlet's feminine side 'that is very intuitive, intelligent and sensitive' but that he had to reconcile this with the character's 'active, decisive hard side' (qtd in Schagerl 2002: 163). Schagerl points out the importance of this actor's movement on stage; 'Feore's physicality was displayed in novel ways: by twisting his limbs around a chair, balancing on the upper level of the tiered set while taunting Polonius, quickly confronting Claudius after the "The Mousetrap," and dancing exuberantly on the upper platform rail' (2002: 165). The opulence of the court was signalled through the costuming, music and spectacle, but this was a thin veneer designed to hide the authoritarian nature of the regime.

Schagerl argues that this production spoke to its political moment within the context of the mounting deficit which was the legacy of William's time in charge. She highlights the paradox which exists when a highly polished, commercially sponsored production attempts to present a social critique, while at the same time being deeply embedded in the act of creating theatre as a consumer product with cultural aspirations. This production, Schagerl asserts, focused on Sidone Boll's Ophelia as a societal disruptor and the source of disquiet for the audience: 'The coming disorder of the kingdom was foreshadowed by Ophelia's veiled sexual behaviour and gestures and her subsequent self-fragmentation' (Schagerl 2002: 167). The backdrop to this production for a Canadian audience was not just the arts funding crisis but also the political wrangling over the constitution and the continued push for sovereignty by Quebec, which would result in the extraordinarily close referendum result of 1995. Schagerl relates this production back to Gurik's adaptation but suggests that here it is Ophelia, rather than her father, who represents Canada's political leadership: 'Ophelia pining for her lost world – her father, Hamlet, society in general – could be transferred to the more general, yet local, concern with the fragility and possible disintegration of Canada.[. . .] Ophelia's madness and death underscored the nation's own fragile psyche and the (as-yet-unrealized) potential for self-destruction' (2002: 167–8). This political reading of the play was not widely adopted and could be seen as evidence that the generational divide within the play was also evident in critical reception of this production. Veteran critic Hayman says that 'Boll gives Ophelia a wonderful little girl quality' (1991) while newcomer Michael Groberman insists 'Ophelia is a quiet, whimpering, weak, mumbling, spineless woman' (1991). At the beginning of the 1990s the Festival's elevated position within the cultural landscape made it difficult for William's political interpretation to be read as such by audiences and critics.

In Schagerl's view Fortinbras's arrival was seen not as the conquest of an invading outsider but as the entrance of a 'much-wished-for figure of stability and compromise'; 'All was not lost: consensus and compromise [. . .] could still be achieved with Fortinbras as the ruler of Denmark' (2002: 168). If it was William's intention to produce an allegory for the country, at this heated moment of national debate, then it seems possible that he was presenting his directorship of the country's flagship classical theatre as a Fortinbras-like leader of compromise and conciliation. As the final English-born director of the Festival, but a landed immigrant in Canada, William was a compromise candidate for the role of artistic director, there to get things ready for the arrival of Monette, the Canadian leader in waiting. The opulence and decadence of the court presented in this production was ready to topple into disarray; as a metaphor for the Festival, as well as for Canada, at this moment it could not have been more apt.

Hamlet, 1994, Richard Monette, Patterson Theatre

Perhaps surprisingly Monette did not hesitate to direct *Hamlet* in his first season but he was very canny in dealing with the Festival's past as he battled for its future. Rather than putting the play on the Festival stage again so soon, he opted for the Patterson Theatre in a move that 'repaired a gap in Stratford history by starring Stephen Ouimette, who had been pencilled in for the role by the Gang of Four thirteen years before' (Cushman 2002: 193). Monette simultaneously directed a new opulent production of *Twelfth Night* on the Festival stage which featured William as 'a fine, purse-lipped Malvolio' (Cushman 2002: 193). The cross-casting of these plays allowed Ouimette to deliver a sweet Sir Andrew Aguecheek alongside a Hamlet who was 'fanged, unromantic, and sardonically eloquent', 'heavy-lidded and dagger-voiced' (Cushman 2002: 193). This *Hamlet* was stripped bare and produced in an intimate and modern way, helping to establish the Patterson Theatre as a space for challenging work. Monette collaborated with his former director Hutt, who also played the Ghost and the Gravedigger in this production, making it a thoroughly Canadian enterprise. The set consisted of chairs and boxes, which could be shifted to create new environments, while allowing the actors freedom of movement on the extended thrust stage. Geoff Chapman recounts 'The action is so breathless, so concentrated, that it generates a sense of insightful tunnel vision' (1994). The costumes were eclectic but generally contemporary and informal. The aim was to move away from a political reading to focus on Monette's preferred psychological and sexual readings of the text, influenced by Phillips. However, the casting of Janet Wright as Gertrude and Peter Donaldson as Claudius, two of the company's actors most associated with contemporary work, with Douglas Rain as Polonius, wearing a turtle-neck beneath his suit, meant that this was to be a production where casual conversation would reign over declaiming the text. This was without any doubt or apology Shakespeare with Canadian accents.

As with the 1976 production, this *Hamlet* investigated the potential for sexual aggression. Schagerl recounts that Ouimette's 'Hamlet was physically rough several times in the production, especially to both Gertrude and Ophelia, suggesting undertones of sexual violence [. . .] in the nunnery scene, Hamlet responded with physical anger to Ophelia, attacking her for Gertrude's betrayal' (2002: 169). This 'clipped and sober production' (Cushman 2002: 193) ended with a sharp final duel between Hamlet and Laertes, played by Cimolino. Again, the generational divide was important in this production, with its focus directed at Festival politics. Horatio, as played by McCamus, had a significant and expanded role at the end of the play. Fortinbras's part was cut, and Horatio was given his lines regarding Hamlet's burial. The production ended with McCamus holding the Danish crown above his head 'suggesting either that he would assume the kingship or that the country would continue even without its royal family' (Schagerl 2002: 170). Monette had not forgotten the promises made and the damage done in the difficult transfer of power in 1980. This ending could be seen as a local statement of intent from the newly appointed artistic director that the future of the Festival would belong to a new group of Canadian actors who had not necessarily grown up in the company. With this production Monette heralded the beginning of a new generation of sensitive, even cynical, interpretations of the play which demonstrated this director's ability to create meaningful work which was both textually nuanced and politically aware in the Patterson Theatre.

Hamlet, 2000, Joseph Ziegler, Festival Theatre

If the Stratford *Hamlets* of the twentieth century were struggling to find a version of the play that would represent the country and the company accurately, then the first decades of the twenty-first century saw a return to looking outside of both for a new definition. Beginning in pitch black with the guards on the watch carrying torches as the only illumination, this production was filled with questioning irony. The sly observational approach taken by Ouimette on the Patterson stage made its way to the Festival Theatre but via an actor and a director whose experience lay predominantly outside of the company's work. Paul Gross as Hamlet was best known for his popular television character Benton Fraser in *Due South*, the fish out of water Mountie fighting crime in downtown Chicago. As a recognized television star and a symbol of Canadian identity, Gross drew new audiences to the theatre, and this helped to breathe life into the play for a new generation. Gross's understanding of the verse and the play's structure were central to his interpretation: 'I started to look at the soliloquies as a progression in the interior state of Hamlet. He gradually becomes much more organized' (Gross qtd in Cushman 2002: 199). (This approach forms the basis of the advice that Gross's character Geoffrey Tennant gives in the first season of *Slings and Arrows* to the young movie star brought in to play the part, referencing both the performance of the part by Keanu Reeves at the Manitoba Theatre Centre in 1995 and Gross's own tackling of the role.) In the press coverage before it opened, Gross points out that his involvement with the Festival spanned twenty-five years, starting at age fifteen when he worked in the box office on a government-sponsored programme during Phillips's directorship, an experience that led him to a career as an actor. Phillips also had a hand in this production's inception since he directed a production of *Hamlet* at the Citadel Theatre which featured both Ziegler and

Gross's wife Martha Burns. When Monette asked Gross about playing the role, he turned to Ziegler for advice.

Ziegler's connections with the Festival were stronger than Gross's. While he was born in the United States, Ziegler moved to Canada to attend the National Theatre School in Montreal after seeing an influential production of Shakespeare at the Guthrie Theatre in Minneapolis, where he grew up and where Langham was working. Ziegler moved to Toronto and became involved in the acting ensemble of the Shaw Festival (1980–2) before joining the Stratford Festival's Young Company with Langham in 1983, graduating to the main company from 1984 to 1987. Ziegler then worked with Phillips at the Citadel Theatre in Edmonton where he directed his first productions. Throughout the 1990s he crisscrossed Canada acting and directing, then moved into film and television, alongside a return to the Toronto theatre. He was a founding member of Soulpepper Theatre and he both acted in and directed many of its productions after its establishment in 1998. Ziegler's career path is not unusual for theatre artists in Canada, and so the aim of bringing him in to direct was to infuse the Festival with some of that diversity of experience.

Reviews of this production make it clear that Gross's Hamlet was not definitive, but this production had a part to play in bringing some of the creative team who had left the Festival back in new roles. Hunter found Gross's Hamlet 'Agile and wily with a spirit that questioned everything, he employed his wit as a probe and included his audience in his jokes almost like a stand-up comic [. . .] in the end he accepted his fate with an amused appreciation of life's overarching irony' (2001: 146). Portman insists that Gross gave 'a performance of intelligence, authority and macabre wit. [. . .] It's a dangerous, edgy, characterization that is flanked by the two contrasting poles of mania and melancholy' (2000). By contrast, John Coulbourn in *The Edmonton Sun* felt that his performance was 'marked by an affable, open charm that too often borders on the manic'; he concludes that 'ultimately his characterization is small' (2000). All of the reviews suggest that the rest of the production lacked focus and energy. Portman reports 'Instead of an atmosphere of murderous scandal and intrigue we get bloodless boredom [. . .] Zeigler's unimaginative use of the Festival Theatre's famous thrust stage doesn't help' (2000). Gross was surrounded by established members of the company who did not inspire much critical praise. Coulbourn calls Benedict Campbell's Claudius 'oily', Domini Blythe's Gertrude 'touching' and Graham Abbey's Laertes 'impressive' (2000) while Portman proclaims that Gross was 'awash in a sea of mediocrity' (2000). The post-Napoleonic setting did nothing to help provide a coherent approach to the play. The sardonic vision of a man out of joint with his surroundings was given a charming presentation on stage but ultimately Gross's frenetic portrayal was seen to lack depth. What this production achieved, however, was to demonstrate the influence of the Festival's former artistic directors, Langham and Phillips, in inspiring and training a new generation of Canadian actors and directors who valued the chance to perform on the Stratford stage.

Hamlet, 2008, Adrian Noble, Festival Theatre

The 2008 *Hamlet* formed part of the only season curated by the triumvirate of Maraden, McAnuff and Shipley. The new leadership was keen to address criticism which was increasingly finding fault with the Festival's inward-looking approach. Taylor indicates a 'general problem with Stratford Festival casting, which has fallen behind the theatrical profession, the academic Shakespeare establishment, and North American culture in the domains of race and gender' (1999: 342). This season involved the return of Plummer in Shaw's *Caesar and Cleopatra* directed by McAnuff, and the casting of Nikki M. James as Cleopatra was designed to bring an actor of colour onto the mainstage in a central role. However, more problematic was the difficulty visiting directors, like Zeigler, had managing the Festival Theatre's thrust stage. Taylor asserts that 'the Stratford company doesn't seem to know what to do anymore with this playing space' (1999: 345). Parolin recounts 'the Festival was so in thrall to the mystique of its premiere stage that what was once radical was now reactionary' (2009: 220). To search for inspiration the artistic directors brought in Adrian Noble (former artistic director at the RSC) to direct *Hamlet*, which starred Ben Carlson in his Festival debut. According to Parolin, 'the new directorate seemed determined to make the Festival Stage work again as a dynamic space that would unleash Stratford's deepest creativity' (2009: 220). However, this production's designer Santo Loquasto altered the stage by simply placing a large asymmetrical stage floor over the thrust.

The production opened with James Blendick's ghost appearing in a cloud of smoke, but this sombre start was followed by a burst of life and activity as the court assembled for a Victorian Christmas party. Ouzounian credits Carlson with 'energy, intelligence, virility, charm and a brilliant way of speaking the text' but also celebrates several other key members of the cast (2008). He praises Geraint Wyn Davies's Polonius as 'a real concerned middle-aged father' and Wentworth's Claudius as 'self-loving and self-loathing at once' (2008). Ouzounian also admires Adrienne Gould's Ophelia for 'creating real romantic and sexual tension with Carlson' (2008). This production was notable for its speed and dramatic use of spotlights, which probed into 'the dark recesses of the souls of Claudius, Gertrude and Prince Hamlet' (Threepwood 2008). According to Clarence Threepwood this *Hamlet* was filled with humour, as well as action. He describes Maria Ricossa's Gertrude as 'trim, brisk', while Gould he felt presented a 'lively, strong willed, Ophelia' (2008). The staging included military uniforms, rifles and a billiard table over which Claudius and Laertes discussed the death of Hamlet. Although Parolin indicates 'the gigantic pool table that occupied centre stage' forced 'Maria Ricossa's Gertrude to deliver her willow speech from the margins of the playing space' (2009: 221). Little was removed from the text, and

Fortinbras came to claim the throne at the end of the play. Running just over three hours, it was a thoughtful execution of the story which demonstrated the abilities of the company but said little about the country or the history of the Festival. Ouzounian claims, 'you couldn't find a better Shakespearean production in all of North America' (2008) and so it seems that imported expertise from Britain enlivened the work of the Festival on this occasion, but the return of 'hired hands' might be an apt description of this production.

Hamlet, 2015, Antoni Cimolino, Festival Theatre

By contrast, Cimolino's production of *Hamlet* in 2015 was both thoroughly rooted in the traditions of the Festival and showed evidence of influence from Noble's and other earlier productions. The 'set consisted of an array of black slabs, made to look like polished granite, evoking tombstones and war memorials' (Cimolino 2019: 16) but also the boxes of Monette's 1994 production. These slabs were arranged to provide different locations but, according to Cimolino, 'everywhere we went in the play, we were in the midst of death' (2019: 17). The characters began the play conventionally in the First World War but their costumes moved forward in time as the play progressed. The play ended with the arrival of Fortinbras in modern military dress. In terms of reach, this production far exceeded those that went before it, given that it was available in three different formats: live, in cinema and online. According to Ouzounian, it was a 'rock-solid production' which presented a 'vision of the play as coherent as it is consistent' (2015). What strikes Ouzounian as extraordinary is the fact that in addition to Jonathan Goad's 'witty, courageous, deeply, philosophical and touchingly human' Hamlet, the company of actors that surrounded him are so accomplished: 'They are all superb and play together like the rarest of teams' (2015). He credits Cimolino with creating a dramatically realistic environment 'in which people really talk to each other with such intensity. Every moment matters, and every moment is played with all reality' (2015). This production provided an excellent example of 'Stratford's signature aesthetic', 'a style of acting know as emotional realism' (Julian and Solga 2021: 197). Ouzounian found it 'the most complete, most fulfilling, most satisfying production of *Hamlet* I can recall in decades of theatregoing, and praise, belongs to everyone. That is the wonder of the Stratford Festival at its best' (2015). Cimolino brought the movement of Guthrie, the ensemble of Langham, the intensity of Phillips and the spontaneity and humour of Monette together in one production.

Portman, another long-time admirer of Stratford, highlights: 'Cimolino, who has himself acted on its famous stage, knows how to draw the audience into its seductive embrace [. . .] This is a production of genuine narrative clarity, but it also has a rare immediacy that brings this dysfunctional household into sharp and resting focus' (2015). The cast was composed of company stalwarts, many of whom had been in Noble's production, who together created a unified production, emphasizing the importance of the ensemble on this stage. Portman describes Geraint Wyn Davies, (Polonius in 2008), as 'oozing hypocrisy and insincerity as the usurping and murderous Claudius' (2015). Of Gould (playing Ophelia for the second time) he writes she 'brings a quiet vulnerability to her early scenes before unleashing a mad scene that is hair-raising in its raw display of unfettered sexual rage' (2015). Tom Rooney's Polonius (Horatio in 2008) was a pedant but also 'the shrewd and caring, elder statesman, whose death becomes an awful absurdity' (Portman 2015). Cimolino chose to make him a Lutheran minister, which 'provided the key to Polonius's tendency to sermonize' (Cimolino 2019: 21). Ouzounian points out: 'Cimolino finds new levels of meaning in the most unexpected places, like underscoring Polonius's boast that he played Julius Caesar once by having various guest members jokingly stab him, only a few scenes before he is actually killed' (2015). Portman writes that Goad's Hamlet 'makes it all so very, very personal'; 'His explosion of rage and anguish, sweeps through the theatre like a flame' (2015). This passion could be seen as a sign of the power of conviction that the company had by this point, knowing that this production would be seen as a marker of the accomplishments of the Festival for the future on film. Cimolino's *Hamlet* was designed to acknowledge and make use of the company's long history of performing this play when it was performed live in the theatre, while creating new audiences through cinema and online distribution.

Hamlet, 2022, Peter Pasyk, Festival Theatre

Young Toronto director Peter Pasyk was originally scheduled to direct *Hamlet* in 2020, but the pandemic closure meant both postponement and a new opportunity to seriously address the issues raised by casting an actor of colour in the title role in the context of the Black Lives Matter movement. Karen Fricker reports on the Festival's response to this crisis: 'The Stratford Festival has started a very public conversation that could change Canadian theatre forever. Last weekend, on June 6, it issued a statement that was unprecedented in admitting its "complicity in unjust systems" and [. . .] acknowledged its own systemic racism "in solidarity with those demonstrating for justice"' (2020a). The Festival's social media channels were then turned over for seventy-two hours to a group of Black company members, resulting in a two-hour online discussion called 'Black Like Me, past present and future: Behind the Stratford Festival Curtain' (Stratford Festival 2020a). The powerful conversation that took place allowed these artists to acknowledge, for the first time, the racist behaviour they had been subjected to throughout their training and professional lives. Fricker explains that the aim of the debate was to work towards concrete change: 'The Stratford social media takeover also pointed toward specific practices that are harmful to actors of colour, in particular the "as cast" contract that allows directors to place actors in smaller roles during a rehearsal process rather than stating roles at the point of hiring' (2020a). The discussion is frank and revealing. When Pasyk's production finally opened in 2022 there was an opportunity to take this discussion forward. Amaka Umeh as Hamlet had the chance to change the way the play was conceived on the Festival stage but the generational divide depicted on stage was again mirrored in the audience and in critical reception.

In her review of the production Fricker proclaims, 'Umeh is a brilliant anchor of a production communicating the paranoia of a contemporary surveillance state' (2022a). Returning to Hirsch's contemporary approach this production was a Denmark where the King ruled through observation, employing technology to keep an eye on everything that happens. Jessica Watson writes, 'The upper level is modelled as a high security facility, complete with glass panels and a walkway that provides a strategic view of the entire set. [. . .] The characters feel trapped, constantly under surveillance in their palace amongst their riches' (2022). This environment provided a sense of claustrophobia despite the spacious nature of the Festival Theatre. Mobile phones were used by the younger generation as part of their natural communications strategies, 'not just to communicate but to eavesdrop and provide video records of events' (Monaghan 2022). By contrast, the older generation used technology as a tool of control; 'Ophelia is made to wear a wire to get the goods on Hamlet' (Monaghan 2022). Watson notes that 'Suited security guards are present throughout the bulk of the show, patrolling the walkway above the stage, standing in the aisles' (2022). The design also allowed references to real-world events; 'Michelle Bohn's costumes reflect the real conversations of the relevance of monarchy in a modern world, with the older characters wearing crisp pressed suits and elegant gowns in muted tones, while the younger players wear brighter colours, wilder patterns and clothing set distinctly in 2022' (Watson 2022). The audience was confronted by a thoroughly recognizable world.

The text was heavily cut, reducing Horatio's part considerably and once again resolving the play without Fortinbras. Unfamiliar or inappropriate language for the updated environment was removed. Umeh played the part as a man; 'The tortured, grieving prince is still referred to as male: the invitation to the audience is to embrace the actor in the role with everything she brings to it' (Fricker 2022a), which included physically threatening behaviour, both towards herself and others. Kelly Monaghan notes the way the generations were divided by acting style as well as dress: 'The elders, Claudius (Graham Abbey), Gertrude (Maev Beatty), and Polonius (Michael Spencer-David) seem to be in a more traditional production and give far more traditional interpretations of their characters' (2022). While issues of race and power were central to this interpretation Watson questions whether gender-blind casting could be productive in a play that 'comments on gender' when 'Hamlet himself blames women for his predicament' (2022). She focuses her thoughts about the 'missed opportunity' of this production on the moment when Claudius accuses Hamlet of 'unmanly grief' in Act 1 scene 2; 'Upon hearing the word "unmanly," Umeh, in all her reactive brilliance, gave a small, bitter smirk: a subtle choice that I was excited for the production to build on' (Watson 2022). Watson concludes that 'Stratford's *Hamlet* is best when the actors leave the stage and make use of the audience, making the crowd a part of the action both as spectators and, ultimately, accomplices' (2022). Applebaum's famous Festival fanfare was played as the King and Queen took their seats as part of the theatre audience for the Mousetrap, turning the Stratford tradition of 'in jokes' on its head. As Fricker points out, the characters in this production, like 'the ever present security guards, watch us as we watch them' (2022a). These reviews reinforce the notion that this was a production centred around Hamlet and the importance of casting a Black actor to play the lead, but the focus of critical attention was also on those attending.

Finding a Festival Hamlet

The audience, on arrival at the Festival Theatre in 2022, was greeted by a glass casket containing Hamlet senior. The production was dedicated to Brent Carver and Christopher Plummer, who had both recently died; the spectre of old Hamlets was everywhere. Audiences were also dealing with the consequences of the combined crises of the pandemic and Black Lives Matter. Like Plummer's original performance on the same stage, there was an enormous weight of expectation placed on Umeh's shoulders. Watson suggests that 'Umeh's performance places her among the ranks of past Stratford Hamlets, including Colm Feore' placing her performance in the continuum documented here (2022). For Lauren Gienow, 'Umeh's Hamlet is very much a young adult of these specific times', working with the text she 'leans into the cynicism and dark nihilistic humour of the play' (2022) providing a vision of the production as a valuable cultural comment for the attending audience. But Monaghan points out the conundrum this production posed for the Festival; the 'sparse audience with whom I saw it (25% max of capacity at my estimate) gave it a standing ovation' (2022). While rave reviews and standing ovations justified the risks taken in this production, the empty seats were disastrous for a Festival that relies on box-office returns. The Stratford audiences in 2022 were not prepared to hear this production's call for self-scrutiny on the mainstage, given that this 'Hamlet's insolence to his elders can be breathtaking' (Monaghan 2022), a bit like Monette's in 1976.

Schargerl's question is important here: Can a production of *Hamlet* provide both a social critique and a commercial product? When ticket prices are out of reach for the target audiences sought, the answer is not simple. But this production must be seen as a first step in the much-needed renewal of the Festival's processes and the re-education of its audiences. While the first four decades of performances of the play looked to establish a distinctly Canadian Hamlet, the last three decades have slowly turned the question of what a Canadian Hamlet could or should mean, and more broadly what the Festival's purpose should be, over to the audience. Slow progress towards making the Festival more accessible and inclusive is being made. The Festival learnt from the experience of the 2022 *Hamlet* and in 2023; Pay-What-You-Will tickets were introduced for mainstage productions, including Gross's *King Lear*, directed by Kimberley Rampersad, the first woman of colour to direct at the Festival Theatre. Change at the Festival may be slow, but it is both possible and necessary.

9

Creating a legacy with *The Tempest* at the Festival

While Hamlet's anger with his elders enabled the Festival to question its future, Prospero's release of artistic control and reflection on his past has provided an opportunity for the Festival to consider its own growing legacy. One actor dominates the performance history of this play, while embodying the acting tradition of the Festival. William Hutt's four performances as Prospero spanned forty-three years and together helped to create a sense of a live theatre tradition which was entirely absent before the Festival began. In fact, Hutt's work at the Festival has been so influential that Robert Reid writes in response to his final performance in the role; 'it might be appropriate to subtitle the festival's first half century as the William Hutt era' (2005). However, Hutt's dominance in twentieth-century (he starred in productions in 1962, 1976, 1999 and 2005) is undermined by the existence on film of three of the four productions in which he did not star: John Hirsch's 1982 production, starring Cariou, filmed by the CBC, McAnuff's 2010 production, starring Plummer, filmed by Bravo!, and Cimolino's 2018 production, starring Henry, filmed by the Festival. While the first film was released only on television, the two more recent films were presented to cinema audiences before their television broadcast. All three productions are currently available online, placing them within the expanding global market for Shakespeare on film. As Kidnie notes, 'Stratford Festival HD ensures that [. . .] both within Canada and abroad, [Shakespeare in performance] is available in Canadian accents' (2018: 138). But she also highlights how the Festival's recent filmed productions differ from NTLive, in that they have never been broadcast in real time: 'The Festival thus prioritizes quality control over the simultaneity, and concurrent risk, of live transmission' (2018: 139). This focus on control in reaching much larger audiences is 'not without its cultural politics' (Kidnie 2018: 138). The Festival's programme of filming the entire canon places these Canadian productions alongside their British counterparts for an online audience. Therefore, *The Tempest* viewed live at the Festival, particularly in the twentieth century, was a spectacular event, showcasing the company's skills and the immersive theatrical magic that the play requires and the stages at Stratford allow. Whereas, filmed productions of *The Tempest*, particularly in the twenty-first century, demonstrate both the benefits of extending the work of the Festival to a wider audience and the real problems that exist in retaining the theatrical magic and sense of involvement which have become part of the 'Stratford Experience', highlighting the gap between living memory and preserved history.

The Tempest in Canada

With its complex layering of usurpations and examination of patterns of dominance and submission *The Tempest* has proven fertile ground for adaptation and alteration. While Henry's performance as Prospero was new to the Festival in 2018, Françoise Faucher featured in the leading role at Théâtre Expérimental des Femmes in 1988 in a translation of the play into Québécois French by Alice Ronfard and Marie Cardinal. Robert Lepage has also had an ongoing relationship with this play. His work first appeared on the international stage when he brought his Shakespeare cycle to Paris in 1992, which included productions of *Macbeth*, *Coriolan* and *La Tempête*, all performed in French, using the politically inflected Québécois translations of Michel Garneau. He also directed *The Tempest* at the National Arts Centre in Ottawa in the same year. In 2011 Lepage returned to *La Tempête* to stage the play on the Indigenous land near his home in Quebec. Melissa Poll documents this production and questions its approach to colonial history:

> Staged on the Huron-Wendat reserve outside Québec City, the production brought together Lepage, his collaborators at Ex Machina and a group of ten Indigenous artists, among them Innu singer Kathia Rock (Ariel) [and] Métis actor Marco Paulin (Caliban) [. . .] By overwriting *The Tempest's* island setting with the socio-political context of New France in 1608, Lepage reconfigured power structures in *The Tempest* to re-envision Shakespeare's text. (2018: 124)

Poll asserts that this collaborative production 'gestured towards recognizing the repercussions of colonialism' and 'featured instances of progressive interculturalism' (2018: 124). While Lepage has since been accused of cultural appropriation and faced protests in 2018 in response to his production *Kanata*, a play that represents the history of Canada (see Carson 2021), the 2011 production was an attempt to recognize the physical environment and cultural authority of Huron-Wendat people.

The play presents a real opportunity to reflect on the displacement of Canada's original inhabitants, but the political problems raised by doing so have meant that productions of *The Tempest* at Stratford have largely avoided any real engagement with the issue of the suppression of Indigenous culture. In 2020, following on from the conversation about systemic racism at the Festival by Black theatre artists, the Festival handed its social media channels over to Indigenous artists who were scheduled to work there in that season. 'Ndo-Mshkogaabwimi – We Are Standing Strong' recounted similar incidents of discrimination, exclusion and cultural appropriation (Stratford Festival 2020b). The fact that all performances at the Stratford Festival now begin with a land rights statement illustrates that the Festival has begun a process of acknowledging Canada's colonial history. But it is perhaps not surprising in a country where the mass graves of Indigenous children, taken from their parents to attend residential schools, are still being discovered that this play is produced in a way that does not look too closely at this aspect of Canadian history. Cimolino says, 'I feel that we have a special responsibility to Indigenous people in Canada and that means we would really like to build a stronger relationship with this community of artists' (qtd in Fricker 2020b). However, Jani Lauzon, the moderator of the YouTube panel, reports that there is 'an unfortunate residue of colonial thinking, which is an assumption of superiority' (qtd in Fricker 2020b). In terms of concrete changes to the Festival's working practices Fricker reports that modifications have been made to the pace and approach of rehearsals involving Indigenous artists and Cimolino states 'I feel strongly that, for the remainder of my tenure, I would like a play by an Indigenous writer in each season' (qtd in Fricker 2020b). However, it appears that these productions will continue to be in the smaller theatres. Therefore, the performance history of *The Tempest* at the Festival speaks softly to issues of social, cultural and political usurpation, forgiveness and redemption both within the organization and beyond it. These productions follow the play's ambivalent interrogation of these issues, while displaying spectacular theatrical expertise and elevating the presence and importance of the director and the actor in the central role. As with *Hamlet*, the history of this play is one which debates white male authority and Shakespeare's dominant position but within the context of the restrictive processes of the Festival's repertory training system.

The Tempest, 1962, George McCowan, Festival Theatre

As Langham's *Hamlet* had in 1957, this production provided an opportunity to show off the benefits of the stage arrangement in the recently renovated Festival Theatre. Langham entrusted the direction of the Festival's first *Tempest* to the Canadian director George McCowan, who had been actively involved in the Canadian Players. The storm at the beginning of the play was spectacularly staged; Walter Kerr writes, 'they turned practical theatre into intangible, breath-taking magic' (1962). But the action slowed after the opening. While the reviewers unanimously applauded Hutt's Prospero, he was seen to lack sympathy. Sydney Johnson writes, 'Hutt plays the role as an olympian figure easily moved to wrath. His Prospero has dignity and depth but it seldom suggests tenderness' (1962b). Henry's Miranda also drew critical accolades. According to Peter Bellamy, 'Henry is an actress of breathtaking beauty and charm' (1962),

FIGURE 10 *William Hutt as Prospero and Martha Henry as Miranda in* The Tempest *(Stratford Festival, 1962). Photograph by Peter Smith. Directed by George McCowan. Designed by Desmond Heeley. Courtesy of the Stratford Festival.*

while Kerr calls her Miranda 'a small, clear pool of innocence in an ambiguous world' (1962) (Figure 10). Considering the other key characters Kemp Thompson saw Bruno Gerussi's Ariel as 'a mercurial, clear-spoken, winning sprite', while John Colicos's 'elemental Caliban' provided 'a virtuoso performance by an actor of wonderful vocal accomplishments and great physical ability' (1962). Thompson concludes that the production gave the play 'an honest and serious treatment' (1962) with a strong focus on forgiveness. But it was the development of the father–daughter relationship between Hutt and Henry that would have an incalculable impact on the fortunes of the Festival.

The Tempest, 1976, Robin Phillips and William Hutt, Avon Theatre

In his second season in charge Phillips used this play to develop the skills of his young actors, but he also relied on Hutt as the play's star and co-director. The pre-season tour of the double bill of *Hamlet* and *The Tempest* to the Place des Arts in Montreal and the National Arts Centre in Ottawa promoted the sense that the Festival was for audiences outside Stratford and tested the mettle of the actors in environments where they were compared against other artists of national and international standing, before the run at the Avon Theatre. The leading actors who alternated between parts, Hamlet and Caliban in Monette's case and Hamlet and Ariel in Pennell's case, were given the opportunity to consolidate their interpretations of both roles. Monette's fiery, angry Hamlet had quite a bit of Caliban in him, and Pennell's more reserved and poetic Dane was influenced by his quiet and cool Ariel. But Gina Mallet points out the stereotypical nature of Monette's portrayal. She writes that he plays 'this contradictory and mythopoeic figure, who fulfils so aptly the colonist's bigotry about the natives, as a caricature of the hunchback of Notre Dame' (1976a), giving a sense of the unhelpful politics of the production (supporting the more recent stories of discrimination by Stratford actors (Stratford Festival 2020b)).

It was a production that highlighted its own theatricality right from the beginning, with a storm that was conjured out of nothing. Kevin Kelly in the *Boston Globe* describes how the production began 'with a rip-roaring storm at sea, a simple white sail dangerously flapping in a thundering wind, against flashing lightning, sailors crying out in wild fear' (1976). Hutt in his second outing in the role was considered by Kelly 'a majestic figure' who 'looks like a mix between Moses and the standard fountainhead of a lion' (1976). Miranda and Ferdinand, played by Maraden and Wetherall, were 'so joyously contagious their exuberance makes the audience burst into applause' (Kelly 1976). One key theatrical effect Phillips and Hutt brought to this production was the use of silent spirits attending Ariel. Kelly describes their effect: 'For most of the play the spirits do nothing but trail him, starting, moving, kneeling, oddly paralytic. [. . .] For a long while I found them distracting. Then, as the play continued, they were more effectively used. Strangely, the more I accepted their staring presence, the more mysterious they seemed, the more genuinely airy inhabitants of Prospero's island' (1976). These spirits, who watched but did not speak, could perhaps represent the audience, critical observers of Stratford's development. Phillips had been seen in his first season as a theatrical magician, building up the company and filling the Festival Theatre with dazzling stars and memorable productions. But his stage magic fell flat at the Avon Theatre for Terry Doran, who points out that stage effects 'simply don't work. Even when they are clever or inventive, they lack the power of the simplest tricks of the trade in film' (1976). And so, the limitations of the Avon stage, as well as Phillips, were highlighted by this production. However, Clive Barnes in *The New York Times* concludes, 'It was staged with a loving regard for the ritual aspects of the play and a special feel for the work as ritual' (1976a). The ripples of influence from this production and Phillips's approach to creating a theatrical apprenticeship for company members would prove crucial to the Festival's progress.

The Tempest, 1982, John Hirsch, Festival Theatre

This was Hirsch's first production, staged eighteen months after becoming artistic director, so it was rather unfortunate that Reg Skene saw it as 'an artistic disaster': 'Cariou as Prospero reduces one of Shakespeare's more complex characters into an insensitive, ranting bully [. . .] The role is played without irony and without a clear definition of emotional relationships' (1982). He concludes that Hirsch is the 'undisputed king of kitsch' (1982). Again, there was a dramatic and dazzling opening shipwreck, this time designed by Denis Heeley. Portman writes, 'It is a production which goes in for special effects with a vengeance' but he notes that these 'effects seem all too patently imposed from without by a production concept too clever and contrived for its own good' (1982). Only Robert Fulford, writing in the *Toronto Star*, defended the use of spectacle, calling it 'a showman's *Tempest*': 'Hirsch has taken that part of his artistic personality that responds to show-business dazzle and applied it to Shakespeare's most graceful, delicate and eloquent magic play. And somehow he's made that mixture work' (1982). While critics complained word of mouth about the show spread, and it generated more than C$1 million at the box office, inspiring standing ovations.

The CBC broadcast of this production showed a significant shift towards Phillips's vision for the work of the Festival, giving greater access for audiences not able to travel to Ontario, but the production also presented the play in an extravagant style which appealed to audiences with wide-ranging tastes. Trish Wilson suggests 'the action often teeters between the magical and cruder marshalling of stage hardware that would be more at home in a heavy metal concert than the festival stage' (1982). The glam rock costume worn by Ariel and the opulent operatic masque provided new levels of spectacle. The spirits who arrived with the banquet appeared as giant and terrifying insects, unafraid of the incomers. The silent spirits of the 1976 production had become a threatening presence. As for the other characters, Portman found James Mezon's Ferdinand and Sherry Flett's Miranda 'as bland as pablum' (1982). In the clowning scenes, which featured Pennell as Stephano, critics found compensation in an otherwise overproduced extravaganza, however, even Pennell was seen as 'shipwrecked with the rest of his unhappy crew' (Portman 1982). If Prospero here is seen as Hirsch, rather than Shakespeare, then this production highlights his defiant approach to leadership; using his power as the former head of Drama at the CBC, he was able to expand the remit and reach of the Festival in new ways, despite the critical reception of the work on stage.

The Tempest, 1992, David William, Festival Theatre

A decade later William also took the opportunity provided by this play to defy the expectations of his critics, opening the fortieth anniversary season on 'an eye-and-ear-catching note' (Brown 1992). Scarfe, as Prospero, stood aloft on the stage balcony, orchestrating everything before him. But again, the storm seems to have been the best part of this production: 'Prospero's initial emergence on the balcony, from between the pages of his book of magic, as he summons up the storm in the clearest and most purposeful of invocations, gives way to pure bedlam as the obedient thunder and lightning overwhelm the ship bearing his enemies' (Bale 1992). Bale suggests that while William and Scarfe were 'seeking a judicious, controlled marshalling of effects [. . .] bombast, both verbal and visual, repeatedly carries them away' (1992). *Toronto Sun* reviewer John Coulbourn considered Scarfe's performance 'stilted, self-satisfied and heavy' (1992). He concludes, 'though William tries to find new focus, this is not a *Tempest* with which to conjure, but rather one with which to lecture and instruct – a plodding *Tempest* barely worthy of the Stratford stage' (1992). Considering the other characters Bale notes 'Ariel (a shock-haired Ted Dykstra) shows up as a gigantic feathered harpie, distracting, rather than impressive' and his only praise is saved for Prospero's other servant; 'Caliban (Wayne Best) is a stunningly physical monster, lolloping around on all fours, ape-like, when he is not swinging by one arm from the balcony' (1992). While impressive visually Best perpetuated the stereotypical representation of Prospero's slave started by Monette (who moved into the role of Sebastian in this production). Coulbourn suggests that Ferdinand and Miranda managed merely 'an aura of inoffensiveness' (1992), while Geoff Chapman in the *Toronto Star* calls the production 'workmanlike' (1992). As with his 1991 *Hamlet*, William used this production to highlight the financial pressures facing the Festival at this time. He writes, 'Stratford is only one of many artistic institutions currently experiencing the severe pressure of an economic climate we are powerless to alter' (*The Tempest* programme 1992). Chapman notes the presence of important opening night guests 'with Governor-General Ray Hnatyshyn and festival founder Tom Patterson front and centre' (1992), illustrating the complex position for the artistic director of this government-sponsored institution. Both Hirsch and William used their productions of *The Tempest* to challenge perceived ideas about the creation of cultural capital at the Festival, as well as expectations of their directing styles, in this case largely unsuccessfully, since William's production was a financial as well as a critical disaster.

The Tempest, 1999, Richard Monette, Festival Theatre

The challenge of making Shakespeare profitable as well as accessible to a wide audience fell to Monette since, as Taylor points out, for much of the 1990s, plays by other authors 'consistently outperformed the Festival's patron saint' (1999: 349) in the main house. Approaching *The Tempest* in his sixth season Monette knew the play, the theatre and the audience well and had a longstanding relationship with his star, Hutt. But his own experience of the play was from the position of the characters who challenge the play's hierarchies and magic, Caliban (1976) and Sebastian (1982). This production used spectacle to engage the audience in a debate about the limits of theatrical illusion at the end of the twentieth century, relying on the audience's familiarity with Hutt's other work at the Festival. But the key to this production was the way that it combined spectacle with Hutt's commanding central performance and the audiences' history with the Festival. Sunil Mahtani writes, 'Hutt was the very essence of strength and majesty', he 'is a master of subtle expression and he held the audience in the palm of his hand each time he was on stage' (1999). Ian Gillespie in the *London Free Press* recounts how Hutt entered the stage 'a halting, fragile creature reaching his spiral-bone staff into the heavens as though he were about to gasp his last', but then the actor built in strength and passion until he reached his final speech, which read as 'an autobiographical comment on a life-long devotion to the art of the stage' (1999). This production was constructed to appeal to first-time and loyal audience members alike.

But Doran, in the *Buffalo Evening News*, calls it a 'touristy *Tempest*': 'Some episodes have been turned into production numbers. This only serves to call attention to the fact that we live in the Age of Movies. Strobe lights, stage fog, flash points, explosions and the like aren't going to do it' (1999). When it came to the 'overcostumed and overstaged' masque, Doran opines 'it might as well be Las Vegas [. . .] Hutt and others are rendered spectators in their own magical kingdom': he concludes that the spectacle was designed to 'address the audience not the play' (1999). The success of musicals on the Festival stage may have led Monette to excess on stage, but I suggest that there was another influence. Michèle Willems asks, 'Could we go so far as to say that postmodern re-presentation of Shakespeare, with its self-referential systems of echoes, allusions or even visual quotations, is in part at least the product of our new video culture?' (2000, 2007: 45). The recent release of a string of Shakespeare films, including Baz Luhrmann's extravagant *Romeo + Juliet* (1996) inevitably created a new environment for popular/ist performances of the plays. Monette and Hutt, working together over many years, had learnt to produce an experience that could be read and appreciated by different audiences in the theatre at once.

However, in *Canadian Theatre Review*, Maria DiCenzo, Alan Filewod, Ric Knowles, Harry Lane and Ann Wilson created a collaborative review of this season at the Festival (and its only real rival, the Shaw Festival), in which they suggest the limitations of this approach; 'Stratford continually replays an allegiance to its own history and its acting dynasties that positions the audience as a privileged spectator' (2000: 86). These five noted theatre academics claim, 'the production traded on memories rather than offering any new or engaged reading of the play' (DiCenzo et al. 2000: 87). Their review points out the imperatives of cultural tourism and the 'quasi-religious pilgrimage to the festival [which . . .] frame[s] the theatrical productions mounted' (DiCenzo et al. 2000: 85) suggesting that at the end of the twentieth century, the Festival was searching for its identity. These scholars argue that Monette and Hutt were 'locked in self-referentiality' which proved detrimental for other members of the cast, 'the Festival acting company seemed to disintegrated around' Hutt (DiCenzo et al. 2000: 86–7). This position is supported by reviews that paid little attention to the other characters on stage. Mahtani calls the lovers 'charming' and suggests that 'Caliban is almost like comic relief' although 'the interpretation doesn't quite come off' (1999). According to Gillespie, Peter Hutt (William's nephew) gave 'an amazing portrayal of Caliban who, as a spitting, sputtering, mangy mass of fur and fish scales manages to combine an endearing innocence with some frightening glimpses of deviant danger' (1999). But DiCenzo and company describe 'Stratford's appallingly racist neo-West-Indian reading of the "brute beast" Caliban' (2000: 86) 'as a kind of theatrical sadism' (2000: 88). Caliban's anger, suppressed by his position of servitude in a social hierarchy he cannot control, was presented in a very personal way in this production. Monette seems to have imposed his own experience playing Caliban onto the next generation of Stratford actor, Hutt the younger. However, despite critics finding fault with Monette's extravagant production values and disturbing racial stereotypes, audiences filled the houses, helping to bring the Festival back from the brink financially.

The Tempest, 2005, Richard Monette, Festival Theatre

The end of the career of one of the longest-serving actors at Stratford provided the focus for the remounting of Monette's 1999 production, creating a moment of realization for many in the audience. Noel Gallagher writes, 'The most memorable line in Shakespeare's *The Tempest* boasted a unique emphasis last night in the production launching the 2005 Stratford Festival season and the farewell stage engagement of William Hutt' (2005). His description of Hutt reinforces this point: 'the 85-year-old legend brings a majestic, Moses-like stature to the role of Prospero' (2005). Of 'the reliable supporting cast' Gallagher singles out Gould's 'moving', 'sweet, naïve teenager Miranda, whose relationship with her father creates this show's warmest and most amusing moments' and, importantly, Ouimette who 'offers an intense yet pleasing depiction of Caliban, the half-human half-devil struggling to achieve redemption' (2005). The lightness of Prospero's relationship with his young daughter was contrasted by the intense interaction he had with Caliban, not just as a character but in Hutt's and Ouimette's respective onstage histories. Moving from *Hamlet* (1994) to Caliban, Ouimette's upward movement in the company's hierarchy appears to have stalled, resulting perhaps in real anger in his portrayal. This reverential production highlights the limitation of the company's repertory model, which only allows a handful of actors to access its top positions.

Ouzounian's review is filled with hyperbole about Hutt's performance; 'His diction, posture and vocal control are superb, yet he manages to make every word, every thought seem freshly minted' (2005). Ouzounian marvels that Hutt 'takes some astonishingly unconventional risks. The famous line "Our revels now are ended" erupts in a burst of white-hot anger, rather than the customary haze of regret' (2005). However, he also highlights the fact that 'Ouimette's Caliban is more subtle than many, concentrating on the depth of his inner hatred, rather than its external manifestations' (2005). The long onstage histories of these actors were deeply felt by those in the audience who were aware of these complexities. But the emphasis on Hutt's impending departure took the focus away from the fact that Monette too was coming to the end of his tenure. Only Reid notes this, 'In his penultimate season as festival director, Richard Monette gives us a solid production that echoes his 1999 offering, staged in honour of Hutt's 50th anniversary in theatre' (2005). Reid adds that this production was also 'a tribute to John Hirsch, a former festival artistic director whose views on the late romance influenced Monette' (2005). In bringing up the influence of Hirsch this reviewer shifts the Festival's theatrical legacy away from the British influence of Phillips's pared-back 1976 production, to his Canadian successor's extravagant production of 1982. But when Reid writes, 'In contrast to contemporary directors who weigh *The Tempest* down under post-colonial baggage, Monette remembers the play is a comedy' (2005); it is faint praise which highlights that this director's sensibilities remained very much rooted in Stratford's twentieth-century traditions. Cushman reviewing the opening night was already looking to the future; 'The pause before [Hutt] bows to the inevitable, which is mercy, is going to be legendary' (2005). This production was designed to celebrate the Festival's growth into an institution of considerable size and importance, and it was fitting that Hutt, who had worked with each of the Festival's artistic directors, was given the opportunity to provide a finale for the founding tradition of the repertory model. The death of Hutt in June 2007, followed by the death of Monette in September 2008, resulted in the end of an era, making new approaches to running the Festival inevitable.

The Tempest, 2010, Des McAnuff, Festival Theatre

Following the critical and box-office success of Shaw's *Caesar and Cleopatra* in 2008, McAnuff and Plummer worked together for a second time on *The Tempest* to create both a stage show and a film for broadcast to cinema. J. Kelly Nestruck reviewing the stage production notes that in this production 'there are two magicians at work': 'The first is Christopher Plummer, a true wizard with Shakespeare's words. Prospero's lines always flow with such natural ease from him, sometimes in what seems like spontaneous spurts, other times as if he's tapped into some enchanted well of poetry deep within' (2010). The second magician, of course, was McAnuff as director who filled the stage with real stage magic: 'His production opens with a bright blue Ariel (the tiny and talented Julyana Soelistyo) swimming down from the ceiling to retrieve one of Prospero's books – a move straight out of a Cirque du Soleil spectacular' (Nestruck 2010). This review highlights the elements of the production which drew on the international careers of the director and actor who had made their names outside the country and links them with the success of the Quebec-based Cirque du Soleil, another Canadian contributor to the international entertainment industry of the twenty-first century. This production's success was based on its careful mixing of international influences with the former experience these two 'magicians' had with the Festival Theatre.

The production on stage included swords that magically danced, a cloak that appeared miraculously and even a moment when Plummer appeared to be seated in mid-air. The stage tricks made it clear that this Prospero was a joker as well as a vengeful tyrant. Kate Taylor makes a direct comparison with Hutt, suggesting that Plummer's performance 'was more overtly dramatic' [. . .] 'creating a man more visibly angry than the huge weary intelligence of his predecessor' (2010). Plummer made it clear that this was not going to be his last performance, yet performing the role at the age of eighty meant that his connection with Miranda was more as an indulgent grandfather than an overprotective father. Nestruck suggests that Trish Lindström's Miranda was 'a rather wild looking young woman who genuinely seems to have grown up without female role models' and even showed a hint of sexual interest in 'Dion Johnstone's scaly, spiny Caliban' (2010). This islander was a 'pathetic but sympathetic creature' (Nestruck 2010) who again was not discernibly related to the Indigenous population. As Nestruck points out, 'a scene where he paddles Trinculo and Stephano around in a canoe nods at that popular post-colonial interpretation' (2010) but the casting of a Black actor as Caliban was not seen as problematic, although it potentially fits within the 'sadistic' apprenticeship model suggested by the collaborative review (DiCenzo et al. 2000: 88). Johnstone's costume and make-up covered his entire body and his eye colour was obscured to make him appear as otherworldly as Ariel. Combined with the oblique references, like the canoe, this production provided a subtle but unchallenging approach to the issue of race within the company and colonial power in the play.

The Lords and the comic characters were both seen as unexceptional in this production, although the casting of Peter Hutt as Alonso, the King of Naples, having completed his apprenticeship as Caliban eleven years earlier, is perhaps worth noting. There was consensus among reviewers that the key relationship was between Prospero and Ariel: 'Plummer's real partner in the production was the otherworldly pixie [...] With both her crisp movements and efficient delivery, she created a delightful birdlike counterpoint to Plummer's heavy figure' (Taylor 2010). Nestruck suggests that this relationship was 'part master-slave and part father-daughter. They understand each other because they are both in bondage – Ariel to the whims of her master, Prospero to the churning emotions in his "old troubled mind"' (2010). This pairing, with an Ariel who was played as an androgynous child (but performed by a thirty-nine-year-old Asian actor), created an unusual love story at the centre of the play which moved audiences and critics alike (see cover image): 'her sad childlike smile infuses every scene with a bittersweet melancholy' (Ouzounian 2010). In the theatre the play was embraced for its tender rendering of a story of redemption and forgiveness, welcoming back to the fold two members of the Stratford family.

The filmed version of this production, given its reliance on stage magic, received a more mixed reception: 'in an age where computer animation can produce any magic it wants, the theatrical illusions inevitably can't bear the scrutiny of the close-up'; it is 'a film of many camera angles but little cinematic invention [. . .] that worthy but rather old fashioned (and not very expensive) thing: a filmed stage play rather than a film adaptation' (Taylor 2010). Both Kate Taylor and Peter Howell suggest that the film served to preserve this production and allow those who were not able to attend the sold-out run in person to see something quite special. But Howell goes on to celebrate the ingeniousness of the theatrical illusion: 'We can actually marvel at how simply and cleverly McAnuff and his crew conjure their illusions, without resorting to the computers that rule Hollywood. The opening storm sequences, using only sound and lights and flapping cloth, is as ingenious as the nylon stocking used for the twister in *The Wizard of Oz*' (2010). Howell makes a link to early cinema, rather than the English theatre tradition, which acts to give this filmed production value in a twenty-first-century North American context. This film, released in cinemas across Canada in November 2010, just after the end of the Stratford season, provided an extension of this production's run, for those not able to travel to Ontario, somewhat like the early tours and Hirsch's television broadcast.

However, when this production was streamed free online in December 2020 it was made available to an international audience able to access an array of resources from around the world. The Festival's 'Watch Party', which accompanied the broadcast, included a new interview with Plummer and McAnuff discussing their collaboration a decade later, an instance of using the streaming event to consolidate the Festival's reputation and history. Viewing the production on a computer screen the close-up action seemed to take the grandeur out of the leading performance. For Robert Tanitch, Plummer's Prospero 'is not composed of harshness. He comes across as a fatherly figure, a genial schoolmaster with a sense of humour' who 'knows from the start that the rarer action is in virtue [rather] than vengeance' (2020). The stage magic in the production, when seen online, was less impressive, but what was highlighted instead was the quality of the costumes. In particular, the elaborate Renaissance black and gold outfits of the Lords, and the goddesses of the masques when lit against a dark background, produced the eerie effect of Elizabethan portraiture (Tanitch 2020). The streamed version of this *Tempest* provided global reach for this production, which highlighted the work of the Festival for a new audience but also made connections with the Festival's past and posed questions about its potentially troubled future.

The Tempest, 2018, Antoni Cimolino, Festival Theatre

Cimolino's production of *The Tempest* starring Henry was steeped in collective memory and, like his *Hamlet*, highlighted the work of Stratford veterans, as well as its training programmes. Prospero's magical robe was a physical embodiment of the Festival's past; 'It incorporated the fabric from the robes worn by every actor who has played Prospero here, along with material from the dress worn by Martha when she played Miranda in her first Festival season in 1962, as well as pieces of the original Festival tent' (Stratford Festival 2021). Like Hutt's farewell to the stage, this production acknowledged Henry's long history of service and her devotion to training young actors, some of whom were with her on stage. Portman suggests that Henry brought 'a quiet wisdom to the role' that reflected 'this actress's own decades of service to Canadian theatre' (2018). Carly Maga writes 'Henry delivers the physicality, timing, cynicism, and humour of a woman who is tired – tired of her obvious skill, tired of having to wield it, tired of arguing for her particular place in a world dominated by men' (2018). Tackling the play as a female leader, in a tradition within the Festival of looking at Renaissance women of power (*Elizabeth Rex* and Hennig's trilogy), Cimolino chose to see Prospero as a depiction of Queen Elizabeth at the end of her reign, rather than Shakespeare, given that she was the ruler Shakespeare would have known best. Cimolino points out that despite the successes of Elizabeth's reign, 'there were pamphlets around London saying it's time to put an end to this old woman's government' (Cimolino and Henry 2018). This production was designed to provide the same kind of farewell to the stage that Hutt and Plummer had enjoyed, but as Nestruck highlights, 'The tension in this Prospero [...] is between her art and her child, Miranda' (2018). The tension felt by those on stage and in the audience was in terms of Henry's legacy, a pull between an outdated past and an undefined future.

Portman describes the spectacular opening shipwreck: 'sails flapping and breaking, winds shrieking through the darkness, frantic crew members shouting at each other [... it is] the most visually stunning *Tempest* ever to grace the Festival Theatre stage' (2018). But there was more to appreciate than just the spectacle: 'Stratford's most dependable company members are on hand for this production and that means an abundance of riches' (Portman 2018). Nestruck highlights individual performances; 'Graham Abbey and André Sills are a riveting double act' as Antonio and Sebastian, they 'fill the schemers with uncommon vigour and humour' (2018). He also notes 'stage legend' Ouimette's 'complete comic mastery as the clown Trinculo' and considers the romance between Ferdinand and Miranda 'as sweet as you could wish' (2018). The set drew Joe

FIGURE 11 *Josue Laboucane as Spirit, André Morin as Ariel, Martha Henry as Prospero and Mamie Zwettler as Miranda in* The Tempest *(Stratford Festival, 2018). Photograph by David Hou. Directed by Antoni Cimolino. Designed by Bretta Gerecke. Lighting design by Michael Walton. Courtesy of the Stratford Festival.*

Szekeres's attention: 'Director Antoni Cimolino has created a grand vista of a magical world [. . .] The split-level Festival stage has been raised and, at the top, there is a mighty tree with naked, overhanging branches. The strong, sturdy roots of the tree reach down to the stage below' (2018) (Figure 11). The recurrence of a great gnarled tree onstage could be seen as a visual reference to earlier productions (*As You Like It* 1977, 1990 *Richard III* 2002), and possibly even as a symbol of the Festival's own growth and development. As for the younger generation Szekeres calls Miranda and Ferdinand 'both sweet and whimsical' although it is intriguing that the casting of a mixed-race actor as the Prince of Naples is not mentioned in any of the reviews. Colour-conscious casting may not have been intended but with another actor of colour, Blake, playing

Caliban it raises questions. Like Johnstone's Caliban in 2010, Blake's skin colour was partially hidden in a costume which covered his body in fins and welts. But for a returning audience this second occurrence of a Caliban of colour seemed pointed. Nestruck found Blake's Caliban 'too sympathetic from the get-go' and the cast as a whole, in my view, seemed too reverential, too keen to support rather than challenge the dominance of the frail-looking Henry.

When considered alongside Lepage's colour-conscious *Coriolanus* the cross-casting of Blake as Caliban and Cominius, and Sills as Sebastian and Coriolanus, the two disrupters of the social hierarchy in *The Tempest* and the two men sent off to battle Rome's enemies in *Coriolanus*, the intersection of actors' roles provided a quiet commentary on the worlds of these two plays. The casting of Ouimette as 'a wickedly amusing' (Szekeres 2018) Trinculo and Junius Brutus and McCamus as Stephano and Menenius showed two different sides of these longstanding Stratford actors. In *The Tempest* they played another comic duo; however, in *Coriolanus* despite both being part of the reigning elite, they were on opposing sides when it came to their support of the central character. The modern-day setting of *Coriolanus* considered how current communications strategies harken back to Roman models, making a direct connection between the challenge to democracy we face today and the one addressed in the play. The power that Coriolanus has as a Black general was undermined by his lack of faith in the system which surrounded him, a government of old white men who had sent him to war. In a similar way casting a woman as Prospero challenged earlier approaches to this play. Henry relates, 'Antoni said to me, at one point, Elizabeth used to refer to herself as a prince. [. . .] Prospero refers to her/himself twice as a prince. And that gave me quite a lot of power' (Cimolino and Henry 2018). Cimolino also returns to the text to reinforce the notion of female power in the play; the figures of Juno and Ceres he suggests, 'come and say to Miranda, protect your strength, protect yourself, your virginity and do not give that up until you're ready to give it up, words that Queen Elizabeth lived by, because it maintains their power' (Cimolino and Henry 2018). Henry used her position of authority within the company to produce a Prospero that was 'compose and dignified' (Szekeres 2018) but which lacked the sonorous resonance and commanding presence of her predecessors.

The focus in this production on the power of female leadership was also explored through the relationships Prospero had with the islanders. Szekeres notes, 'André Morin encapsulates a majestic but sometimes hardened Ariel who has also endured challenges and struggles'; he had an 'unsteady relationship first with Caliban's witch mother, Sycorax, and now the former Duchess' (2018). Ariel was joined on stage by a series of silent spirits who impressed Szekeres with 'their complete stillness and quiet focus' (2018). Henry spoke directly to them at the end of the play, potentially acknowledging the power structures of the Festival's past. Nestruck suggests, 'Henry is most moving in the soliloquy where Prospero says goodbye to the magical creatures she has conjured over the many years she's ruled her enchanted island [. . .] a luminous love pouring out of her as a dozen bramble-headed beings gather at her feet' (2018). Only after the onstage community had been acknowledged, and her magic book had been cast away, did Henry speak directly to the devoted Stratford audience who surrounded her on three sides. Complicity and forgiveness were both addressed in a way that spoke to the attending audience.

Pandemic presentations

The link between Canadian culture and technology came into its own in 2020. The response of the Stratford Festival to the pandemic shut down was more robust, more determined and more open than many other theatres operating at this time. The Festival made an enormous effort to maintain its connection with its audiences, and this online activity, which included discussions from a range of perspectives involving participants in and around the productions, best replicates the feeling of excitement and engaged debate which takes place in Stratford most summers. The online screening schedule began with a trio of productions which featured leadership and social order and included Cimolino's productions of *King Lear*, starring Feore, and *Macbeth* starring Ian Lake, alongside Lepage's *Coriolanus* with Sills in the lead. *The Tempest* (2018) was the first in the second trio of films released focusing on isolation, which also included Cimolino's 2015 production of *Hamlet*, co-locating these two plays for Festival audiences for the first time since 1976. *Timon of Athens*, directed by Ouimette and starring Ziegler, was the third production screened. Other material was added online at that time to augment the viewing experience for audiences. *The Tempest* of 2018 is currently accompanied on the Stratfest@home platform by a virtual roundtable with the cast, and three conversations with Cimolino: one with the designer, Bretta Gerecke; one with academic Stephen Greenblatt; and one with Margaret Atwood discussing her novel *Hag-Seed* (2016) which is based on the play.

In Margaret Atwood's novel Felix, the artistic director of a Festival that is suspiciously like the Stratford Festival is ousted by his second in command (Tony) on the eve of his production of *The Tempest*. Felix retreats to the woodlands of Canada and works 'off grid' until he is given the opportunity to return and seek his revenge through staging the play in a prison setting, in front of his former rival, who is by this point a visiting government official. The novel involves an examination not only of the Festival but of Shakespeare's work and the position both hold in Canadian life, linked as they are in the story to other public structures including the prison system and the government. *Hag-Seed* considers the implications for Canadians of elevating not only a British playwright, but the cultural institution most associated with his work, to a position of pre-eminence in the country. The inclusion of Atwood in the material which supports Cimolino's production online illustrates how the discussions instigated by the plays and their performance at the Festival are amplified and extended through other creative forms. Perhaps the most extraordinary thing about the Stratford Festival is that it is both the source of a national theatre tradition and the centre for debate about alternatives to its position of authority.

In the twenty-first century, with the online presence of Festival productions on three different digital platforms, there is a danger that the debate around the plays will become diffuse and the identity of the organization will unravel. The end of the magic moments of recognition and interconnectivity, which have made the Festival such a special place for its live audiences, may be replaced by something new, but equally they may not. The question of Stratford's place in the international Shakespeare world of online resources is provoked by the simultaneous availability of the 2016 all-female production of *The Tempest* at the Donmar Warehouse, directed by Phyllida Lloyd, starring Harriet Walter, and Greg Doran's 2016 production for the Royal Shakespeare Company, starring Simon Russell Beale, which used image capture technology to create avatars on stage. The Stratford Festival online, a bit like Prospero, has re-entered a cosmopolitan world from which it has been excluded for many years. Thankfully the Festival, like the restored Duke of Milan, has introduced restorative processes to address the colonial approaches of the past and has young offspring, with different backgrounds and perspectives, who will help to steer a new course for the future.

Conclusion – A moment of reorientation for the company (2022–3)

All's Well That Ends Well, 2022, Scott Wentworth, Tom Patterson Theatre

The second play to open in the new Tom Patterson Theatre in June 2022 was, naturally, *All's Well*, this time featuring Jessica B. Hill as Helen (as she was called in this production) and Jordin Hall as Bertram, both graduates of the Birmingham Conservatory and actors of colour. The plot of this play centres around the ideas of family, loyalty and lineage, involving and even contrasting the connections that are created through biology with those that are forged through hard work and affection. In the programme notes Kidnie emphasizes the importance of the play's 'conspicuous generational divide': 'There are young adults leaving their families and trying to find their place in the world, and there are superannuated parents and guardians who seem like relics of another time. This older generation have made their names and established their wealth through feats and adventures that belong to the past' (*All's Well* programme 2022a: 7). While she is not directly addressing the working conditions of the Festival, Kidnie's remarks are a fitting description of the expectations, but also the possibilities, available to the younger generation: the 'power and authority this older generation still wields [...] is immense' (*All's Well* programme 2022a: 7). In the context of this production the implications of casting young Black actors in the roles of the younger generation seem significant. McKenna as the Countess and Carlson as the King of France were on hand as mentors, as well as established Stratford stars, but the focus of this production was on creating future opportunities for the young actors on stage. Hill shone when she was given scope to interact with the audience. This Helen was clear-sighted about the obstacles in her way, but she was convinced that through diligence and persistence she could triumph. She won over the audience, not with a misplaced sense of romanticism, or her overwhelming love for Bertram, but through her sense of outrage at the limitations placed on her because of her status. Her desire to challenge the social order was not merely for personal gain but because it was the right thing to do (Figure 12). As a result, she earned the

FIGURE 12 *Jessica B. Hill as Helen in* All's Well That Ends Well *(Stratford Festival, 2022). Photograph by David Hou. Directed by Scott Wentworth, Designed by Michelle Bohn. Lighting design by Louise Guinand. Courtesy of the Stratford Festival.*

affection of the Countess, and the audience, who had no trouble seeing Bertram's limitations.

While the costumes and minimal set pieces indicated that the production was taking place in and around the First World War in Europe (again), the sensibility was centred on the company in the present moment. Director Wentworth insists: 'The play we are hearing today is very different from the one Tyrone Guthrie and his company heard in 1953. And that's as it should be. The play our company is hearing, with all its contradictions, seems very much a play for our world as it is today' (*All's Well* programme 2022a: 5). Wentworth, in his twenty-seventh season with the Festival, was very much part of the establishment that Helen/Hill may want to displace, but the institution which has supported him in both his acting and directing endeavours, also provided this opportunity for the younger generation to enter a debate about its future. Quite poignantly he writes 'it is a play of hope, of paradise lost and the cost of paradise regained' (*All's Well* programme 2022a: 5) which again could be referring as much to the Festival's post-pandemic recovery as to the long-term happiness of Helen and Bertram. Ultimately, the future of the Festival rests with a new generation and their ability to continue to find ways to engage audiences in the questions and problems put forward by the plays. The Patterson stage, with its extremely long thrust, invites the audience to participate across the space. The steps down into the auditorium and the entrances through the vomitoria between and underneath audience members mirror the original Festival stage but the space is entirely flexible and is supported by a range of technical additions which could not have been achieved in the larger hall. This theatre has been created as a space for experimentation, drawing together the old and the new to make something fresh for the future. While there were teething problems with the first two productions, this space has the potential to change the focus of the Festival. The 'Miracle' of the first season was a collective act of faith. At the end of the performance I attended, Helen seemed as amazed as the audience that her mad plan had succeeded. And that is the magic formula which defines the work of the Stratford Festival; it is a combination of hard work and familiarity with the plays and the players in an intimate environment that allows everyone in the space to create something new together in the present moment out of Shakespeare's plays.

Coming full circle

The Stratford Festival has spent the past seventy years balancing ingenuity and convention, innovation and industry, creativity and commerce. It has nurtured Canadian talent, but it has also been accused of hoarding the limited public arts funding available in the country, thereby curtailing creativity elsewhere. The fact that the Festival has produced a body of internationally renowned actors and directors is balanced by the criticism it faces in the national media and in scholarly debates about the detrimental role of Shakespeare in forming a unique Canadian theatrical identity. The Stratford Festival set out to reinvent Shakespeare's work on a new stage for a new audience, but it also wanted to reinvent Canada's vision of itself and give the country an international presence culturally. Is there a performance style created by the Festival which is uniquely Canadian? If there is, it is the energetic relationship between theatre architecture and Shakespeare's texts, realized by a dedicated company in the presence of a knowledgeable recurring audience over time. Combining the lessons taught by well-established British theatre artists with a Canadian perspective resulted in a house style that utilizes exuberant physical action to enliven the plays' debates about social hierarchies and generational divides. But more than just a style, the initial goal of the Festival was to give Canada a theatre tradition it could be proud of and in that it must be seen as a success. Not through every production or through the work of any one artistic director, but instead through the cumulative effort of hundreds of actors, directors, designers, playwrights, musicians, technicians, administrative staff, archivists and, most importantly, audiences, the majority of whom have been Canadian. In many ways the Stratford Festival is more like Shakespeare's Globe than the RSC, in its experimental approach to theatre architecture and its exploration of the relationship between theatre spaces and audience interaction. Like Sam Wannamaker at the Globe, Tom Patterson, the instigator of the Stratford Festival, stands for a set of pioneering ideals which are the responsibility of all future members of the company to maintain. The renovated Tom Patterson Theatre, which is devoted to educational outreach and experimental work, is a testament to those ideals and to the notion that the company is an important part of Canada's theatrical culture, not removed from it.

Epilogue: Martha Henry Memorial, 13 November 2021

Martha Henry passed away just twelve days after her final performance in the Studio Theatre of Edward Albee's *Three Tall Women* on 9 October 2021. A month later the Festival Theatre was reopened for the first time since the pandemic closure to honour her extraordinary contribution. Henry's career, and its marking in a public but intimate event, sums up the spirit of the Stratford Festival in ways few other single afternoons in the theatre could. In addition to the spoken and sung live contributions, there were clips from video performances and testimonials which were recorded for Henry's receipt of the Stratford Festival Legacy Award in 2014. But behind and above all of this was a silent record of her many performances projected onto a screen at the back of the stage on which she had performed so many times. Three of the costumes from her most notable roles stood on either side of the screen, including Prospero's robe, as a quiet reminder of where she had been standing herself for fifty-six years. The Memorial Tribute ended with an invitation to the audience to look beneath our seats. There every member of the audience found a volume from Henry's personal library. My prize was an early edition of the collected works of Anton Chekhov, a playwright whose work she both acted in and directed. My mother received Antony Sher's *The Year of the King* (2004) a fitting connection with Stratford-upon-Avon and another actor whose work was synonymous with the activity of a company dedicated to Shakespeare's work. My father's volume was the RSC edition of *King John* and *Henry VIII* (2012), another link between the two Stratfords, but also between the academic and theatrical worlds. The hierarchy of learning that has been established both in the academic world and in the theatre world, through companies like the Stratford Festival and the RSC, provides structures of learning that aim to train young people to take over the work of their elders. For those who can embrace the opportunity, and better the instruction of their teachers, this model can produce astonishing results. For those who find their work does not fit within the confines of the apprenticeship structure of a repertory company, the experience can be detrimental, even destructive. It is somewhat ironic that the Stratford Festival, which was set up, and often moved forward, by theatre artists who did not feel their work fit within the British hierarchies of learning and performance, created its own set of parameters which put in place a similar sense of inclusion and exclusion.

Henry's legacy was her work as an actor, a director but most importantly as a mentor and teacher of the next generation of Canadian theatre artists. Naturally not every actor who has wanted to enter the Stratford Festival has been given the opportunity to do so, and there are many who could claim, with justification, that they were excluded from promotion within the company. But the sense of the Festival as a family is one that is supported not only by the actors who have worked there over many seasons but by the fact that those working backstage and in administration, as well as many audience members, have multi-generational attachments to it. As a member of the regular audience, I have been given the opportunity to watch actors and directors work their way through the plays over their careers, providing me with a depth of understanding of these works which is unmatched in other places. But the Stratford Festival has also always had a very clear sense of its history and has been careful to promote and preserve its legacy. The digital world is making archival material more accessible, and the Festival is now very well placed to make its story available to a wider audience.

To be involved in the Stratford Festival requires a certain commitment to the cause of creating a future for Canadian theatre. As an institution this Festival has succeeded in creating a sense of what the pinnacle of Canadian Shakespeare achievement might look like. While it often misses the mark, the Festival has provided sufficient evidence of what it can produce to keep its audiences engaged in the ongoing work of making Shakespeare speak to Canadians. Chris Wiegand's review of the 2023 season in *The Guardian* illustrates that the Festival's appetite for experimentation with repertoire and its commitment to live theatre continues: 'With three plays performed in rotation on its main stage, the festival leaves you in no doubt of a production's ephemeral nature [. . .] And who knew that Larson's musical [*Rent*] has so much in common with Lear?' (2023). Combining contemporary work that looks at life and love in the shadow of disease, with Shakespeare's great tragedy of the Early Modern plague era, demonstrates how the Festival is facing the post-pandemic world. In many ways 2023 was the 'New Beginning' of Cimolino's imagining, instigating the next phase of the Stratford Festival, as a centre of international importance which promotes inclusive approaches to Shakespeare's work for future generations, both within and beyond Canada's borders.

REFERENCES

Note: All references to Shakespeare's plays refer to Ann Thompson, David Scott Kastan, H. R. Woudhuysen and Richard Proudfoot, eds (2021), *Arden Shakespeare Third Series Complete Works*, London: The Arden Shakespeare.

Adams, David (2022), 'Financial Report 69th Annual Meeting of Members, The Stratford Shakespearean Festival of Canada', 2 April.

Atkinson, Brooks (1953), '"All's Well That Ends Well" Opens at the Stratford Festival', *New York Times*, 16 July.

Atkinson, Brooks (1956), 'Theatre: Bard in Canada', *New York Times*, 20 June.

Atkinson, Brooks (1957), 'Hamlet at Stratford Found Spirited, Modern', *Globe and Mail* (*New York Times Service*), 3 July: 3.

Atwood, Margaret (2016), *Hag-seed*, London: Hogarth Press.

Bainbridge, Roger (1976), 'Nicholas Pennell in Two Roles: Brooding Hero to Mischievous Sprite', *Kingston Whig Standard*, 6 February.

Bale, Doug (1976), 'Pennell's more Compelling: Hamlet Given Two Interpretations', *London Free Press*, 8 March.

Bale, Doug (1986), 'Unity, Coherence Missing in Stratford's Hamlet', *London Free Press*, 21 May.

Bale, Doug (1992), '*Tempest* Starts, Ends Well, but Sailing is Rough in Middle', *London Free Press*, 3 June.

Barber, John (1979), 'Shakespeare Locked in Deep-Freeze of Ritual', *Daily Telegraph*, 9 June.

Barnes, Clive (1976a), 'Stage: Two at Stratford', *New York Times*, 10 June.

Barnes, Clive (1976b), 'Stage: "Cleopatra" and "Earnest" in Canada', *New York Times*, 12 July.

Bellamy, Peter (1962), '"Tempest" Is a Gale of Beaty', *Ohio Plain Dealer*, 22 June.

Bennett, Susan (2022), 'Afterword', in Robert Ormsby and Valerie Clayman Pye (eds), *Shakespeare and Tourism*, 285–91, London: Routledge.
Berry, R. (1979), 'Stratford Festival Canada', *Shakespeare Quarterly*, 30 (2): 167–75.
Brown, Stewart (1992), 'A Fine *Tempest* Blows into Stratford', *Hamilton Spectator*, 4 June.
Brydon, Diana and Irena R. Makaryk, eds (2002), *Shakespeare in Canada: A World Elsewhere?*, Toronto: University of Toronto Press.
Brydon, Ronald (1964), *New Statesman*, 10 April.
Buccalo, Regina (2019), *Haunting History Onstage: Shakespeare in the USA and Canada*, Cambridge: Cambridge University Press.
Campbell, Nora René (1982), 'The Stratford Festival of Canada: Evolution of an Artistic Policy (1953–1980) as Basis for Success', PhD diss., University of Wisconsin-Madison.
Canadian Press (1976), 'Two Actors Portray Different Hamlets', *Vancouver Sun*, 8 March.
Canadian Press (1986), 'Carver Portrays Passionate Hamlet', *Guelph Mercury*, 21 May.
Carson, Christie (2021), *Robert Lepage's Intercultural Encounters*, Cambridge: Cambridge University Press.
Carson, Neil (1974), 'Some Textual Implications of Tyrone Guthrie's 1953 Production of *All's Well That Ends Well*', *Shakespeare Quarterly*, 25 (Winter): 52–60.
Carson, Neil (2010), 'A Fresh Advance in Shakespearean Production: Tyrone Guthrie in Canada', in Christine Dymkowski and Christie Carson (eds), *Shakespeare in Stages: New Theatre Histories*, 57–70, Cambridge: Cambridge University Press.
Chapman, Geoff (1992), '*Tempest* in a Textbook Empty without Scarfe', *Toronto Star*, 2 June.
Chapman, Geoff (1994), 'Ouimette's Mad Hamlet becomes Vividly Accessible', *Toronto Star*, 6 June.
Cimolino, Antoni (2019), 'The Play's Not the Only Thing', in Kenneth Graham and Alysia Kolentsis (eds), *Shakespeare on Stage and Off*, 15–24, Montreal & Kingson: McGill-Queens University Press.
Cimolino, Antoni (2022), 'Antoni Cimolino on the Stratford Festival', *Shakespeare Alive*, 9 August. Available online https://shakespearealive.buzzsprout.com/1438858/11035514 (accessed 15 July 2023).

Cimolino, Antoni and Martha Henry (2018), 'Insights from the Director and this Production's Prospero' Performance Plus', Stratfest@home.ca Available online https://www.stratfordfestival.ca/Learn/Teachers/TeachingResources/PerformancePlus/The-Tempest (accessed 15 July 2023).
Conlogue, Ray (1998), 'Troubled Times for Classical Theatre', *The Globe and Mail*, 11 July.
Coulbourn, John (1992), 'Plodding *Tempest* Unworthy of Bard', *Toronto Sun*, 3 June.
Coulbourn, John (2000), 'Going Mad for Hamlet', *The Toronto Sun*, 30 May.
Crew, Robert (1986a), 'High Jinks with Hamlet', *Toronto Star*, 23 May.
Crew, Robert (1986b), 'Daring *Cymbeline* a Winner', *Toronto Sunday Star*, 3 August.
Cushman, Robert (1977), 'Flying the Flag', *The Observer*, 19 July.
Cushman, Robert (2002), *Fifty Seasons at Stratford*, Toronto: McClelland & Stewart.
Cushman, Robert (2005), 'The Difficulties of Playing Opposite a Stage Legend', *National Post*, 2 June.
DeVine, Lawrence (1986), '"Henry VIII": A Rousing Resurrection', *Detroit Free Press*, 25 May.
DiCenzo, Maria, Alan Filewod, Ric Knowles, Harry Lane and Ann Wilson (2000), 'Cultural Tourism at Shaw and Stratford: The Shaw Festival and the Stratford Festival 1999', *Canadian Theatre Review*, Spring: 85–8.
Dobson, Michael and Stanley Wells, eds (2001), *Oxford Companion to Shakespeare*, Oxford: Oxford University Press.
Doran, Terry (1976), 'Straining for Effects Puts Damper on Magic of "The Tempest"', *Buffalo Evening News*, 24 June.
Doran, Terry (1999), 'At Stratford, a Touristy "Tempest"', *Buffalo Evening News*, 3 June: D-5.
Edinborough, A. (1957), 'Canada's Permanent Elizabethan Theatre', *Shakespeare Quarterly*, 8: 511–14.
Edinborough, A. (1969), 'The Director's Role at Canada's Stratford', *Shakespeare Quarterly*, 20 (4): 443–6.
Everett-Green, Robert (2016), 'The Tragicomedy of Shakespeare in Quebec', *The Globe and Mail*, 21 May: R11.
Filewod, Alan (1987), *Collective Encounters: Documentary Theatre in English Canada*, Toronto: University of Toronto Press.

Fraser, John (1976), 'On the Road with Hamlet(s): Not Hamstrung, Still Hampered', *The Globe and Mail*, 20 March.

Fricker, Karen (2020a), 'The Stratford Festival Admitted Its Own Systemic Racism and Gave Black Artists a Chance to Speak Out', *Toronto Star*, 10 June.

Fricker, Karen (2020b), 'Indigenous Voices Take the Lead on Stratford Festival's Social Media', *Toronto Star*, 18 June.

Fricker, Karen (2022a), 'Amaka Umeh is Engrossing and Revelatory in the Stratford Festival's *Hamlet*', *Toronto Star*, 3 June.

Fricker, Karen (2022b), 'Two Very Different Hamlets Open a Conversation about Where the Stratford Festival is Heading', *Toronto Star*, 2 August.

Fulford, Robert (1982), 'Others Storm, but One Man has Big Hurrah for Hirsch's *Tempest*', *Toronto Star*, 28 August.

Gallagher, Noel (2005), 'Hutt's Prospero Fitting Swansong', *London Free Press*, 1 June.

Galloway, Myron (1976a), 'Monette's Hamlet Intense, Sharp', *Montreal Star*, 18 March.

Galloway, Myron (1976b), 'Second Hamlet Excels as Troubled Dane', *Montreal Star*, 19 March.

Gienow, Lauren (2022), 'Hamlet at the Stratford Festival is Fresh and Brilliant and Amaka Umeh is a Star', 3 June. Available online https://www.broadwayworld.com/toronto/article/BWW-Review-HAMLET-at-the-Stratford-Festival-is-Fresh-and-Brilliant-and-Amaka-Umeh-is-a-Star-20220603 (accessed 15 July 2023).

Gillespie, Ian (1999), 'Actor Comes Close to Writer's Genius', *London Free Press*, 1 June.

Groberman, Michael (1991), 'Horror Style Hamlet just doesn't Work', *Ottawa Citizen*, 29 May.

Groome, Margaret (2002), 'Stratford and the Aspirations for a Canadian National Theatre', in Diana Brydon and Irena R. Makaryk (eds), *Shakespeare in Canada: A World Elsewhere?*, 108–36, Toronto: University of Toronto Press.

Guthrie, Tyrone (1959, 1987), *A Life in the Theatre*, London: Columbus Books Ltd.

Guthrie, Tyrone and Robertson Davies with drawings by Grant Macdonald (1953), *Renown at Stratford*, Toronto: Clarke, Irwin & Company.

Guthrie, Tyrone and Robertson Davies with drawings by Grant Macdonald (1954), *Twice the Trumpets Sounded*, Toronto: Clarke, Irwin & Company.

Guthrie, Tyrone, Robertson Davies, Boyd Neel and Tanya Moiseiwitsch (1955), *Thrice the Brinded Cat Mew'd*, Toronto: Clarke, Irwin & Company.

Hayman, Edward (1986), '"Hamlet" Comes Off "Taut, Eloquent"', *The Detroit News*, 21 May.

Hayman, Edward (1991), 'Alas By-the-Book "Hamlet" Lacks Humanity', *The Detroit News*, 28 May.

Hirsch, John (1981), 'John Hirsch on Stratford', *Canada Today/ D'Aujourd'hui*, 12, no. 4 (April): 7.

Hirsch, John (1988), 'Directing Shakespeare: Celia O'Neal in conversation with John Hirsch', *Canadian Theatre Review*, 54: 46–51.

Howell, Peter (2010), 'Grand Acting in a *Tempest* that Tickles', *Toronto Star*, 5 November.

Hunter, Martin (2001), *Romancing the Bard: Stratford at Fifty*, Toronto: Dundurn Press.

Jackson, Berners A. W. (1968), 'Retrospective/ the Stratford Festival 1958–1968', in Peter Raby (ed.), *The Stratford Scene 1958–68*, 13–25, Toronto: Clarke, Irwin & Company.

Jackson, Berners A. W. (1973), 'Powerful *Pericles* a Revelation', *Hamilton Spectator*, 8 August.

Jackson, Berners A. W. (1975), 'Stratford Festival Canada', *Shakespeare Quarterly*, 27 (1): 24–32.

Jenstad, Janelle Day (2003), 'The Stratford, Ontario, 2002 Season: A Canadian's Overview', *Shakespeare Bulletin*, 21 (2): 48–50.

Johnson, Sydney (1962a), 'Peter Coe Revolutionises "Macbeth"', *Montreal Star*, 19 June.

Johnson, Sydney (1962b), 'A Faint Aura of Disappointment', *Montreal Star*, 21 June.

Julian, Erin and Kim Solga (2021), 'Ethics: The Challenge of Practising (and not just representing) Diversity at the Stratford Festival of Canada', in Peter Kirwan and Kathryn Prince (eds), *The Arden Research Handbook of Shakespeare and Contemporary Performance*, 192–210, London: Bloomsbury Publishing.

Karr, Jack (1957), 'New Theatre, Hamlet vie for Audience, Plummer Compelling', *Toronto Daily Star*, 2 July.
Kelly, Kevin (1976), 'Powerful "Tempest" Grips Stratford', *Boston Globe*, 11 June.
Kennedy, Dennis (1993), *Looking at Shakespeare: A Visual History of Twentieth-Century Performance*, Cambridge: Cambridge University Press.
Kennedy, Dennis (2017), 'Global Shakespeare and Globalized Performance' in James Bulman (ed.), *The Oxford Handbook of Shakespeare and Performance*, 441–57, Oxford: Oxford University Press.
Kerr, Walter (1953), '"All's Well": Old Comedy is Very Much Alive', *New York Herald Tribune*, 16 July.
Kerr, Walter (1956), '*Henry V* is Presented at Canada's Stratford', *New York Herald Tribune*, 20 June.
Kerr, Walter (1962), 'The Tempest', *New York Herald Tribune*, 22 June.
Kerr, Walter (1968), 'Stratford *Tartuffe* Greater than Superb', *New York Times*, 23 June.
Kidnie, Margaret Jane (2004), '"What World Is This?" *Pericles* at the Stratford Festival of Canada, 2003', *Shakespeare Quarterly*, 55: 307–19.
Kidnie, Margaret Jane (2016), 'Proximal Dreams: Peter Sellars at the Stratford Festival Canada', in Susan Bennett (ed.), *The Shakespearean International Yearbook 16: Special Section, Shakespeare on Site*, 11–28, Abingdon: Routledge.
Kidnie, Margaret Jane (2018), 'The Stratford Festival of Canada: Mental Tricks and Archival Documents in the Age of NTLive', in P. Aebischer, S. Greenhalgh and L. Osborne (eds), *Shakespeare and the 'Live' Theatre Broadcast Experience*, 133–46, London: The Arden Shakespeare.
Kidnie, Margaret Jane (2020), personal correspondence, email.
Knelman, Martin (1982), *A Stratford Tempest*, Toronto: McClelland and Stewart.
Knowles, Richard Paul (1994), 'Shakespeare, 1993, and the Discourses of the Stratford Festival, Ontario', *Shakespeare Quarterly*, 45 (2): 211–25.
Knowles, Richard Paul (2004), *Shakespeare and Canada: Essays on Production, Translation and Adaptation*, Brussels: P.I.E – Peter Lang.

Knowles, Richard Paul (2005), 'Encoding/Decoding Shakespeare: *Richard III* at the 2002 Stratford Festival', in Barbara Hodgdon and W. B. Worthen (eds), *A Companion to Shakespeare and Performance*, 297–318, Oxford: Wiley-Blackwell.

Kroker, Arthur (1984), *Technology and the Canadian Mind: Innis/McLuhan/Grant*, Montreal: New World Perspectives.

Kuling, Peter (2017), 'Counterfactual History at the Stratford Festival: Timothy Findley's *Elizabeth Rex* and Peter Hinton's *The Swanne*', in Irena R. Makaryk and Kathryn Prince (eds), *Shakespeare in Canada: Remembrance of Ourselves*, 72–8, Ottawa: University of Ottawa Press.

Langham, Michael (1968), 'Introduction/Twelve Years at Stratford', in Peter Raby (ed.), *The Stratford Scene 1958–68*, 6–12, Toronto: Clarke, Irwin & Company.

Langham, Michael (1982), 'Interview', in Nora René Campbell, 'The Stratford Festival of Canada: Evolution of an Artistic Policy (1953–1980) as Basis for Success', PhD diss., University of Wisconsin-Madison, 418–20.

Lieblein, Leanore (2002), '"Le Re-making" of le grand Will: Shakespeare in Francophone Quebec', in Diana Brydon and Irena R. Makaryk (eds), *Shakespeare in Canada: A World Elsewhere?*, 174–91, Toronto: University of Toronto Press.

Mackintosh, Iain (2011), *The Guthrie Thrust Stage: A Living Legacy*, Association of British Theatre Technicians.

Maga, Carly (2018), 'As Stratford's Prospero, Martha Henry has Firm Grasp on Her Magic', *Toronto Star*, 12 June. Available online https://www.thestar.com/entertainment/stage/review/2018/06/12/as-stratfords-prospero-martha-henry-has-firm-grasp-on-her-magic.html (accessed 15 July 2023).

Mahtani, Sunil (1999), 'Stratford's Tempest Soars', *The Record Sherbrooke*, 3 September.

Makaryk, Irena R. (2001), 'Canada', in Michael Dobson and Stanley Wells (eds), *Oxford Companion to Shakespeare*, 64–5, Oxford: Oxford University Press.

Makaryk, Irena R. (2002), 'Introduction', in Diana Brydon and Irena R. Makaryk (eds), *Shakespeare in Canada: A World Elsewhere?*, 3–41, Toronto: University of Toronto Press.

Makaryk, Irena R. and Kathryn Prince, eds (2017), *Shakespeare in Canada: Remembrance of Ourselves*, Ottawa: University of Ottawa Press.

Mallet, Gina (1976a), 'Two Directors Put Emphasis on Romance', *Toronto Star*, 28 June.
Mallet, Gina (1976b), 'Stratford's Young Hamlets Worthy Contenders Both', *Toronto Star*, 19 August.
Mallet, Gina (1977), '*Much Ado about Nothing* is Embalmed Shakespeare', *Toronto Star*, 17 August.
McGee, C. E. (2002), 'Shakespeare *Canadiens* at the Stratford Festival' in Diana Brydon and Irena R. Makaryk (eds), *Shakespeare in Canada: A World Elsewhere?*, 141–58, Toronto: University of Toronto Press.
Mietkiewicz, Henry (1986), 'Hutt a Mesmerizing Man for All Seasons', *Toronto Star*, 25 July.
Monaghan, Kelly (2022), '*Hamlet* at the Stratford Festival', Ontariostage.com, 3 June. Available online https://ontariostage.com/hamlet-at-the-stratford-festival/ (accessed 15 July 2023).
Moore, Don (2017), 'Race, National Identity, and the Hauntological Ethics of Slings and Arrows', in Irena R. Makaryk and Kathryn Prince (eds), *Shakespeare in Canada: Remembrance of Ourselves*, 97–110, Ottawa: University of Ottawa Press.
Nestruck, J. Kelly (2010), 'Plummer, McAnuff Take Two Paths to Pleasure', *The Globe and Mail*, 27 June. Available online https://www.theglobeandmail.com/arts/theatre-and-performance/mcanuff-plummer-find-two-paths-to-magic/article4083566/ (accessed 15 July 2023).
Nestruck, J. Kelly (2018), 'Review: Art More Powerful than Bomb Threats in Stratford Festival's *The Tempest*', *The Globe and Mail*, 11 June. Available online https://www.theglobeandmail.com/arts/theatre-and-performance/reviews/article-review-art-more-powerful-that-bomb-threats-in-stratford-festivals/ (accessed 15 July 2023).
Ormsby, Robert (2010), '"This Famous Duke of Milan of Whom So Often I have Heard Renown": William Hutt at The Stratford and New Burbage Festivals', *Canadian Theatre Review*, 141: 10–15.
Ormsby, Robert (2017), 'Global Cultural Tourism at Canada's Stratford Festival: *The Adventures of Pericles*', in James Bulman (ed.), *The Oxford Handbook of Shakespeare and Performance*, 568–83, Oxford: Oxford University Press.
Ouzounian, Richard, ed. (2002), *Stratford Gold: 50 years, 50 Stars, 50 Conversations*, Toronto: McArthur & Company.

Ouzounian, Richard (2005), 'Hutt Magical to the Last Line', *Toronto Star*, 1 June.
Ouzounian, Richard (2008), 'A Prince among Hamlets', *Toronto Star*, 29 May.
Ouzounian, Richard (2010), 'Legit Review: *The Tempest*', *Variety*, 30 June.
Ouzounian, Richard (2015), 'Stratford's *Hamlet* Reveals the Festival at its Best', *Toronto Star*, 25 May.
Parolin, Peter (2009), '"What Revels Are in Hand?" A Change of Direction at the Stratford Shakespeare Festival of Canada', *Shakespeare Quarterly*, 60: 197–224.
Patterson, Tom and Allan Gould (1987), *First Stage: The Making of the Stratford Festival*, Toronto: McClelland & Stewart.
Pennington, Bob (1986), 'An Enchanting Fairy Story', *Toronto Sun*, 23 May.
Pettigrew, John and Jamie Portman (1985a), *Stratford: The First Thirty Years Vol. I 1953–1967*, Toronto: Macmillan of Canada.
Pettigrew, John and Jamie Portman (1985b), *Stratford: The First Thirty Years Vol. II 1968–1982*, Toronto: Macmillan of Canada.
Poll, Melissa (2018), *Robert Lepage's Scenographic Dramaturgy*, Cham, Switzerland: Palgrave Macmillan.
Portman, Jamie (1976a), 'Twin Hamlets a Reward for Play-Goers', Southam News Service: *Montreal Gazette*, 9 March.
Portman, Jamie (1976b), 'New *Tempest* Offers Shimming Imagery', Southam News Service: *Calgary Herald*, 10 March.
Portman, Jamie (1977), 'Production of Unforgettable Beauty', Southam News Service: *The Brantford Expositor*, 19 August.
Portman, Jamie (1982), 'Hirsch's *Tempest* a Disappointment', Southam News Service: *Ottawa Citizen*, 10 June.
Portman, Jamie (1986), '*Cymbeline* is a Triumph', Southam News Service: *Calgary Herald*, 6 August.
Portman, Jamie (2000), 'Gross's Hamlet a Blazing Comet', *Ottawa Citizen*, 31 May.
Portman, Jamie (2015), 'Stratford's Latest *Hamlet* is a Triumph', *Capital Critics' Circle*, 15 June. Available online https://capitalcriticscircle.com/stratfords-latest-hamlet-triumph/ (accessed 15 July 2023).
Portman, Jamie (2018), 'Acting Legend Martha Henry Triumphs as Prospero at Stratford', *Capital Critics' Circle*, 30 June. Available online https://capitalcriticscircle.com/acting-legend-martha-henry-triumphs-prospero-stratford/ (accessed 15 July 2023)

Posner, Michael (2008), 'Former Stratford Director Cites Creative Interference as Reason for Stepping Aside', *The Globe and Mail*, 24 March. Available online https://www.theglobeandmail.com/news/national/former-stratford-director-cites-creative-interference-as-reason-for-stepping-aside/article669552/ (accessed 15 July 2023).

Raby, Peter, ed. (1968), *The Stratford Scene 1958–68*, Toronto: Clarke, Irwin & Company.

Rae, Ian (2017), 'Stratford, Shakespeare, and J. D. Barnett', in Irena R. Makaryk and Kathryn Prince (eds), *Shakespeare in Canada: Remembrance of Ourselves*, 49–69, Ottawa: University of Ottawa Press.

Reid, Robert (2005), 'Hutt Shines in *The Tempest*, his Final Stratford Play', *The Record*, 1 June.

Reid, Barbara and Thelma Morrison (1994), *A Star Danced: The Story of how Stratford Started the Stratford Festival*, Stratford: Beacon Herald.

Report (1951), *Royal Commission on National Development in the Arts, Letter and Sciences 1949–1951*, Ottawa: King's Printer.

Riedstra, Lutzen H. (2010), *Tom Patterson, 1920–2005*, Toronto: Ontario Heritage Trust.

Robertson, Campbell (2008), 'At Stratford Last Man Standing Runs Show', *The New York Times*, 18 March. Available online https://www.nytimes.com/2008/03/18/theater/18stratford.html (accessed 15 July 2023).

Schagerl, Jessica (2002), 'A National *Hamlet*? Stratford's Legacy of Twentieth-Century Productions', in Diana Brydon and Irena R. Makaryk (eds), *Shakespeare in Canada: A World Elsewhere?*, 159–73, Toronto: University of Toronto Press.

Seddon, George (1964), 'Canadian Capers: Theatre in Chichester', *Observer*, 14 April.

Shaughnessy, Robert (2002), *The Shakespeare Effect: A History of Twentieth-Century Performance*, London: Palgrave.

Skene, Reg (1982), 'Hirsch *Tempest* a Disaster', *Winnipeg Free Press*, 30 June.

Slings and Arrows (2003–6), [TV series], Dir. Peter Wellington, created and written by Susan Coyne, Bob Martin and Mark McKinney, CAN: Acorn Media, first broadcast 3 November 2003.

Speaight, Robert (1973), *Shakespeare on Stage: An illustrated History of Shakespearian Performance*, London: William Collins, Sons and Company.
Stanton, Victor (1973), 'Stratford's *Othello* a Travesty', *Kitchner-Waterloo Record*, 7 June.
Stratford Beacon Herald (1952), 'Council Told of Idea to Make Stratford World Famous Shakespeare Centre', 22 January.
Stratford Festival (1959), *The Stratford Shakespearean Festival of Canada, 1953–1959*, Stratford: Stratford Festival.
Stratford Festival (1962), 'Artistic Director Michael Langham on the 1962 Stage Changes', Source Festival Press Release.
Stratford Festival (1977), Festival Press Release, 23 July.
Stratford Festival (1992), programme for *The Tempest*, Stratford: Stratford Festival.
Stratford Festival (2010), programme for *The Tempest*, Stratford: Stratford Festival.
Stratford Festival (2020a), 'Black Like Me, Past, Present and Future: Behind the Stratford Festival Curtain', YouTube, 8 June. Available online: Black Like Me, past, present and future: Behind the Stratford Festival Curtain – YouTube. https://www.youtube.com/watch?v=xJK85IRtzYM.
Stratford Festival (2020b), 'Ndo-Mshkawgaabwimi – We All Are Standing Strong', YouTube, 20 June. https://www.youtube.com/watch?v=jHzm7sbJ6Ck.
Stratford Festival (2021), Martha Henry Memorial Programme, 13 November.
Stratford Festival (2022a), programme for *All's Well that Ends Well*, Stratford: Stratford Festival of Canada.
Stratford Festival (2022b), programme for *Richard III*, Stratford: Stratford Festival of Canada.
Szekeres, Joe (2018), '*The Tempest* at the Stratford Festival', *The Theatre Times*, 6 September. Available online https://thetheatretimes.com/the-tempest-at-the-stratford-festival/ (accessed 15 July 2023).
Tanitch, Robert (2020), 'Stream Review: *The Tempest* at Stratford Festival Theatre, Ontario', britishtheatreguide.info, 4 December. Available online https://www.britishtheatreguide.info/reviews/the-tempest-stratford-festi-19612 (accessed 15 July 2023).

Tanya Moiseiwitsch: A Celebration (2003), Stratford: Stratford Festival of Canada, 12 July.
Taylor, Gary (1999), 'Theatre Proximities: The Stratford Festival 1998', *Shakespeare Quarterly*, 50 (3): 334–54.
Taylor, Kate (1998), 'Saving Stratford from the Excesses of Success', *The Globe and Mail*, 18 July: C1.
Taylor, Kate (2010), '*The Tempest*'s Static Transition from Stage to Film', *The Globe and Mail*, 6 November.
Thompson, Kemp (1962), '*Tempest* Reveals Forgiveness Theme', *Kitchener-Waterloo Record*, 21 June.
Threepwood, Clarence (2008), '*Hamlet* at the Stratford Festival', Ezine@articles, 1 August.
The Times (1953), 'Shakespeare in Canada: A Festival in the Making', 22 July: 11.
Tinker, Jack (1977), 'How Wrong I was about Maggie Smith', *Daily Mail*, 13 June.
Tracy, Marc (2022) 'Who Can Play the King? Questions of Representation Fuel Casting Debates', *The New York Times*, 28 July. Available online https://www.nytimes.com/2022/07/28/theater/richard-iii-casting-debates.html (accessed 15 July 2023).
Tynan, Kenneth (1956), *Observer*, 9 September.
Wagner, Anton (1989), 'Ontario, Theatre In', in Eugene Benson and L.W. Conolly (eds), *The Oxford Companion to Canadian Theatre*, 397–400, Toronto: Oxford University Press.
Wallace, Robert (1990), *Producing Marginality: Theatre and Criticism in Canada*, Saskatoon, Saskatchewan: Fifth House Publishers.
Watson, Jessica (2022), '*Hamlet* at Stratford Festival', Intermissionmagazine.ca, 29 June. Available online https://www.intermissionmagazine.ca/reviews/review-hamlet-at-stratford-festival/ (accessed 15 July 2023).
Whittaker, Herbert (1957), 'Hamlet Death Scene Magnificent Climax at Stratford Opening', *The Globe and Mail*, 1 July.
Whittaker, Herbert (1958), 'Introduction', in *The Stratford Festival 1953–1957: A Record in Pictures and Text of the Shakespearean Festival in Canada*, ix–xxix, Toronto: Clarke, Irwin & Company.
Whittaker, Herbert (1972), 'An Imposing, Old Style King Lear', *Globe and Mail*, 8 June.

Wiegand, Chris (2023), 'Richard II in a Hot Tub, Much Ado Done Anew: Canada's Stratford Festival Puts Shocks into Shakespeare', *The Guardian*, 4 July. Available Online https://www.theguardian.com/stage/2023/jul/04/richard-ii-much-ado-canada-stratford-festival-shakespeare (accessed 15 July 2023)

Willems, Michèle (2000, 2007), 'Video and Its Paradoxes', in Russell Jackson (ed.), *The Cambridge Companion to Shakespeare on Film*, 35–46, Cambridge: Cambridge University Press.

Wilson, Jane (1986), 'Stratford's *Pericles* Stirring Theatre', *Kitchener-Waterloo Record*, 23 May.

Wilson, Trish (1982), *Kitchener-Waterloo Record*, 10 June.

Wright, Kailin (2017), '"Who's There?": *Slings and Arrows*' Audience Dynamics', in Irena R. Makaryk and Kathryn Prince (eds), *Shakespeare in Canada: Remembrance of Ourselves*, 79–98, Ottawa: University of Ottawa Press.

INDEX

Note: This volume and its index have been created to highlight patterns and connections across the Festival's complex seventy-year history; as a result people, places and plays mentioned only once have largely been omitted in what follows.

Abbey, Graham   132, 136, 181, 187, 208
Abraham, Chris   155–6
Albee, Edward   160, 219
Allied Forces   20, 33, 42
All's Well That Ends Well
   1953 production   28, 33–4, 39–44, 46
   1977 production   95
   1988 production   118
   2002 production   138
   2008 production   151
   2022 production   1, 215–18
American
   audiences   33, 88, 102, 123, 127, 139, 143
   North American premières   71–2, 84
   North American setting   46, 90, 116–18, 132
   plays   106, 127, 129, 145
   South American setting   147
Antony and Cleopatra
   1967 production   73–83
   1976 production   93
   1993 production   127
   2003 production   146
   2014 production   155–6
Applebaum, Louis   48–50, 137, 187
Assembly Hall (Edinburgh)   19, 24
As You Like It
   1959 production   62
   1972 production   83, 85
   1977 production   96, 138, 209
   1978 production   98
   1983 production   108
   1987 production   117
   1990 production   126, 132, 138, 209
   1996 production   131
   2000 production   131
   2005 production   147
   2010 production   153
   2016 production   156
Atienza, Edward   110, 116
Atkinson, Brooks   39–40, 43, 55, 168
Atwood, Margaret   212

Avon Theatre 14, 49, 53, 56, 61, 63–4, 67, 69–71, 73–4, 81–3, 85, 87, 90–1, 93, 99, 101, 102, 111, 114–16, 118, 120, 123, 127, 139, 147, 151, 153, 155, 157, 170, 173–4, 194–6

Bale, Doug 171–3, 198
Barnes, Clive 93, 196
Bawtree, Michael 85, 87
Beard, Robert 116, 118, 124
Beckett, Samuel *Waiting for Godot* 81–2, 129, 134, 152
Bedford, Brian 90–1, 95–6, 98–102, 124–5, 129–30, 134, 137, 147
Benson, Susan 90, 111
Bentley-Fisher, Patrica 170–1
Best, Wayne 134, 199
Birmingham Conservatory 136, 150–1, 215
Birmingham Repertory Theatre 52, 113
Blake, Michael 158–9, 209–10
Blendick, James 119, 132, 173, 182
Blyth, Domini 100, 181
board of directors 25, 30–1, 47, 52, 54, 59, 62, 67, 72–3, 77–8, 81, 83, 87–9, 97–9, 101, 104–6, 150, 160; *see also* Festival committee
Bohn, Michelle 186, 216
Boll, Sidone 175–6
Brecht, Bertold

Brechtian 72
Mother Courage and Her Children 116, 155
The Resistible Rise of Arturo Ui 115
Rise and Fall of the City of Mahogonny 71
Threepenny Opera 137
Trumpets and Drums 91, 113
Brighton, Pam 100–1, 104–5
British theatre 10, 21–2, 68, 218
Broadway 57, 107, 112, 130
Bryden, Ronald 68–9
Brydon, Diana 12, 161
Burge, Stuart 69–70

Caldwell, Zoe 64, 73, 99–100
Campbell, Benedict 111, 134, 136, 181
Campbell, Douglas 30, 48–9, 61–4, 70–1, 82, 108, 111, 120, 134, 136, 168
Canada Council 9, 52, 59, 62, 88
Canadian
  actors 20–1, 25, 27–8, 43, 54, 56, 102, 112, 160, 162, 169, 178, 181
  Actor's Equity (ACTRA) 95–6
  alternative theatre 12–13, 77–81, 87, 89, 92, 151
  audience interaction 35, 109, 219
  cultural critics 73, 77, 128
  culture 8–9, 20, 160, 211
  early theatre development 8–10

identity 14, 20, 25, 53, 149, 179, 218–19, 221
nationalism/ists 13, 25, 27, 48, 57, 72–3, 77–9, 81, 88, 90, 95–6, 102, 123, 144
national theatre 10, 13, 20, 22, 44, 59, 89, 213
National Theatre School 95, 180
plays at Stratford 20, 81, 99, 124, 128, 146, 153
professional theatre 8–10, 12, 20, 22, 49, 58, 102, 129, 160, 185
Shakespeare 6–7, 13, 32, 52, 220–1
Canadian Broadcasting Corporation (CBC) 9, 127, 135, 156, 190, 197–8
Canadian Players 49, 61, 169, 194
Canadian Theatre Review 89, 201
Cariou, Len 104, 107, 190, 197
Carlson, Ben 182, 216
Carroll, Tim 155
Carson, Neil 35–6, 40, 42–3
Carver, Brent 115, 120, 173–5, 188
Chapman, Geoff 177, 199
Charlesworth, Marigold 96
Chekhov, Anton 220
 The Cherry Orchard 71
 The Seagull 82, 101
 Three Sisters 94, 120, 153
 Uncle Vanya 71, 99, 101
Chichester Theatre 53, 68–71, 89
Ciceri, Leo 69–70, 72, 169
Cimolino, Antoni 1, 3–7, 11, 113, 127, 130, 136, 143–7, 152–61, 164, 178, 183–5, 190, 193, 207–12, 221
Citadel Theatre (Edmonton) 113, 179–80
Clarke, Cecil 28–9, 31–2, 45, 48
Coe, Peter 65, 68
Colicos, John 66, 68, 70, 194
colonial/ism 12, 62, 80, 88, 102, 132, 143–4, 157, 192–3, 203, 205, 213
Comedy of Errors, *The*
 1963 production 67–8
 1975 production 89–90
 1981 production 107
 1989 production 119
 1994–5 production 131
 2007 production 147
 2018 production 158
Conelly, Patricia 108, 111
Coriolanus 15
 1961 production 64
 1981 production 107
 1992 production of *Coriolan* in Paris 191
 1997 production 132
 2006 production 147
 2018 production 157–8, 210–12
Coulbourn, John 180–1, 198–9
Covid (pandemic) crisis 1, 8, 14, 21, 143–4, 158–60, 185, 188, 211, 217, 219, 221

Coward, Noël   110, 125
Coyne, Susan   110, 117
Crest Theatre   49, 129
Crew, Robert   114, 174
Cronyn, Hume   83, 93–4
Cronyn, Tandy   116
cultural capital   2, 199
Cushman, Robert   11, 19, 25–7, 38, 45–6, 64, 82, 95, 108, 112, 131–3, 156, 169–70, 173, 175, 177–9, 203
Cymbeline
  1970 production   77, 84
  1986 production   114, 116
  2004 production   146
  2012 production   154

Dare, Daphne   90, 92, 100, 114
Davies, Geraint Wyn   114, 119, 138, 182, 184
Davies, Robertson   11, 20, 31, 42, 112, 128
Dews, Peter   87, 107
Dexter, John   78, 105
DiCenzo, Maria   201, 205
Dilworth, Alan   156–7, 159
Donaldson, Peter   129, 178
Doran, Greg   7, 213
Doran, Terry   196, 200
Dumas, Alexandre, *The Three Musketeers*   82, 118

Edinborough, Arnold   58, 167–8, 170
Edinburgh Festival   19, 24–5, 54, 57–8
Edwardian setting   116–17, 124

Elizabethan stage   27, 91
Ellington, Duke   2, 61, 68, 125

Fairfield, Robert   31, 51, 54, 59, 65
Feore, Colm   1, 4–5, 109, 114, 116, 118, 124, 127, 130, 138, 175, 188, 212
Filewod, Alan   12, 79, 201
Findley, Timothy
  Elizabeth Rex   135, 149
  The Stillborn Lover   135
First World War   91, 117, 119, 125, 130, 132, 136, 157, 183, 217
French Canada   9, 86
French Canadian actors   54–6
Fricker, Karen   185–7, 193
Frye, Northrop   112, 161–2

Gabourie, Dean   153, 155
Gaffney, Anita   155
Gaffney, Oliver   30
Galloway, Pat   101, 128, 170–2
Gang of Four   105–6, 129, 152, 173, 177
Garneau, Michel   88, 192
Gascon, Jean   56, 62, 68, 70–4, 77, 80–8, 107, 110, 120
Gélinas, Gratien   56, 166
Gereckc, Brctta   209, 212
Gilbert and Sullivan   46, 66, 70, 109, 111, 113, 120, 135
Giles, David   83, 109
Gill, Peter   84–5
Gillespie, Ian   200–1
Goad, Jonathan   183–5

Gogol, Nikolai, *The Government Inspector* 73–4, 110
Goldby, Derek 107, 130
Gould, Adrienne 182, 184, 202
Gould, Glenn 48, 135
government funding 2, 8–9, 98, 100, 143, 150, 175–6, 179, 218
Grand Theatre (London, Ontario) 127, 152, 173
Grey, Earle 20–1
Groome, Margaret 20–1, 42, 44, 57–60
Gross, Paul 162, 179–81, 189
Guinness, Alec 1, 4, 26, 28, 30–2, 34, 37–8, 41–3, 57, 137–8
Gurik, Robert 78, 165, 176
Guthrie, Tyrone 1, 7, 10–11, 19–50, 56–74, 80, 85, 95, 103, 106, 112, 124, 134, 136, 139, 146, 154, 162, 180, 184, 217
Guthrie Theatre (Minneapolis) 53, 70–1, 74, 81, 85, 180

Hamlet 14, 23, 65, 129
 1937 Elsinore production 23
 1957 production 23, 60, 167–9, 193
 1969 production 82, 169–70
 1976 production 93, 170–3, 194–5
 1986 production 115, 120, 173–4
 1991 production 124, 174–7, 199
 1994 production 130, 177–8, 202
 2000 production 179–81
 2008 production 151, 181–3
 2015 production 156, 164, 183–5, 207, 212
 2022 production 185–9
 history of in Canada 163–7, 188–90, 193
Hamlet, Prince du Québec 78, 165–7
Hayman, Edward 173–6
Heeley, Desmond 60, 62, 68, 84, 107–8, 110, 119, 195, 197
Hennig, Kate 156–7, 159, 208
Henry IV 1958 production Part 1 61
 1965 production Parts 1&2 70
 1984 production Part 1 111
 2001 production Parts 1&2 136
 2006 production Part 1 147
 2016 production Parts 1&2 with *Henry V* (*Breath of Kings: Rebellion, Breath of Kings: Redemption*) 156
Henry V
 1956 production 52, 54–7, 158, 167
 1966 production 5, 71, 73
 1980 production 5, 101
 1989 production 119
 2001 production 136
 2012 production 154

2016 production (*Breath of Kings: Rebellion, Breath of Kings: Redemption*) 156
Henry VI
  1966 production 72
  1980 production Parts 1–3 101
  2002 production (*Revenge in France, Revolt in England*) 137
Henry VIII
  1949 and 1950 production Stratford-upon-Avon 27
  1953 production Old Vic 27–8, 34
  1961 production 64
  1986 production 114–15
  2004 production 146
  2019 production 159
Henry, Martha 14, 72, 91–2, 94–5, 114, 127, 129, 130, 132–3, 135, 137–8, 146, 153, 155, 157, 159, 194–5, 207–11, 219–20
Hill, Jessica B. 215–17
Hinton, Peter 151
  The Swanne 146, 149, 159
Hirsch, John 71–4, 77, 80–3, 94, 103–13, 119, 121, 154, 197–9, 203
Holliday, Billie 2, 61
Hopkins, Bernard 120, 124, 128
Hunter, Martin 11, 48, 56, 68, 69, 80, 87, 106, 169, 172–3, 180
Hutt, Peter 201–2, 205
Hutt, William 14, 69, 82–3, 85–93, 99–101, 103–4, 106–8, 110, 114–17, 127, 129–31, 135, 138, 147, 162–3, 169–73, 177, 190, 193–6, 200–5, 207–8
Hyland, Frances 60, 62, 72, 100, 168

Ibsen, Henrik 39–40
  The Enemy of the People 127
  Hedda Gabler 84
Indigenous (people and artists) 160, 192–3, 205
international; *see also* touring
  audiences 14, 34, 69, 144–5, 157, 160, 162
  critical debate 6, 29, 31, 55
  influences 81, 100, 112, 152, 204
  perspectives 30, 33, 42, 139, 144, 151–2, 154, 163, 195
  reputation 11, 13, 15–16, 20, 28, 32, 44, 52, 59, 69, 93, 102, 151, 156–7, 161–2
  stars 24–5, 28, 49, 53, 93, 100, 105

Jackson, Berners 61, 70, 87, 90–1
Jackson, Brian 63–5, 71, 84, 118
Johnson, Geordie 120, 133–4
Johnson, Sydney 65, 194
Johnstone, Dion 147–8, 205, 210
Jonson, Ben, *The Alchemist* 82–3
  Volpone 85
Julian, Erin 144, 157–9, 184

Julius Caesar
   1950 production
      Shakespeare Memorial
      Theatre 52
   1955 production 47
   1965 production 71
   1978 production 99
   1998 production 134
   2009 production 153
   2018 production 158

Kareda, Urjo 91, 93, 99, 101, 104–5
Karr, Jack 167–8
Kennedy, Dennis 27–8, 35, 46–7, 77, 91, 148
Kerr, Walter 40, 55, 82, 194
Kidnie, Margaret Jane 117, 144, 147–8, 156, 190–1, 215
King John
   1960 production 63
   1974 production 87
   1993 production 125, 127
   2004 production 146
   2014 production 155–6
King Lear
   1964 production 70
   1972–3 production 86, 123
   1979–80 production 99–100, 102, 108
   1985 production 108, 110
   1988 production 117, 132
   1996 production 130
   2002 production 138
   2007 production 147
   2014 production 155
   2023 production 189
   Slings and Arrows Episode
      featuring 162

Knowles, Richard Paul 12, 44, 57, 88, 125, 127, 133, 137–8, 144, 148, 201
Kuling, Peter 149, 162

Lambermont, Jeannette 119, 131, 136
Langham, Michael 47–74, 80, 82, 84–7, 99, 103, 110–12, 119–20, 125, 129–30, 151–2, 154, 157–8, 167–9, 180–1, 184, 193–4
Latham, David 139, 146
Leblanc, Diana 4–5, 133, 153, 160
Lepage, Robert 82, 157–8, 191–2, 210, 212
Lévesque, René 78, 168
Lieblein, Leanore 78–9, 88
Loughran, Kiera 157–8
Love's Labour's Lost
   1961 production 64
   1964 production 68
   1974 production 87
   1979 production 99
   1983/4 production 111
   1989 production 120
   1992 production 124
   2003 production 146
   2008 production 151
   2015 production 156

McAnuff, Des 108, 143, 145, 150–5, 181, 190
Macbeth
   1962 production 65–6
   1971 production 85
   1978 production 98
   1983 production 108

1986 production 115
1990 production 124
1995 production 133
2004 production 146
2009 production 153
2016 production 156, 212
Garneau translation of 88, 191
McCamus, Tom 129, 132, 134, 137–8, 158, 167, 178, 210
McCowan, George 61–2, 64, 66, 193–5
Macdonald, Brian 111, 120, 124, 135–6
McGee, C. E. 126, 131–2, 162
McKenna, Seana 4, 109, 133–4, 149, 154, 158, 216
Mackintosh, Iain 10, 19, 23–4
Mahtani, Sunil 200–1
Major, Leon 67, 111
Makaryk, Irena R. 9, 11–13, 44, 161, 163
Mallet, Gina 94, 96, 172, 195
Manitoba Theatre Centre (Winnipeg) 71, 74, 81, 179
Maraden, Marti 94, 96, 124, 127–8, 133, 145, 150–3, 172, 181, 196
Mason, James 45–6, 48
Massey Report (1951) 10, 20–2, 34, 44
Maxwell, Roberta 101, 108
Measure for Measure
 1954 production 45
 1969 production 83
 1975/6 production 91–2, 94
 1985 production 109

1992 production 125
2005 production 147
2013 production 155
Merchant of Venice, The
 1955 production 48
 1970 production 83
 1976 production 93
 1984 production 108
 1989 production 118
 1996 production 133
 2007 production 147
 2013 production 155
Merry Wives of Windsor, The
 1956 production 54
 1967 production 73, 123
 1978 production 98
 1990 production 124
 1995 production 130
 2011 production 153
 2019 production 158
Midsummer Night's Dream, A
 1960 production 63
 1968 production 82
 1976/7 production 94, 96
 1984 production 108
 1989 production 119
 1999 production 130
 2004 production 146–7
 2009 production 153
 2014 production 155–6
 2014 production
  (A Chamber play) 156
 2021 production 160
Miller, Arthur 91, 106, 112
 The Crucible 91
 Death of a Salesman 110
Moiseiwitsch, Tanya 24, 26–8, 30–2, 34, 37, 39, 41, 44–6, 49–51, 55, 61, 64–5, 70, 84, 95, 110, 134

Molière 9, 56, 81, 124
  Le Bourgeois Gentilhomme 68, 70
  Husbands and Cuckolds 129
  The Imaginary Invalid 87, 127
  The Misanthrope 107
  The Miser 130
  Tartuffe 82–4, 110
Monaghan, Kelly 186–8
Monette, Richard 73, 92–3, 96, 101, 108, 116, 118–19, 122, 124, 126–39, 143–50, 152, 154–5, 159, 167, 170–3, 176–8, 180, 183–4, 188, 195, 199–204
Moore, Don 162–3
Moore, Dora Mavor 20, 23
Morin, André 209, 211
Moss, Peter 98–9, 101, 104–5, 118, 135
Much Ado about Nothing
  1958 production 61
  1971 production 85
  1977 production 96
  1980 production 100
  1983 production 111
  1987 production 116
  1998 production 130
  2006 production 147
  2012 production 154
Murrell, John 99, 101, 155

National Arts Centre (Ottawa) 73, 83–5, 96, 98, 150, 192, 194
National Film Board (Canada) 30
National Theatre (UK) 34
  Olivier Theatre 10
Needles, William 49, 111, 119, 134
Negin, Mark 68
Nestruck, J. Kelly 204–5, 208, 210–11
Neville, John 103–4, 108, 110–21, 123, 136, 173–4
New Play Society 20
Noble, Adrian 151, 181–4

Old Vic Theatre 23–4, 27–8, 34, 57, 64, 113, 123, 169
Olivier, Laurence 23, 71, 118
O'Neill, Eugene 152
  Ah Wilderness 127
  Long Day's Journey into Night 101, 129, 138, 158
Open Air Theatre, Regent's Park (UK) 113, 129
Ormsby, Robert 114–15, 147–8, 162–3
Othello; *see also* Djanet Sears *Harlem Duet*
  1959 production 62
  1973 production 86–7, 123
  1987 production 116
  1994 production 134
  2013 production 155
  2019 production 158–9
Ouimette, Stephen 125, 130–1, 134, 146–7, 157–8, 177–9, 202–3, 208, 210, 212
Ouzounian, Richard 11, 113–14, 119, 136, 182–4, 203, 206

Parolin, Peter   146–8, 151–2, 182
Pasyk, Peter   160, 185–7
Patterson, Tom   1, 10, 22–6, 29–30, 32, 34, 47, 49, 83, 199, 219
Patterson, Tom and Allan Gould, *First Stage*   11, 26, 29
Peacock, Lucy   4–5, 111, 115, 118, 120, 131, 160, 173
Pearson, Lester   165–6
Pennell, Nicholas   93, 100, 108–9, 118–19, 170–2, 195, 198
Pericles
   1973/4 production   77, 87
   1986 production   114
   2003 *The Adventure of* production   146–8
   2015 *The Adventure of* production   156
Pettigrew, John and Jamie Portman, *Stratford: The First Thirty Years*   11, 36, 38, 43, 49, 54, 57, 63, 66, 70–1, 83–4, 86, 91, 94, 97–8, 100–1, 104, 170
Phillips, Robin   77–8, 89–120, 149, 152, 162, 170–3, 178–81, 184, 194–7, 203
Plummer, Christopher   14–15, 51, 55, 60–1, 65–6, 73–83, 86, 130, 138, 151, 153–4, 165, 167–9, 181, 188, 204–8
Portman, Jamie   98, 114, 171, 180–1, 184, 197–8, 208
Potter, Miles   134, 146, 149, 154, 158

Pownall, Leon   115, 175
Prévost, Robert   62, 68
Prince, Kathryn   13, 163
proscenium arch   14, 24, 27, 36, 39, 49, 53, 157

Québéc/ois   56–7, 78–81, 88, 105, 122–3, 126, 128, 165–6, 176, 191–2, 204
Queen Elizabeth I   4, 96, 135, 149, 157, 208, 210–11
Queen Elizabeth II   6, 27–8, 32–4, 36–7, 39, 43, 60, 62, 95, 122

Raby, Peter   11, 82
Rae, Ian   13, 162
Rain, Douglas   49, 62, 70, 72, 133–4, 178
Rampersad, Kimberley   160, 189
Reaney, James, *Colours in the Dark*   74
Reid, Barbara and Thelma Morrison, *A Star Danced*   11, 29, 32
Reid, Kate   62, 66, 95
Reid, Robert   190, 203
repertory theatres/model   9, 13–14, 24, 88, 158, 193, 202, 204, 220
Richard II
   1964 production   69–70
   1979 production   99
   1999 production   133, 136
Richard III   1, 4, 8
   1953 production   1, 4, 28, 31–2, 34–9, 42–4, 60
   1967 production   73

1977 production   95–6, 98
1988 production   5, 118
2002 *Reign of Terror*
  production   8, 133, 137, 209
2011 production   4–5, 154
2022 production   1–8
2022 Royal Shakespeare
  production   5, 7
Richard III (historical king)   3, 5
Rintoul, Brian   114, 118
Robinson, Kelly   136, 146
Romeo and Juliet
  1960 production   63
  1968 production   82
  1977 production   96, 123
  1984 production   109
  1987 production   116
  1992 production   127
  1997 production   133
  2008 production   151
  2013 production   155
  2017 production   156
Rose, Richard   128, 131–2, 134
Rostand, Edmond *Cyrano
  de Bergerac*   66, 68, 129–30, 153
Royal Shakespeare Company
  (RSC)   2, 5, 90, 96, 213, 219–20; *see also*
  Stratford-upon-Avon
Royal Shakespeare Theatre
  (RST)   10, 19
Rubin, Leon   110–11, 137, 146–8

Scarfe, Alan   100, 109, 124, 198
Schagerl, Jessica   164, 174–6, 178, 188

school performances   61–4, 82–3, 87
Schulman, Susan H.   136, 146
Scofield, Paul   64
Sears, Djanet, *Harlem Duet*   146, 148
Second World War   9, 21, 23, 52, 80, 114
Shakespeare's Globe   7, 10, 217
Shatner, William   47
Shaughnessy, Robert   10, 36, 38–41
Shaw, George Bernard   39–40, 106
  Arms and the Man   110
  Caesar and Cleopatra   151, 181, 204
  Saint Joan   90
Shaw Festival   150, 180, 201
Shepherd, Elizabeth   115, 173
Shipley, Don   145, 150, 152, 181
Shultz, Albert   117
Sills, André   158, 208, 210, 212
Slings and Arrows   162, 179
Smith, Maggie   93–6, 98, 100–2, 109, 137, 153
Solga, Kim   144–5, 157–9, 184
Sophocles *Oedipus Rex*
  1954/5 production   45–6, 48
  1988 production   118
  1997 production   134
Soulpepper Theatre   118, 162, 180
Speaight, Robert   46, 48
Stoppard, Tom, *Rosencrantz
  and Guildenstern Are
  Dead*   115, 174

Stratford Beacon Herald 23, 32
Stratford City Council 23, 30
Stratford community 14, 22–3, 26, 29–30, 32
Stratford Festival actor training 8, 20, 43–4, 48, 53, 61, 80, 88, 97, 106, 111, 136, 160, 181, 185, 193, 207–8
Stratford Festival audiences 14, 49–50, 90, 105, 109, 212
Stratford Festival committee 22–7; *see also* board of directors
Stratford Festival Concert Hall 1–2, 85
Stratford Festival Theatre 1, 5, 10, 19, 24, 50
  audience relationship/ interaction 21, 35, 50, 109, 219
  balcony (auditorium) 58, 168
  permanent theatre building 57–61
  productions in 73–4, 83–4, 89–91, 114, 116, 124, 138, 146, 151–3, 160, 167, 169–70, 174, 179, 181, 183, 185–6, 188–9, 193–4, 196–9, 202, 204, 207–8, 219
  renovations in 1962 65–7
  stage balcony 4, 38, 40, 65, 90, 93, 95–6, 110, 116–17, 198–9
  thrust stage 1, 4, 10, 14, 19, 23–4, 26, 33–5, 43, 46, 48, 71, 90, 102, 109, 129, 134, 147, 162, 170, 177, 181
Stratford Music Festival 1, 48–9, 53, 65
Stratford-upon-Avon, (UK) 27, 52, 54, 60, 64, 130, 149, 220; *see also* Royal Shakespeare Company
Shakespeare Memorial Theatre 27, 52
Strindberg, August *The Dance of Death* 73, 81
Studio Theatre 14, 97, 139, 148–50, 153–60, 219
Swerdfager, Bruce 94
Szekeres, Joe 209–11

Taming of the Shrew, *The*
  1954 production 45
  1962 production 66
  1973 production 86
  1979 production 100
  1981 production 107
  1988 production 118
  1997 production 131
  2003 production 146
  2008 production 151
  2015 production 156
Tandy, Jessica 93–4, 96
Taylor, Gary 104, 111, 115–16, 125, 132, 134–6, 181, 199
Taylor, Kate 135, 146, 204–5
Tempest, *The* 14–15, 163
  1962 production 15, 66, 190, 193–4
  1976 production 93, 170, 190, 194–6

1982 production 107, 190, 197–8
1992 production 124, 198–9
1999 production 147, 190, 199–202
2005 production 149, 190, 202–4
2010 production 153–4, 190, 204–7
2018 production 157–8, 190, 201–13
2016 Donmar Warehouse production 213
2016 RSC production 213
in Canada 190–3
Théâtre du Nouveau Monde (TNM) 56, 80
Thiessen, Vern *Shakespeare's Will* 146, 148–9, 154
Third Stage 2, 85–7, 90, 92, 99–100, 102, 110, 113, 116, 124; see also Tom Patterson Theatre
Timon of Athens
1963/4 production 67–8, 157
1991 production 125, 157
2004 production 146
2017 production 156–7, 212
Titus Andronicus
1978/80 production 99–100
1989 production 119
2000 production 132–3
2011 production 154
Tom Patterson Theatre 1–7, 14, 124–5, 129–38, 146–7, 149, 151, 153–60, 177–9, 215, 217, 219; see also Third Stage
tour/ing 7, 49, 52, 61, 63, 67, 80–1, 83, 169
Australia 87
Canada 71, 73, 83, 89, 93, 97, 170, 194
Chichester 53, 68–9, 157
Europe and Russia 86
London 102
New York 54, 63, 85
North America 81–2, 85, 110, 112, 170, 206
Tremblay, Michel 78, 128–9
Troilus and Cressida
1963 production 67–8
1987 production 116
2002 production 146
Trudeau, Pierre Elliot 122, 166
Twelfth Night
1957 production 60
1966/7 production 72–4, 123
1975 production 90
1980 production 100
1985 production 109–10
1988 production 117
1991 production 124
1994 production 130, 177
2001 production 136
2006 production 147
2011 production 153–4
2017 production 156
Two Gentlemen of Verona, The
1958 production 61
1975 production 89
1984 production 111
1988 production 118

1992 production   128
1998 production   131–2
2010 production   153
Two Noble Kinsmen, The
   2002 production   138

Umeh, Amaka   165, 186–8
Ustinov, Peter   99–100, 108, 150

Victorian period   19, 39–40, 100, 119, 130, 174, 182
vomitoria   40, 65, 217

Wallace, Robert   12, 79–80
Watson, Jessica   186–8
Welsh, Kenneth   82, 169–70
Wentworth, Scott   110, 133–4, 136, 156, 158, 174, 182, 215–17
Wetherall, Jack   101, 196
Whittaker, Herbert   11, 25, 34, 45–6, 86, 168
Wilde, Oscar   39–40, 93
   An Ideal Husband   147
   The Importance of Being Earnest   92–3, 99, 124
William, David   72–4, 85–6, 96, 109–11, 114, 116, 119–20, 122–30, 174–7, 198–9
Williams, Tennessee   106
   Cat on a Hot Tin Roof   120, 145
   The Glass Menagerie   110, 145
   Streetcar Named Desire   110
Winter's Tale, The
   1958 production   61
   1978 production   98
   1986 production   114
   1998 production   134
   2010 production   153
Wood, John   91, 99, 115, 119, 131, 146, 174
Worth, Irene   30–2, 40–1, 138
Wright, Janet   125, 178
Wright, Susan   114, 116
Wylie, William T.   74, 81

Young Company   89, 91, 93, 102, 111–13, 115–18, 120, 127, 131–2, 136, 162, 180

Ziegler, Joseph   157, 179–80, 212
Zwettler, Mamie   160, 209

www.ingramcontent.com/pod-product-compliance
Lightning Source LLC
Chambersburg PA
CBHW071816300426
44116CB00009B/1343